C. E. Graves

The Clouds of Aristophanes

C. E. Graves

The Clouds of Aristophanes

ISBN/EAN: 9783337008420

Printed in Europe, USA, Canada, Australia, Japan

Cover: Foto ©Thomas Meinert / pixelio.de

More available books at **www.hansebooks.com**

Pitt Press Series.

THE
CLOUDS OF ARISTOPHANES

EDITED

WITH INTRODUCTION AND NOTES

BY

C. E. GRAVES, M.A.

FELLOW AND LECTURER OF ST JOHN'S COLLEGE, CAMBRIDGE

CAMBRIDGE:
AT THE UNIVERSITY PRESS.
1898

[*All Rights reserved.*]

Cambridge:
PRINTED BY J. & C. F. CLAY,
AT THE UNIVERSITY PRESS.

PREFACE

THIS edition of the *Clouds* follows the lines of my edition of the *Wasps* (Pitt Press, 1894); but, in accordance with the wish of the publishers, the notes are shorter, and there are fewer passages cited in illustration. In striving to be brief I hope I shall not be found obscure.

For the notes I am largely indebted to the labours of Dr Blaydes, and the editions of Teuffel (Kaehler, 1887) and Green are referred to throughout. I have also to thank Mr Green for valuable suggestions which he has lately sent me. Rutherford's *New Phrynichus* I have found of the greatest use; it is essential to every student of Aristophanes. The grammatical references are mainly to the last edition of Goodwin's *Greek Moods and Tenses*.

ST JOHN'S COLLEGE, CAMBRIDGE.
September, 1898.

CONTENTS

	PAGE
INTRODUCTION	vii
THE CLOUDS OF ARISTOPHANES	1
NOTES ON THE ARGUMENTS	71
NOTES	73
INDEX I	167
II	168

INTRODUCTION

THE Comedy of the *Clouds* was exhibited at the Great or City Dionysia in the year 423. The year before Aristophanes had brought out the *Knights*, assailing Cleon, the popular patriot and hero, at the height of his power and success, with equal audacity, wit and virulence. The play was a splendid triumph; but it naturally brought some trouble and danger to the poet. Cleon, it is plain, struck back and struck hard; probably by impeaching his antagonist as an alien, as we gather from sundry hints in the *Wasps*. A compromise of some sort seems to have been made; Aristophanes held his hand from Cleon, and he produced his next plays in another name. It was better too to hold aloof from public men and public matters, and not to meddle too directly with the burning questions of the day.

There was a safer subject to hand, tempting to any satirist, and thoroughly congenial to Aristophanes. There was a dragon with poisonous breath, calling for his sharpest spear. The new learning, he felt, was corrupting and killing the moral and social life of Athens. The latter part of the fifth century was a time of scepticism and free thought. Old beliefs in matters of religion, old principles of government, old canons of morality and conduct, were no longer to be accepted without question. They were arraigned at the bar of intellectual and logical inquiry, and called on to answer for themselves.

All this Aristophanes hated. 'It is against this growing tone,' says Dr Merry, 'that Aristophanes, as an uncompromising conservative, fights with desperate energy. It seemed to him at once impious and immoral; and, above all, it represented a deep disloyalty to that glorious Athenian past, in the foreground of which he seemed to see the men who had fought at Marathon as the only true type of national virtue.'

Consequently he regarded with deep dislike and suspicion the professors, the Sophists or 'teachers of wisdom,' mostly foreigners, who descended on Athens and reaped a harvest from the instruction of wealthy or ambitious young men. They undertook to fit their pupils for the duties of practical and public life; to train their minds indeed with scientific theories and enlarge their mental horizon; but above all to impart the faculty of convincing argument and persuasive speech.

This is not the place to enter on a discussion of the Sophists and their teaching. Enough to say that to a prejudiced and hostile eye they might easily seem to teach a system of juggling with words, of using logic to confound right and wrong, and of questioning every accepted truth in morals and religion. The old citizen's conception of a Sophist was like the typical British sailor's notion of a lawyer. Thus Aristophanes hated and feared the new teachers, and attacked them with the full conviction of righteous wrath. Strange indeed it seems to us that he should have taken Socrates as their representative, and grossly unfair; for Socrates as we know him was the very opposite of the quibbling and equivocating pedant. He was a diligent searcher after truth at any cost; a man of hardy outdoor life, at home in every company, grudging his teaching to none, and utterly indifferent to gain. Still he was known as a daring inquirer, a perpetual questioner and arguer, a friend of Euripides and other dangerous men. There was too, as Mr Green shows in his Introduction, an element of actual enmity and dislike. Socrates was not merely taken as representing a school; the attack on him was personal, and felt to be so. Years afterwards, in his defence on his trial, Socrates declared that his most dangerous enemies were not those who actually accused him in court, but those who had learned from Aristophanes to regard him as an idle speculator on things above and beneath the earth, and a perverter of right and wrong.

The *Clouds* proved unsuccessful when placed on the stage, Cratinus winning the first prize with the Πυτίνη, and Ameipsias being second with the Κόννος. The verdict of the judges was plainly backed by the general voice, for the poet reproaches the spectators with rejecting and misunderstanding him, both in the revised Parabasis of the *Clouds*, and in the *Wasps* which came out the following year. This failure was a surprise and a severe disappointment. Aristophanes declares that this was the best and the most carefully written of his plays; it was indeed too subtle and refined for the bulk of the audience; vulgar farce and coarse personalities were what they liked, and they had no taste for higher art. Making every allowance for the self-laudation which is habitual with Aristophanes, it is clear that he aimed high in the *Clouds*, and believed himself to have achieved a work admirable in its purpose and conception, and dignified and charming in its style.

The Greek argument pronounces the play to be τῶν πάνυ δυνατῶς πεποιημένων, 'a most able writing'; and critics generally have echoed the judgment. It has always been the favourite of the student and the scholar. It is certainly unsurpassed for delicate touches of wit and irony, and the earlier songs of the chorus are of exquisite beauty. The opening scene is excellent, ἁρμοδίωτα καὶ δεξιώτατα συγκείμενος, as the old commentator says.

There is not much likelihood in the tradition that the failure of the *Clouds* was brought about by the friends of Socrates. It is more probable that the bulk of the spectators did not care about philosophy, however amusingly travestied. And on the whole I suspect that it was not a good acting play. For one thing the subject was too 'thin.' Scraps of science and snippets of grammar could not be invested with an interest which would carry away an audience, and the lessons which Socrates gives his pupil are dull and tedious. Again there is a deficiency in the characters. The chief personage indeed, Strepsiades, the coarse blundering burgess, has life and individuality; but Socrates is a lay-figure labelled, and the other characters are lifeless dummies. In fact Aristophanes was dealing with people and things that he only knew from report and prejudice, and with which he had no sympathy. He was not at home in the school of philosophy as he was in the assembly and the law courts. So the play is too ideal for the stage, without the strong personal feeling which was looked for in comic scenes, and without the broad and sustained farce which gives 'go' to a comedy.

Convinced of the merit of his work, Aristophanes determined to remodel it. Of this we have the traditional account in Argument IV. The play as we have it is the second *Clouds*; to which alone belong lines 518—562 in the Parabasis, the contest between the two Causes, and the final destruction of the φροντιστήριον. It is noticeable that the additions greatly add to the violence with which Socrates is assailed. The older play burlesqued him as an idle pedant; the later attacks him as a teacher of injustice and impiety. Probably Aristophanes did not reproduce the *Clouds*, for the statement that it reappeared in 422, and failed more utterly than before, is plainly wrong. Nor was the remodelling complete, for we still have repetitions and omissions, and passages disjointed and unconnected—all which a final revision would have removed.

MANUSCRIPTS REFERRED TO (FROM BLAYDES).

A. Par. Nation. 2712.
C. Par. Nation. 2717.
G. Par. Nation. 2827.
R. Ravennas.

S. Ven. Marc. 475.
T. Ven. Marc. 472.
U. Ven. Marc. 473.
V. Ven. Marc. 474.

ΑΡΙΣΤΟΦΑΝΟΥΣ ΝΕΦΕΛΑΙ

ΤΑ ΤΟΥ ΔΡΑΜΑΤΟΣ ΠΡΟΣΩΠΑ

ΣΤΡΕΨΙΑΔΗΣ
ΦΕΙΔΙΠΠΙΔΗΣ
ΘΕΡΑΠΩΝ ΣΤΡΕΨΙΑΔΟΥ
ΜΑΘΗΤΑΙ ΣΩΚΡΑΤΟΥΣ
ΣΩΚΡΑΤΗΣ
ΧΟΡΟΣ ΝΕΦΕΛΩΝ
ΔΙΚΑΙΟΣ ΛΟΓΟΣ
ΑΔΙΚΟΣ ΛΟΓΟΣ
ΠΑΣΙΑΣ, δανειστής
ΑΜΥΝΙΑΣ
ΜΑΡΤΥΣ
ΧΑΙΡΕΦΩΝ

The parts were thus assigned, according to Teuffel:

Protagonist, Strepsiades and Just Cause.
Deuteragonist, Socrates, Unjust Cause and Pasias.
Tritagonist, Pheidippides, Disciple, Amynias and Chaerephon.

ΥΠΟΘΕΣΕΙΣ

I

Τὸ δρᾶμα τὸ τῶν Νεφελῶν κατὰ Σωκράτους γέγραπται τοῦ φιλοσόφου ἐπίτηδες ὡς κακοδιδασκαλοῦντος τοὺς νέους Ἀθήνησι, τῶν κωμικῶν πρὸς τοὺς φιλοσόφους ἐχόντων τινὰ ἀντιλογίαν· οὐχ, ὥς τινες, δι' Ἀρχέλαον τὸν Μακεδόνων βασιλέα, ὅτι προέκρινεν αὐτὸν Ἀριστοφάνους. ὁ χορὸς δὲ ὁ κωμικὸς εἰσήρχετο ἐν 5 τῇ ὀρχήστρᾳ τῷ νῦν λεγομένῳ λογίῳ. καὶ ὅτε μὲν πρὸς τοὺς ὑποκριτὰς διελέγετο, εἰς τὴν σκηνὴν ἑώρα· ὅτε δὲ ἀπελθόντων τῶν ὑποκριτῶν τοὺς ἀναπαίστους διεξῄει, πρὸς τὸν δῆμον ἀπεστρέφετο· καὶ τοῦτο ἐκαλεῖτο στροφή. ἦν δὲ τὰ ἰαμβεῖα τετράμετρα. εἶτα τὴν ἀντίστροφον ἀποδόντες, πάλιν τετράμετρον 10 ἐπέλεγον ἴσων στίχων. ἦν δὲ περὶ τὸ πλεῖστον ιϛ′. ἐκαλεῖτο δὲ ταῦτα ἐπιρρήματα. ἡ δὲ ὅλη πάροδος τοῦ χοροῦ ἐκαλεῖτο παράβασις. Ἀριστοφάνης ἐν Ἱππεῦσιν,

ἦν μέν τις ἀνὴρ τῶν ἀρχαίων κωμῳδοδιδάσκαλος, ὃς ἡμᾶς
ἠνάγκαζε λέξοντας ἔπη πρὸς τὸ θέατρον παραβῆναι. 15

5. αὐτὸν om. V. qu. Εὐριπίδην.   6. λογίῳ· qu. λογείῳ.
10. ἀντίστροφον· qu. ἀντιστροφήν.

II

Φασὶ τὸν Ἀριστοφάνην γράψαι τὰς Νεφέλας ἀναγκασθέντα ὑπὸ Ἀνύτου καὶ Μελήτου, ἵνα διασκέψαιντο ποῖοί τινες εἶεν Ἀθηναῖοι κατὰ Σωκράτους ἀκούοντες. ηὐλαβοῦντο γάρ, ὅτι πολλοὺς εἶχεν ἐραστάς, καὶ μάλιστα τοὺς περὶ Ἀλκιβιάδην, οἳ
5 καὶ ἐπὶ τοῦ δράματος τούτου μηδὲ νικῆσαι ἐποίησαν τὸν ποιητήν. ὁ δὲ πρόλογός ἐστι τῶν Νεφελῶν ἁρμοδιώτατα καὶ δεξιώτατα συγκείμενος. πρεσβύτης γάρ ἐστιν ἄγροικος ἀχθόμενος παιδὶ ἀστικοῦ φρονήματος γέμοντι καὶ τῆς εὐγενείας εἰς πολυτέλειαν ἀπολελαυκότι. ἡ γὰρ τῶν Ἀλκμαιωνιδῶν οἰκία, ὅθεν ἦν τὸ πρὸς
10 μητρὸς γένος ὁ μειρακίσκος, ἐξ ἀρχῆς, ὥς φησιν Ἡρόδοτος, τεθριπποτρόφος ἦν, καὶ πολλὰς ἀνῃρημένη νίκας, τὰς μὲν Ὀλυμπίασι, τὰς δὲ Πυθοῖ, ἐνίας δὲ Ἰσθμοῖ καὶ Νεμέᾳ καὶ ἐν ἄλλοις πολλοῖς ἀγῶσιν. εὐδοκιμοῦσαν οὖν ὁρῶν ὁ νεανίσκος ἀπέκλινε πρὸς τὸ ἦθος τῶν πρὸς μητρὸς προγόνων.

III

Πρεσβύτης τις Στρεψιάδης ὑπὸ δανείων καταπονούμενος διὰ τὴν ἱπποτροφίαν τοῦ παιδός, δεῖται τούτου φοιτήσαντα ὡς τὸν Σωκράτη μαθεῖν τὸν ἥττονα λόγον, εἴ πως δύναιτο τὰ ἄδικα λέγων ἐν τῷ δικαστηρίῳ τοὺς χρήστας νικᾶν καὶ μηδενὶ τῶν
5 δανειστῶν μηδὲν ἀποδοῦναι. οὐ βουλομένου δὲ τοῦ μειρακίσκου, διαγνοὺς αὐτὸς ἐλθὼν μανθάνειν, μαθητὴν τοῦ Σωκράτους ἐκκαλέσας τινὰ διαλέγεται. ἐκλυθείσης δὲ τῆς διατριβῆς, οἵ τε

7. ἐκλυθείσης· qu. ἐκκυκληθείσης.

ΥΠΟΘΕϹΕΙϹ 3

μαθηταὶ κύκλῳ καθήμενοι πιναροὶ συνορῶνται, καὶ αὐτὸς ὁ Σωκράτης ἐπὶ κρεμάθρας αἰωρούμενος καὶ ἀποσκοπῶν τὰ μετέωρα θεωρεῖται. μετὰ ταῦτα τελεῖ παραλαβὼν τὸν πρεσβύτην, καὶ τοὺς νομιζομένους παρ' αὐτῷ θεούς, Ἀέρα, προσέτι δὲ καὶ Αἰθέρα καὶ Νεφέλας κατακαλεῖται. πρὸς δὲ τὴν εὐχὴν εἰσέρχονται Νεφέλαι ἐν σχήματι χοροῦ, καὶ φυσιολογήσαντος οὐκ ἀπιθάνως τοῦ Σωκράτους ἀποκαταστᾶσαι πρὸς τοὺς θεατὰς περὶ πλειόνων διαλέγονται. μετὰ δὲ ταῦτα ὁ μὲν πρεσβύτης διδασκόμενος ἐν τῷ φανερῷ τινὰ τῶν μαθημάτων γελωτοποιεῖ· καὶ ἐπειδὴ διὰ τὴν ἀμαθίαν ἐκ τοῦ φροντιστηρίου ἐκβάλλεται ἄγων πρὸς βίαν τὸν υἱὸν συνίστησι τῷ Σωκράτει. τούτου δὲ ἐξαγαγόντος αὐτῷ ἐν τῷ θεάτρῳ τὸν ἄδικον καὶ τὸν δίκαιον λόγον, διαγωνισθεὶς ὁ ἄδικος πρὸς τὸν δίκαιον λόγον νικᾷ, καὶ παραλαβὼν αὐτὸν ὁ ἄδικος λόγος ἐκδιδάσκει. κομισάμενος δὲ αὐτὸν ὁ πατὴρ ἐκπεπονημένον ἐπηρεάζει τοῖς χρήσταις, καὶ ὡς κατωρθωκὼς εὐωχεῖ παραλαβών. γενομένης δὲ περὶ τὴν εὐωχίαν ἀντιλογίας, πληγὰς λαβὼν ὑπὸ τοῦ παιδὸς βοὴν ἵστησι, καὶ προσκαταλαλούμενος ὑπὸ τοῦ παιδὸς ὅτι δίκαιον τοὺς πατέρας ὑπὸ τῶν υἱῶν ἀντιτύπτεσθαι, ὑπεραλγῶν διὰ τὴν πρὸς τὸν υἱὸν σύγκρουσιν ὁ γέρων, κατασκάπτει καὶ ἐμπίπρησι τὸ φροντιστήριον τῶν Σωκρατιστῶν. τὸ δὲ δρᾶμα τῶν πάνυ δυνατῶς πεποιημένων.

12. κατακαλεῖται· qu. ἀνακαλεῖται.

IV

Τὸ δὲ δρᾶμα τοῦτο τῆς ὅλης ποιήσεως κάλλιστον εἶναί φησι καὶ τεχνικώτατον.

Αἱ πρῶται Νεφέλαι ἐν ἄστει ἐδιδάχθησαν ἐπὶ ἄρχοντος Ἰσάρχου, ὅτε Κρατῖνος μὲν ἐνίκα Πυτίνῃ, Ἀμειψίας δὲ Κόννῳ.

1—2

5 διόπερ Ἀριστοφάνης διαρριφθεὶς παραλόγως ᾠήθη δεῖν ἀναδιδάξας τὰς δευτέρας ἀπομέμφεσθαι τὸ θέατρον. ἀποτυχὼν δὲ πολὺ μᾶλλον καὶ ἐν τοῖς ἔπειτα οὐκέτι τὴν διασκευὴν εἰσήγαγεν. αἱ δὲ δεύτεραι Νεφέλαι ἐπὶ Ἀμεινίου ἄρχοντος. Τοῦτο ταυτόν ἐστι τῷ προτέρῳ. διεσκεύασται δὲ ἐπὶ μέρους, 10 ὡς ἂν δὴ ἀναδιδάξαι μὲν αὐτὸ τοῦ ποιητοῦ προθυμηθέντος, οὐκέτι δὲ τοῦτο δι' ἥν ποτε αἰτίαν ποιήσαντος. καθόλου μὲν οὖν σχεδὸν παρὰ πᾶν μέρος γεγενημένη διόρθωσις. τὰ μὲν γὰρ περιῄρηται, τὰ δὲ πέπλεκται, καὶ ἐν τῇ τάξει καὶ ἐν τῇ τῶν προσώπων διαλλαγῇ μετεσχημάτισται· τὰ δὲ ὁλοσχερους τῆς 15 διασκευῆς [τοιαῦτα ὄντα] τετύχηκεν· αὐτίκα ἡ παράβασις τοῦ χοροῦ ἤμειπται, καὶ ὅπου ὁ δίκαιος λόγος πρὸς τὸν ἄδικον καλεῖ, καὶ τελευταῖον ὅπου καίεται ἡ διατριβὴ Σωκράτους.

Τὴν μὲν κωμῳδίαν καθῆκε κατὰ Σωκράτους, ὡς τοιαῦτα νομίζοντος, καὶ Νεφέλας καὶ Ἀέρα καὶ τί γὰρ ἀλλ' ἢ ξένους 20 εἰσάγοντος δαίμονας. χορῷ δὲ ἐχρήσατο Νεφελῶν πρὸς τὴν τοῦ ἀνδρὸς κατηγορίαν, καὶ διὰ τοῦτο οὕτως ἐπεγράφη. διτταὶ δὲ φέρονται Νεφέλαι. οἱ δὲ κατηγορήσαντες Σωκράτους Μέλητος καὶ Ἄνυτος.

12. γεγενημένη· qu. γεγένηται ἡ.   13. πέπλεκται· παραπέπλεκτεν V.   14. τὰ .. ὁλοσχερους· ἃ ... ὁλοσχερῆ vulg.

V

ΘΩΜΑ ΤΟΥ ΜΑΓΙΣΤΡΟΥ

Ἄνυτος καὶ Μέλητος Σωκράτει τῷ Σωφρονίσκου βασκήναντες καὶ αὐτὸν μὴ δυνάμενοι βλάψαι ἀργύριον ἱκανὸν Ἀριστοφάνει δεδώκασιν, ἵνα δρᾶμα κατ' αὐτοῦ συστήσηται. καὶ ὃς πεισθεὶς γέροντά τινα Στρεψιάδην καλούμενον ἐπλάσατο ὑπὸ χρεῶν 5 πιεζόμενον, ἃ δὴ ἀνηλώκει περὶ τὴν τοῦ παιδὸς Φειδιππίδου ἱπποτροφίαν. οὕτω δὲ τούτων ἐχόντων, μὴ ἔχων ὁ Στρεψιάδης

ΥΠΟΘΕCΕΙC 5

τί ποιήσει περὶ τὰ χρέα, βουλεύεται προσαγαγεῖν τῷ Σωκράτει τὸν ἑαυτοῦ παῖδα, ἵνα παρ' αὐτοῦ τὸν ἄδικον μάθῃ λόγον, καὶ οὕτω τοὺς δανειστὰς ἀποκρούσηται. Φειδιππίδης μὲν οὖν, πολλὰ δεηθέντος τοῦ πατρός, προσελθεῖν οὐκ ἐπείσθη· ἀποτυχὼν δὲ ὁ 10 πρεσβύτης τῆς ἐπ' ἐκείνου ἐλπίδος καὶ οὐκ ἔχων ὅστις καὶ γένηται, εἰς δεύτερον εἶδε πλοῦν. οὐδὲν γὰρ τῆς ἡλικίας φροντίσας οὐδ' ἐνθυμηθεὶς εἴ τισιν ἄτοπος δόξειεν ἀνὴρ ἐπὶ γήραος οὐδῷ μανθάνειν καθάπερ κομιδῇ νέος ἀρχόμενος, ἀλλ' εἰς ἓν ἀφεωρακὼς μόνον ἐκεῖνο, ἐὰν ἄρα οἷός τε γένηται τοὺς 15 δανειστὰς διὰ πειθοῦς ἀποστερῆσαι τὰ χρήματα, αὐτὸς πρόσεισι τῷ Σωκράτει. οὐκ ἔχων δὲ ὑπηρετοῦντα τῇ νοήσει τὸν νοῦν, ἀλλὰ τοιοῦτος ὢν οἷς ἐμάνθανεν, οἷος καὶ πρὶν τῆς παιδείας ἐφῆφθαι, αὐτὸς μὲν ἀπέγνω παιδεύεσθαι, προσελθὼν δὲ τῷ παιδὶ καὶ αὖθις πολλαῖς πέπεικε ταῖς δεήσεσιν ἕνα τῶν Σωκράτους 20 ὁμιλητῶν γενέσθαι. ὁ δὲ καὶ γέγονε καὶ μεμάθηκε. συνίσταται δὲ τὸ δρᾶμα ἐκ χοροῦ Νεφελῶν. ἔχει δὲ κατηγορίαν τοῦ Σωκράτους, ὅτι τοὺς συνήθεις θεοὺς ἀφεὶς καινὰ ἐνόμιζε δαιμόνια, Ἀέρα καὶ Νεφέλας καὶ τὰ τοιαῦτα.

VI

Πρεσβύτης τις Στρεψιάδης ὑπὸ δανείων καταπονούμενος διὰ τὴν ἱπποτροφίαν τοῦ παιδὸς δεῖται τούτου φοιτήσαντα εἰς τὸν Σωκράτην μαθεῖν τὸν ἄδικον λόγον, ὅπως μηδενὶ τῶν δανειστῶν μηδὲν ἀποδώσῃ. μὴ βουλομένου δὲ τοῦ παιδὸς εἰσέρχεται αὐτός. καὶ μὴ δυνάμενος μαθεῖν διὰ τὸ γῆρας ἐκδιώκεται. ὑποστρέψας 5 δὲ καὶ τῷ υἱῷ πείσας ἤγαγεν αὐτὸν τῷ Σωκράτει, ὃς καλέσας τὸν δίκαιον λόγον καὶ ἄδικον καὶ αἵρεσιν τῷ νέῳ δοὺς ἐκλέξασθαι, διδάσκει ἐκεῖνον τὸν ἄδικον λόγον. μαθὼν δὲ ὁ υἱὸς ὅπερ ἐβούλετο ὁ πατὴρ καὶ τὴν παχύτητα ἐκείνου καταγνοὺς τύπτει τὸν πατέρα αὐτὸν ἑστιῶντα. ὁ δὲ ἀλγήσας διὰ τὴν τοῦ παιδὸς 10

ἀσέβειαν ἀπελθὼν κατακαίει τὸ φροντιστήριον, νομίσας Σωκράτην αἴτιον τῆς ἀσεβείας τοῦ παιδὸς εἶναι. κατηγορεῖ δὲ ἐνταῦθα τοῦ Σωκράτους ὡς ἀσεβοῦς καὶ ξένους θεοὺς ἐπεισάγοντος, ἀφέντος τοὺς συνήθεις. ἐπιγράφεται δὲ Νεφέλαι, διότι παρεισάγεται
15 χορὸς Νεφελῶν ὁμιλῶν Σωκράτει, ἃς ἐνόμιζε θεάς, ὡς Ἀριστοφάνης κατηγορεῖ. ὁ γὰρ Ἄνυτος καὶ Μέλητος φθονοῦντες Σωκράτει καὶ μὴ δυνάμενοι ἄλλως βλάψαι ἢ φανερῶς κατηγορῆσαι μεγάλου ὄντος ἱκανὸν ἀργύριον δεδώκασιν Ἀριστοφάνει ταύτην τὴν κωμῳδίαν κατ' ἐκείνου γράψαι. τὰ δὲ πρόσωπα
20 Στρεψιάδης, Φειδιππίδης, μαθητὴς Σωκράτους, Σωκράτης, χορὸς Νεφελῶν, δίκαιος λόγος, ἄδικος λόγος, Πασίας δανειστής, μάρτυς.

VII

(ΑΡΙΣΤΟΦΑΝΟΥΣ ΓΡΑΜΜΑΤΙΚΟΥ)

Πατὴρ τὸν υἱὸν σωκρατίζειν βούλεται·
καὶ τῆς περὶ αὐτὸν ψυχρολογίας διατριβὴ
ἱκανή, λόγων ἀπόνοια πρὸς τοὐναντίον.
χορὸς δὲ Νεφελῶν ὡς ἐπωφελῆ λέγων,
5 καὶ τὴν ἀσέβειαν Σωκράτους διεξιών·
ἄλλαι θ' ὑπ' ἀνδρός...κατηγορίαι πικραί,
καὶ τῶν μαθητῶν εἰς πατραλοίας ἐκτόπως.
εἶτ' ἐμπυρισμὸς τῆς σχολῆς τοῦ Σωκράτους.

ΑΡΙΣΤΟΦΑΝΟΥΣ ΝΕΦΕΛΑΙ

ΣΤΡΕΨΙΑΔΗΣ. ΦΕΙΔΙΠΠΙΔΗΣ. ΘΕΡΑΠΩΝ

ΣΤ. Ἰοὺ ἰού·
ὦ Ζεῦ βασιλεῦ, τὸ χρῆμα τῶν νυκτῶν ὅσον·
ἀπέραντον. οὐδέποθ᾽ ἡμέρα γενήσεται;
καὶ μὴν πάλαι γ᾽ ἀλεκτρυόνος ἤκουσ᾽ ἐγώ.
οἱ δ᾽ οἰκέται ῥέγκουσιν· ἀλλ᾽ οὐκ ἂν πρὸ τοῦ. 5
ἀπόλοιο δῆτ᾽, ὦ πόλεμε, πολλῶν οὕνεκα,
ὅτ᾽ οὐδὲ κολάσ᾽ ἔξεστί μοι τοὺς οἰκέτας.
ἀλλ᾽ οὐδ᾽ ὁ χρηστὸς οὑτοσὶ νεανίας
ἐγείρεται τῆς νυκτός, ἀλλὰ πέρδεται
ἐν πέντε σισύραις ἐγκεκορδυλημένος. 10
ἀλλ᾽ εἰ δοκεῖ ῥέγκωμεν ἐγκεκαλυμμένοι.
ἀλλ᾽ οὐ δύναμαι δείλαιος εὕδειν δακνόμενος
ὑπὸ τῆς δαπάνης καὶ τῆς φάτνης καὶ τῶν χρεῶν
διὰ τουτονὶ τὸν υἱόν. ὁ δὲ κόμην ἔχων

2. ὅσον· ἀπέραντον A etc. Mein. Green Blaydes. ὅσον ἀπέραντον R Dind. al.
3. ἀπέραντον AR al. ἀπέρατον V.
7. κολάσ᾽ ἔξεστι GU al. Dind. Mein. Blaydes. κολάσαι ἔξεστι RV al. κολάσαι ᾽ξεστι A Gr.

ΑΡΙΣΤΟΦΑΝΟΥΣ

ἱππάζεταί τε καὶ ξυνωρικεύεται
ὀνειροπολεῖ θ' ἵππους· ἐγὼ δ' ἀπόλλυμαι
ὁρῶν ἄγουσαν τὴν σελήνην εἰκάδας·
οἱ γὰρ τόκοι χωροῦσιν. ἅπτε, παῖ, λύχνον,
κἄκφερε τὸ γραμματεῖον, ἵν' ἀναγνῶ λαβὼν
ὁπόσοις ὀφείλω καὶ λογίσωμαι τοὺς τόκους.
φέρ' ἴδω τί ὀφείλω; δώδεκα μνᾶς Πασίᾳ.
τοῦ δώδεκα μνᾶς Πασίᾳ; τί ἐχρησάμην;
ὅτ' ἐπριάμην τὸν κοππατίαν. οἴμοι τάλας,
εἴθ' ἐξεκόπην πρότερον τὸν ὀφθαλμὸν λίθῳ.
ΦΕ. Φίλων, ἀδικεῖς· ἔλαυνε τὸν σαυτοῦ δρόμον.
ΣΤ. τοῦτ' ἔστι τουτὶ τὸ κακόν, ὅ μ' ἀπολώλεκεν·
ὀνειροπολεῖ γὰρ καὶ καθεύδων ἱππικήν.
ΦΕ. πόσους δρόμους ἐλᾷ τὰ πολεμιστήρια;
ΣΤ. ἐμὲ μὲν σὺ πολλοὺς τὸν πατέρ' ἐλαύνεις δρόμους.
ἀτὰρ τί χρέος ἔβα με μετὰ τὸν Πασίαν;
τρεῖς μναῖ διφρίσκου καὶ τροχοῖν Ἀμυνίᾳ.
ΦΕ. ἄπαγε τὸν ἵππον ἐξαλίσας οἴκαδε.
ΣΤ. ἀλλ', ὦ μέλ', ἐξήλικας ἐμέ γ' ἐκ τῶν ἐμῶν,
ὅτε καὶ δίκας ὤφληκα, χἄτεροι τόκου
ἐνεχυράσεσθαί φασιν. ΦΕ. ἐτεόν, ὦ πάτερ,
τί δυσκολαίνεις καὶ στρέφει τὴν νύχθ' ὅλην;
ΣΤ. δάκνει μέ τις δήμαρχος ἐκ τῶν στρωμάτων.
ΦΕ. ἔασον, ὦ δαιμόνιε, καταδαρθεῖν τί με.
ΣΤ. σὺ δ' οὖν κάθευδε· τὰ δὲ χρέα ταῦτ' ἴσθ' ὅτι
ἐς τὴν κεφαλὴν ἅπαντα τὴν σὴν τρέψεται.

24. ἐξεκόπην libri Ko. Gr.   ἐξεκόπη Kust. Herm. Mein. al.
28. ἐλᾷ libri vulg.   ἐλᾷς Herm. prob. Mein.
35. ἐνεχυράσεσθαι U Mein. al.   ἐνεχυράσασθαι RV cet. Herm.
39. σὺ δ' οὖν R al.   σὺ μὲν οὖν V.
40. τρέψεται vulg.   στρέψεται V.   στρέψαί R.

ΝΕΦΕΛΑΙ 9

φεῦ.
εἴθ' ὤφελ' ἡ προμνήστρι' ἀπολέσθαι κακῶς,
ἥτις με γῆμ' ἐπῆρε τὴν σὴν μητέρα·
ἐμοὶ γὰρ ἦν ἄγροικος ἥδιστος βίος,
εὐρωτιῶν, ἀκόρητος, εἰκῆ κείμενος,
βρύων μελίτταις καὶ προβάτοις καὶ στεμφύλοις.
ἔπειτ' ἔγημα Μεγακλέους τοῦ Μεγακλέους 46
ἀδελφιδῆν ἄγροικος ὢν ἐξ ἄστεως,
σεμνήν, τρυφῶσαν, ἐγκεκοισυρωμένην.
ταύτην ὅτ' ἐγάμουν, ξυγκατεκλινόμην ἐγὼ
ὄζων τρυγός, τρασιᾶς, ἐρίων περιουσίας, 50
ἡ δ' αὖ μύρου, κρόκου, καταγλωττισμάτων,
δαπάνης, λαφυγμοῦ, Κωλιάδος, Γενετυλλίδος.
οὐ μὴν ἐρῶ γ' ὡς ἀργὸς ἦν, ἀλλ' ἐσπάθα.
ἐγὼ δ' ἂν αὐτῇ θοἰμάτιον δεικνὺς τοδὶ
πρόφασιν ἔφασκον, ὦ γύναι, λίαν σπαθᾷς. 55
ΘΕ. ἔλαιον ἡμῖν οὐκ ἔνεστ' ἐν τῷ λύχνῳ.
ΣΤ. οἴμοι· τί γάρ μοι τὸν πότην ἧπτες λύχνον;
δεῦρ' ἔλθ' ἵνα κλάῃς. ΘΕ. διὰ τί δῆτα κλαύσομαι;
ΣΤ. ὅτι τῶν παχειῶν ἐνετίθεις θρυαλλίδων.
μετὰ ταῦθ', ὅπως νῷν ἐγένεθ' υἱὸς οὑτοσί, 60
ἐμοί τε δὴ καὶ τῇ γυναικὶ τἀγαθῇ,
περὶ τοὐνόματος δὴ 'νταῦθ' ἐλοιδορούμεθα·
ἡ μὲν γὰρ ἵππον προσετίθει πρὸς τοὔνομα,

47. ἄστεως Dind. al. ἄστεος libri.
50. ἐρίων περιουσίας vulg. ἐρίων, περιουσίας Reisk. σιρῶν, ἐριουργίας Naber.
61. ἐμοί τε δὴ καὶ τῇ vulg. ἐμοί τε καὶ τἠμῇ Blaydes.
62. δὴ 'νταῦθ' Reisig Seager Blaydes. δὴ ταῦτ' AG al.
δ' ἠντεῦθεν R. δὴν ἐντεῦθεν V. δὴ 'ντεῦθεν Herm. Dind. al.

Ξάνθιππον ἢ Χαίριππον ἢ Καλλιππίδην,
ἐγὼ δὲ τὸ τοῦ πάππου 'τιθέμην Φειδωνίδην. 65
τέως μὲν οὖν ἐκρινόμεθ'· εἶτα τῷ χρόνῳ
κοινῇ ξυνέβημεν καθέμεθα Φειδιππίδην.
τοῦτον τὸν υἱὸν λαμβάνουσ' ἐκορίζετο,
ὅταν σὺ μέγας ὢν ἅρμ' ἐλαύνῃς πρὸς πόλιν,
ὥσπερ Μεγακλέης, ξυστίδ' ἔχων. ἐγὼ δ' ἔφην,
ὅταν μὲν οὖν τὰς αἶγας ἐκ τοῦ φελλέως, 71
ὥσπερ ὁ πατήρ σου, διφθέραν ἐνημμένος.
ἀλλ' οὐκ ἐπίθετο τοῖς ἐμοῖς οὐδὲν λόγοις,
ἀλλ' ἵππερόν μου κατέχεεν τῶν χρημάτων.
νῦν οὖν ὅλην τὴν νύκτα φροντίζων ὁδοῦ 75
μίαν εὗρον ἀτραπὸν δαιμονίως ὑπερφυᾶ,
ἢν ἢν ἀναπείσω τουτονί, σωθήσομαι.
ἀλλ' ἐξεγεῖραι πρῶτον αὐτὸν βούλομαι.
πῶς δῆτ' ἂν ἥδιστ' αὐτὸν ἐπεγείραιμι; πῶς;
Φειδιππίδη, Φειδιππίδιον. ΦΕ. τί ὦ πάτερ; 80
ΣΤ. κύσον με καὶ τὴν χεῖρα δὸς τὴν δεξιάν.
ΦΕ. ἰδού. τί ἔστιν; ΣΤ. εἰπέ μοι, φιλεῖς ἐμέ;
ΦΕ. νὴ τὸν Ποσειδῶ τουτονὶ τὸν ἵππιον.
ΣΤ. μή μοί γε τοῦτον μηδαμῶς τὸν ἵππιον·
οὗτος γὰρ ὁ θεὸς αἴτιός μοι τῶν κακῶν. 85
ἀλλ' εἴπερ ἐκ τῆς καρδίας μ' ὄντως φιλεῖς,
ὦ παῖ, πιθοῦ. ΦΕ. τί οὖν πίθωμαι δῆτά σοι;

64. Χαίριππον V Bergk Blaydes Gr. Χάριππον AG al. Dind. al.
Χάλιππον R.
65. τὸ τοῦ πάππου Cobet. τοῦ πάππου vulg.
74. ἵππερον vulg. Herm. Ko. Teuf. Blaydes. ἵππερων Dind.
Mein.
75. ὁδοῦ, μίαν A al. Herm. Mein. Ko. Teuf. φροντίζων, ὁδοῦ G
Reis. Dind. Green.
87. πιθοῦ AUV al. πιθοῦ μοι RS al. τί οὖν πίθωμαι Bodl. 6.

ΝΕΦΕΛΑΙ 11

ΣΤ. ἔκστρεψον ὡς τάχιστα τοὺς σαυτοῦ τρόπους,
καὶ μάνθαν' ἐλθὼν ἂν ἐγὼ παραινέσω.
ΦΕ. λέγε δή, τί κελεύεις; ΣΤ. καί τι πείσει;
ΦΕ. πείσομαι 90
νὴ τὸν Διόνυσον. ΣΤ. δεῦρό νυν ἀπόβλεπε.
ὁρᾷς τὸ θύριον τοῦτο καὶ τᾠκίδιον;
ΦΕ. ὁρῶ. τί οὖν τοῦτ' ἐστὶν ἐτεόν, ὦ πάτερ;
ΣΤ. ψυχῶν σοφῶν τοῦτ' ἐστὶ φροντιστήριον.
ἐνταῦθ' ἐνοικοῦσ' ἄνδρες, οἳ τὸν οὐρανὸν 95
λέγοντες ἀναπείθουσιν ὡς ἔστιν πνιγεύς,
κἄστιν περὶ ἡμᾶς οὗτος, ἡμεῖς δ' ἄνθρακες.
οὗτοι διδάσκουσ', ἀργύριον ἤν τις διδῷ,
λέγοντα νικᾶν καὶ δίκαια κἄδικα.
ΦΕ. εἰσὶν δὲ τίνες; ΣΤ. οὐκ οἶδ' ἀκριβῶς τοὔνομα·
μεριμνοφροντισταὶ καλοί τε κἀγαθοί. 101
ΦΕ. αἰβοῖ πονηροί γ', οἶδα. τοὺς ἀλαζόνας,
τοὺς ὠχριῶντας, τοὺς ἀνυποδήτους λέγεις·
ὧν ὁ κακοδαίμων Σωκράτης καὶ Χαιρεφῶν.
ΣΤ. ἢ ἢ σιώπα· μηδὲν εἴπῃς νήπιον. 105
ἀλλ', εἴ τι κήδει τῶν πατρῴων ἀλφίτων,
τούτων γενοῦ μοι σχασάμενος τὴν ἱππικήν.
ΦΕ. οὐκ ἂν μὰ τὸν Διόνυσον, εἰ δοίης γέ μοι
τοὺς φασιανοὺς οὓς τρέφει Λεωγόρας.
ΣΤ. ἴθ' ἀντιβολῶ σ', ὦ φίλτατ' ἀνθρώπων ἐμοί, 110
ἐλθὼν διδάσκου. ΦΕ. καὶ τί σοι μαθήσομαι;
ΣΤ. εἶναι παρ' αὐτοῖς φασὶν ἄμφω τὼ λόγω,

πιθοῦμαι STV. τί οὖν πείθομαι RST al. ὦ παῖ, πιθοῦ. ΦΕ. τί οὖν
πίθωμαι; Dawes, Herm. Dind. Blaydes. ὦ παῖ, πιθοῦ μοι. ΦΕ. τί δὲ
πίθωμαι; C. F. Herm. Bergk Kock.
90. καί τι vulg. κᾆτα Elmsl. Cobet. καὶ σύ F. W. Schmidt.
104. deest in R et revera emblema sapit.

ΑΡΙΣΤΟΦΑΝΟΥΣ

τὸν κρείττον᾽, ὅστις ἐστί, καὶ τὸν ἥττονα.
τούτοιν τὸν ἕτερον τοῖν λόγοιν, τὸν ἥττονα,
νικᾶν λέγοντά φασι τἀδικώτερα. 115
ἢν οὖν μάθῃς μοι τὸν ἄδικον τοῦτον λόγον,
ἃ νῦν ὀφείλω διὰ σέ, τούτων τῶν χρεῶν
οὐκ ἂν ἀποδοίην οὐδ᾽ ἂν ὀβολὸν οὐδενί.
ΦΕ. οὐκ ἂν πιθοίμην· οὐ γὰρ ἂν τλαίην ἰδεῖν
τοὺς ἱππέας τὸ χρῶμα διακεκναισμένος. 120
ΣΤ. οὔκ ἄρα μὰ τὴν Δήμητρα τῶν γ᾽ ἐμῶν ἔδει,
οὔτ᾽ αὐτὸς οὔθ᾽ ὁ ζύγιος οὔθ᾽ ὁ σαμφόρας·
ἀλλ᾽ ἐξελῶ σ᾽ ἐς κόρακας ἐκ τῆς οἰκίας.
ΦΕ. ἀλλ᾽ οὐ περιόψεταί μ᾽ ὁ θεῖος Μεγακλέης
ἄνιππον ὄντ᾽. ἀλλ᾽ εἶμι, σοῦ δ᾽ οὐ φροντιῶ. 125
ΣΤ. ἀλλ᾽ οὐδ᾽ ἐγὼ μέντοι πεσών γε κείσομαι·
ἀλλ᾽ εὐξάμενος τοῖσιν θεοῖς διδάξομαι
αὐτὸς βαδίζων ἐς τὸ φροντιστήριον.
πῶς οὖν γέρων ὢν κἀπιλήσμων καὶ βραδὺς
λόγων ἀκριβῶν σχινδαλάμους μαθήσομαι; 130
ἰτητέον. τί ταῦτ᾽ ἔχων στραγγεύομαι,
ἀλλ᾽ οὐχὶ κόπτω τὴν θύραν; παῖ, παιδίον.

ΜΑΘΗΤΗΣ

βάλλ᾽ ἐς κόρακας, τίς ἐσθ᾽ ὁ κόψας τὴν θύραν;
ΣΤ. Φείδωνος υἱὸς Στρεψιάδης Κικυννόθεν.
ΜΛ. ἀμαθής γε νὴ Δί᾽, ὅστις οὑτωσὶ σφόδρα 135
ἀπεριμερίμνως τὴν θύραν λελάκτικας

115. τἀδικώτερα RV plures libri. τἀδικώτατα U al.; cf. 657.
121. οὐκ ἄρα vulg. οὔτἄρα Cobet.
125. ἄνιππον ὄντ᾽· ἀλλ᾽ εἶμι Cobet (εἶμι Bodl. 7). ἄνιππον· ἀλλ᾽
εἴσειμι libri vulg.

ΝΕΦΕΛΑΙ

  καὶ φροντίδ' ἐξήμβλωκας ἐξηυρημένην.
ΣΤ. σύγγνωθί μοι· τηλοῦ γὰρ οἰκῶ τῶν ἀγρῶν.
  ἀλλ' εἰπέ μοι τὸ πρᾶγμα τοὐξημβλωμένον.
ΜΑ. ἀλλ' οὐ θέμις πλὴν τοῖς μαθηταῖσιν λέγειν. 140
ΣΤ. λέγε νυν ἐμοὶ θαρρῶν· ἐγὼ γὰρ οὑτοσὶ
  ἥκω μαθητὴς ἐς τὸ φροντιστήριον.
ΜΑ. λέξω. νομίσαι δὲ ταῦτα χρὴ μυστήρια.
  ἀνήρετ' ἄρτι Χαιρεφῶντα Σωκράτης
  ψύλλαν ὁπόσους ἄλλοιτο τοὺς αὐτῆς πόδας· 145
  δακοῦσα γὰρ τοῦ Χαιρεφῶντος τὴν ὀφρὺν
  ἐπὶ τὴν κεφαλὴν τὴν Σωκράτους ἀφήλατο.
ΣΤ. πῶς δῆτα τοῦτ' ἐμέτρησε; ΜΑ. δεξιώτατα.
  κηρὸν διατήξας εἶτα τὴν ψύλλαν λαβὼν
  ἐνέβαψεν ἐς τὸν κηρὸν αὐτῆς τὼ πόδε, 150
  κᾆτα ψυχεῖσι περιέφυσαν περσικαί.
  ταύτας ὑπολύσας ἀνεμέτρει τὸ χωρίον.
ΣΤ. ὦ Ζεῦ βασιλεῦ, τῆς λεπτότητος τῶν φρενῶν.
ΜΑ. τί δῆτ' ἄν, ἕτερον εἰ πύθοιο Σωκράτους
  φρόντισμα; ΣΤ. ποῖον; ἀντιβολῶ, κάτειπέ μοι.
ΜΑ. ἀνήρετ' αὐτὸν Χαιρεφῶν ὁ Σφήττιος 156
  ὁπότερα τὴν γνώμην ἔχοι, τὰς ἐμπίδας
  κατὰ τὸ στόμ' ᾄδειν ἢ κατὰ τοὐρροπύγιον.
ΣΤ. τί δῆτ' ἐκεῖνος εἶπε περὶ τῆς ἐμπίδος;
ΜΑ. ἔφασκεν εἶναι τοὔντερον τῆς ἐμπίδος 160
  στενόν· διὰ λεπτοῦ δ' ὄντος αὐτοῦ τὴν πνοὴν

  137. ἐξηυρημένην Mein. Hold. Blaydes. ἐξευρημένην libri et vulg.
  148. τοῦτ' ἐμέτρησε V al. libri vulg. τοῦτο διεμέτρησε R. διεμέτρησε (sine τοῦτο) A al. libri Teuf. Hold. Blaydes. τοῦτο δὴ 'μέτρησε Cobet Kock Mein.
  151. ψυχεῖσι Blaydes. ψυχείσῃ Dind. Hold. ψυγείσῃ vulg.; vid. com.
  157. ἔχοι R al. ἔχει AG al.

ΑΡΙΣΤΟΦΑΝΟΥΣ

βία βαδίζειν εὐθὺ τοὐρροπυγίου·
ἔπειτα κοῖλον πρὸς στενῷ προσκείμενον
τὸν πρωκτὸν ἠχεῖν ὑπὸ βίας τοῦ πνεύματος.
ΣΤ. σάλπιγξ ὁ πρωκτός ἐστιν ἄρα τῶν ἐμπίδων. 165
ὢ τρισμακάριος τοῦ διεντερεύματος.
ἢ ῥᾳδίως φεύγων ἂν ἀποφύγοι δίκην
ὅστις δίοιδε τοὔντερον τῆς ἐμπίδος.
ΜΑ. πρώην δέ γε γνώμην μεγάλην ἀφῃρέθη
ὑπ' ἀσκαλαβώτου. ΣΤ. τίνα τρόπον; κάτειπέ
μοι. 170
ΜΑ. ζητοῦντος αὐτοῦ τῆς σελήνης τὰς ὁδοὺς
καὶ τὰς περιφοράς, εἶτ' ἄνω κεχηνότος,
ἀπὸ τῆς ὀροφῆς νύκτωρ γαλεώτης κατέχεσεν.
ΣΤ. ἥσθην γαλεώτῃ καταχέσαντι Σωκράτους.
ΜΑ. ἐχθὲς δέ γ' ἡμῖν δεῖπνον οὐκ ἦν ἑσπέρας. 175
ΣΤ. εἶεν· τί οὖν πρὸς τἄλφιτ' ἐπαλαμήσατο;
ΜΑ. κατὰ τῆς τραπέζης καταπάσας λεπτὴν τέφραν,
κάμψας ὀβελίσκον, εἶτα διαβήτην λαβών,
ἐκ τῆς παλαίστρας θυμάτιον ὑφείλετο.
ΣΤ. τί δῆτ' ἐκεῖνον τὸν Θαλῆν θαυμάζομεν; 180
ἄνοιγ' ἄνοιγ' ἀνύσας τὸ φροντιστήριον,
καὶ δεῖξον ὡς τάχιστά μοι τὸν Σωκράτη·
μαθητιῶ γάρ· ἀλλ' ἄνοιγε τὴν θύραν.
ὦ Ἡράκλεις, ταυτὶ ποδαπὰ τὰ θηρία;
ΜΑ. τί ἐθαύμασας; τῷ σοι δοκοῦσιν εἰκέναι; 185
ΣΤ. τοῖς ἐκ Πύλου ληφθεῖσι, τοῖς Λακωνικοῖς.
ἀτὰρ τί ποτ' ἐς τὴν γῆν βλέπουσιν οὑτοιί;

179. θυμάτιον Herm. plerique edd. θοἰμάτιον libri. θοινημάτιον Bergk.
182. Σωκράτη Mein. Dind. al. Σωκράτην plerique libri; vid. com.
185. εἰκέναι SV edd. ἐοικέναι plerique libri.

ΝΕΦΕΛΑΙ 15

ΜΑ. ζητοῦσιν οὗτοι τὰ κατὰ γῆς. ΣΤ. βολβοὺς ἄρα
ζητοῦσι. μή νυν τουτογὶ φροντίζετε·
ἐγὼ γὰρ οἶδ' ἵν' εἰσὶ μεγάλοι καὶ καλοί. 190
τί γὰρ οἵδε δρῶσιν οἱ σφόδρ' ἐγκεκυφότες;
ΜΑ. οὗτοί γ' ἐρεβοδιφῶσιν ὑπὸ τὸν Τάρταρον.
ΣΤ. τί δῆθ' ὁ πρωκτὸς ἐς τὸν οὐρανὸν βλέπει;
ΜΑ. αὐτὸς καθ' αὑτὸν ἀστρονομεῖν διδάσκεται.
ἀλλ' εἴσιθ', ἵνα μὴ 'κεῖνος ὑμῖν ἐπιτύχῃ. 195
ΣΤ. μήπω γε μήπω γ'· ἀλλ' ἐπιμεινάντων, ἵνα
αὐτοῖσι κοινώσω τι πραγμάτιον ἐμόν.
ΜΑ. ἀλλ' οὐχ οἷόν τ' αὐτοῖσι πρὸς τὸν ἀέρα
ἔξω διατρίβειν πολὺν ἄγαν ἐστὶν χρόνον.
ΣΤ. πρὸς τῶν θεῶν, τί γὰρ τάδ' ἐστίν; εἰπέ μοι. 200
ΜΑ. ἀστρονομία μὲν αὐτηί. ΣΤ. τουτὶ δὲ τί;
ΜΑ. γεωμετρία. ΣΤ. τοῦτ' οὖν τί ἐστι χρήσιμον;
ΜΑ. γῆν ἀναμετρεῖσθαι. ΣΤ. πότερα τὴν κληρουχικήν;
ΜΑ. οὔκ, ἀλλὰ τὴν σύμπασαν. ΣΤ. ἀστεῖον λέγεις.
τὸ γὰρ σόφισμα δημοτικὸν καὶ χρήσιμον. 205
ΜΑ. αὕτη δέ σοι γῆς περίοδος πάσης. ὁρᾷς;
αἵδε μὲν Ἀθῆναι. ΣΤ. τί σὺ λέγεις; οὐ πείθομαι,
ἐπεὶ δικαστὰς οὐχ ὁρῶ καθημένους.
ΜΑ. ὡς τοῦτ' ἀληθῶς Ἀττικὸν τὸ χωρίον.
ΣΤ. καὶ ποῦ Κικυννῆς εἰσὶν οὑμοὶ δημόται; 210
ΜΑ. ἐνταῦθ' ἔνεισιν. ἡ δέ γ' Εὔβοι', ὡς ὁρᾷς,

189. τουτογί Pors. Dind. Mein. Blaydes. τοῦτό γε MR al. τοῦτ'
ἔτι AV al. τοῦτό γ' ἔτι Reisig Herm. Kock al.
192. γ' ACV al. δ' GR al.
195. ὑμῖν Bergk Kock Mein. al. ἡμῖν vulg.
203. ἀναμετρεῖσθαι libri. ἀναμετρῆσαι Cobet frustra, vid. Blaydes.

ἡδὶ παρατέταται μακρὰ πόρρω πάνυ.
ΣΤ. οἶδ'· ὑπὸ γὰρ ἡμῶν παρετάθη καὶ Περικλέους.
ἀλλ' ἡ Λακεδαίμων ποῦ 'στιν; ΜΑ. ὅπου 'στίν;
αὑτηί.
ΣΤ. ὡς ἐγγὺς ἡμῶν. τοῦτο πάνυ φροντίζετε, 215
ταύτην ἀφ' ἡμῶν ἀπαγαγεῖν πόρρω πάνυ.
ΜΑ. ἀλλ' οὐχ οἷόν τε. ΣΤ. νὴ Δί' οἰμώξεσθ' ἄρα.
φέρε τίς γὰρ οὗτος οὑπὶ τῆς κρεμάθρας ἀνήρ;
ΜΑ. αὐτός. ΣΤ. τίς αὐτός; ΜΑ. Σωκράτης. ΣΤ.
ὦ Σώκρατες.
ἴθ' οὗτος, ἀναβόησον αὐτόν μοι μέγα. 220
ΜΑ. αὐτὸς μὲν οὖν σὺ κάλεσον· οὐ γάρ μοι σχολή.
ΣΤ. ὦ Σώκρατες,
ὦ Σωκρατίδιον.

ΣΩΚΡΑΤΗΣ
τί με καλεῖς ὦφήμερε;
ΣΤ. πρῶτον μὲν ὅ τι δρᾷς, ἀντιβολῶ, κάτειπέ μοι.
ΣΩ. ἀεροβατῶ καὶ περιφρονῶ τὸν ἥλιον. 225
ΣΤ. ἔπειτ' ἀπὸ ταρροῦ τοὺς θεοὺς ὑπερφρονεῖς,
ἀλλ' οὐκ ἀπὸ τῆς γῆς, εἴπερ; ΣΩ. οὐ γὰρ ἄν ποτε
ἐξηῦρον ὀρθῶς τὰ μετέωρα πράγματα,
εἰ μὴ κρεμάσας τὸ νόημα καὶ τὴν φροντίδα
λεπτὴν καταμίξας ἐς τὸν ὅμοιον ἀέρα. 230
εἰ δ' ὦν χαμαὶ τἄνω κάτωθεν ἐσκόπουν,
οὐκ ἄν ποθ' ηὗρον· οὐ γὰρ ἀλλ' ἡ γῆ βίᾳ

215. πάνυ AR al. Kock Mein. Blaydes. πάλιν V. μέγα Δ Herm.
Teuf. μεταφροντίζετε Bentl.
226. ὑπερφρονεῖς libri et vulg. σὺ περιφρονεῖς Blaydes.
232. ηὗρον Dind. Mein. Blaydes. εὗρον vulg.

ΝΕΦΕΛΑΙ

ἕλκει πρὸς αὑτὴν τὴν ἰκμάδα τῆς φροντίδος.
πάσχει δὲ ταὐτὸ τοῦτο καὶ τὰ κάρδαμα.
ΣΤ. τί φῄς; 235
ἡ φροντὶς ἕλκει τὴν ἰκμάδ' ἐς τὰ κάρδαμα;
ἴθι νυν κατάβηθ', ὦ Σωκρατίδιον, ὡς ἐμέ,
ἵνα με διδάξῃς ὦνπερ ἕνεκ' ἐλήλυθα.
ΣΩ. ἦλθες δὲ κατὰ τί; ΣΤ. βουλόμενος μαθεῖν λέγειν.
ὑπὸ γὰρ τόκων χρήστων τε δυσκολωτάτων 240
ἄγομαι, φέρομαι, τὰ χρήματ' ἐνεχυράζομαι.
ΣΩ. πόθεν δ' ὑπόχρεως σαυτὸν ἔλαθες γενόμενος;
ΣΤ. νόσος μ' ἐπέτριψεν ἱππικὴ δεινὴ φαγεῖν.
ἀλλά με δίδαξον τὸν ἕτερον τοῖν σοῖν λόγοιν,
τὸν μηδὲν ἀποδιδόντα. μισθὸν δ' ὅντιν' ἂν 245
πράττῃ μ' ὀμοῦμαί σοι καταθήσειν τοὺς θεούς.
ΣΩ. ποίους θεοὺς ὀμεῖ σύ; πρῶτον γὰρ θεοὶ
ἡμῖν νόμισμ' οὐκ ἔστι. ΣΤ. τῷ γὰρ ὄμνυτ'; ἢ
σιδαρέοισιν ὥσπερ ἐν Βυζαντίῳ;
ΣΩ. βούλει τὰ θεῖα πράγματ' εἰδέναι σαφῶς 250
ἅττ' ἐστὶν ὀρθῶς; ΣΤ. νὴ Δί', εἴπερ ἔστι γε.
ΣΩ. καὶ ξυγγενέσθαι ταῖς νεφέλαισιν ἐς λόγους,
ταῖς ἡμετέραισι δαίμοσιν; ΣΤ. μάλιστά γε.
ΣΩ. κάθιζε τοίνυν ἐπὶ τὸν ἱερὸν σκίμποδα.
ΣΤ. ἰδοὺ κάθημαι. ΣΩ. τουτονὶ τοίνυν λαβὲ 255
τὸν στέφανον. ΣΤ. ἐπὶ τί στέφανον; οἴμοι,
Σώκρατες,
ὥσπερ με τὸν Ἀθάμανθ' ὅπως μὴ θύσετε.
ΣΩ. οὔκ, ἀλλὰ ταῦτα πάντα τοὺς τελουμένους

238. ἵνα με διδάξῃς GR al. edd. ἵνα μ' ἐκδιδάξῃς complures libr. Herm. Bergk.
248. τῷ γὰρ ὄμνυτ'; ἢ vulg. τῷ νόμιζετ'; ἢ conj. Göttling; vid. com.
251. ὀρθῶς vulg. ὄντως Herw.
258. ταῦτα πάντα libri vulg. πάντας ταῦτα Reisk. al.

ΑΡΙΣΤΟΦΑΝΟΥΣ

ἡμεῖς ποιοῦμεν. ΣΤ. εἶτα δὴ τί κερδανῶ;
ΣΩ. λέγειν γενήσει τρίμμα κρόταλον παιπάλη. 260
ἀλλ' ἔχ' ἀτρεμεί. ΣΤ. μὰ τὸν Δί' οὐ ψεύσει γέ με·
καταπαττόμενος γὰρ παιπάλη γενήσομαι.
ΣΩ. εὐφημεῖν χρὴ τὸν πρεσβύτην καὶ τῆς εὐχῆς
ἐπακούειν.
ὦ δέσποτ' ἄναξ ἀμέτρητ' ἀήρ, ὃς ἔχεις τὴν γῆν
μετέωρον,
λαμπρός τ' αἰθήρ, σεμναί τε θεαὶ νεφέλαι βροντη-
σικέραυνοι, 265
ἄρθητε φάνητ', ὦ δέσποιναι, τῷ φροντιστῇ με-
τέωροι.
ΣΤ. μήπω μήπω γε πρὶν ἂν τουτὶ πτύξωμαι, μὴ
καταβρεχθῶ.
τὸ δὲ μηδὲ κυνῆν οἴκοθεν ἐλθεῖν ἐμὲ τὸν κακο-
δαίμον' ἔχοντα.
ΣΩ. ἔλθετε δῆτ', ὦ πολυτίμητοι νεφέλαι, τῷδ' εἰς
ἐπίδειξιν·
εἴτ' ἐπ' Ὀλύμπου κορυφαῖς ἱεραῖς χιονοβλήτοισι
κάθησθε, 270
εἴτ' Ὠκεανοῦ πατρὸς ἐν κήποις ἱερὸν χορὸν
ἵστατε νύμφαις,
εἴτ' ἄρα Νείλου προχοαῖς ὑδάτων χρυσέαις ἀρύτεσθε πρόχοισιν,

261. ἀτρεμεί Herm. al. ἀτρέμας vulg. ἀτρεμί R Dind.
263. ἐπακούειν RV Dind. al. ὑπακούειν AG al.
268. μηδὲ κυνῆν Herm. Dind. al. μὴ κυνῆν libri. μὴ κινέην
Bentl. Blaydes ; vid. com.
272. Νείλου· Νείλου 'ν Mein. Blaydes. προχοαῖς R vulg. προχοὰς
V Dind. χρυσέαις RV al. χρυσέοις aliquot libri. ἀρύτεσθε Herm.
Dind. Blaydes. ἀρύεσθε R vulg. πρόχοισιν Herm. Mein. al. προχόοισιν RV al. πρόχουσιν aliquot libri.

ΝΕΦΕΛΑΙ 19

ἢ Μαιῶτιν λίμνην ἔχετ᾽ ἢ σκόπελον νιφόεντα
Μίμαντος·
ὑπακούσατε δεξάμεναι θυσίαν καὶ τοῖς ἱεροῖσι
χαρεῖσαι.

ΧΟΡΟΣ
Strophe (275—290)
ἀέναοι Νεφέλαι, 275
ἀρθῶμεν φανεραὶ δροσερὰν φύσιν εὐάγητον,
πατρὸς ἀπ᾽ ὠκεανοῦ βαρναχέος
ὑψηλῶν ὀρέων κορυφὰς ἐπὶ
δενδροκόμους, ἵνα 280
τηλεφανεῖς σκοπιὰς ἀφορώμεθα,
καρπούς τ᾽ ἀρδομέναν ἱερὰν χθόνα,
καὶ ποταμῶν ζαθέων κελαδήματα,
καὶ πόντον κελάδοντα βαρύβρομον·
ὄμμα γὰρ αἰθέρος ἀκάματον σελαγεῖται 285
μαρμαρέαισιν αὐγαῖς.
ἀλλ᾽ ἀποσεισάμεναι νέφος ὄμβριον
ἀθανάτας ἰδέας ἐπιδώμεθα
τηλεσκόπῳ ὄμματι γαῖαν. 290
ΣΩ. ὦ μέγα σεμναὶ νεφέλαι, φανερῶς ἠκούσατέ μου
καλέσαντος.
ἤσθου φωνῆς ἅμα καὶ βροντῆς μυκησαμένης
θεοσέπτου;
οὐ μὴ σκώψει μηδὲ ποιήσεις ἅπερ οἱ τρυγοδαίμονες οὗτοι;
ἀλλ᾽ εὐφήμει· μέγα γάρ τι θεῶν κινεῖται σμῆνος
ἀοιδαῖς. 297

274. ὑπακούσατε AV al. Kock Cobet Blaydes. ουπακουσατε R.
ἐπακούσατε aliquot libri Dind. Mein. al. χαρεῖσαι R. φανεῖσαι V.
289. ἀθανάτας ἰδέας R Dind. Mein. al. ἀθανάταις ἰδέαις plur. libri.
296. σκώψει· σκώψῃς...ποιήσῃς libri.

2—2

Antistrophe (299—313)

ΧΟ. παρθένοι ὀμβροφόροι,
ἔλθωμεν λιπαρὰν χθόνα Παλλάδος, εὔανδρον
   γᾶν   300
Κέκροπος ὀψόμεναι πολυήρατον·
οὗ σέβας ἀρρήτων ἱερῶν, ἵνα
μυστοδόκος δόμος
ἐν τελεταῖς ἁγίαις ἀναδείκνυται,
οὐρανίοις τε θεοῖς δωρήματα,   305
ναοί θ' ὑψερεφεῖς καὶ ἀγάλματα,
καὶ πρόσοδοι μακάρων ἱερώταται,
εὐστέφανοί τε θεῶν θυσίαι θαλίαι τε,
παντοδαπαῖς ἐν ὥραις,   310
ἦρί τ' ἐπερχομένῳ Βρομία χάρις,
εὐκελάδων τε χορῶν ἐρεθίσματα,
καὶ μοῦσα βαρύβρομος αὐλῶν.

ΣΤ. πρὸς τοῦ Διὸς ἀντιβολῶ σε, φράσον, τίνες εἴσ',
   ὦ Σώκρατες, αὗται
αἱ φθεγξάμεναι τοῦτο τὸ σεμνόν; μῶν ἡρῶναί
   τινές εἰσιν;   315

ΣΩ. ἥκιστ', ἀλλ' οὐράνιαι νεφέλαι, μεγάλαι θεαὶ
   ἀνδράσιν ἀργοῖς·
αἵπερ γνώμην καὶ διάλεξιν καὶ νοῦν ἡμῖν παρέ-
   χουσιν,
καὶ τερατείαν καὶ περίλεξιν καὶ κροῦσιν καὶ
   κατάληψιν.

ΣΤ. ταῦτ' ἄρ' ἀκούσασ' αὐτῶν τὸ φθέγμ' ἡ ψυχή
   μου πεπότηται,

306. ὑψερεφεῖς· ὑψηρεφεῖς R.
307. πρόσοδοι· πρόδομοι RV.
310. παντοδαπαῖς ἐν· παντοδαπαῖσιν Blaydes.

καὶ λεπτολογεῖν ἤδη ζητεῖ καὶ περὶ καπνοῦ
στενολεσχεῖν, 320
καὶ γνωμιδίῳ γνώμην νύξασ' ἑτέρῳ λόγῳ ἀντι-
λογῆσαι·
ὥστ' εἴ πως ἔστιν ἰδεῖν αὐτὰς ἤδη φανερὰς
ἐπιθυμῶ.

ΣΩ. βλέπε νυν δευρὶ πρὸς τὴν Πάρνηθ'· ἤδη γὰρ
ὁρῶ κατιούσας
ἡσυχῇ αὐτάς. ΣΤ. φέρε ποῦ; δεῖξον. ΣΩ.
χωροῦσ' αὗται πάνυ πολλαὶ
διὰ τῶν κοίλων καὶ τῶν δασέων, αὗται πλάγιαι.
ΣΤ. τί τὸ χρῆμα; 325
ὡς οὐ καθορῶ. ΣΩ. παρὰ τὴν εἴσοδον. ΣΤ.
ἤδη νυνὶ μόλις οὕτως.

ΣΩ. νῦν γέ τοι ἤδη καθορᾷς αὐτάς, εἰ μὴ λημᾷς
κολοκύνταις.

ΣΤ. νὴ Δί' ἔγωγ', ὦ πολυτίμητοι. πάντα γὰρ ἤδη
κατέχουσιν.

ΣΩ. ταύτας μέντοι σὺ θεὰς οὔσας οὐκ ᾔδησθ' οὐδ'
ἐνόμιζες;

ΣΤ. μὰ Δί', ἀλλ' ὁμίχλην καὶ δρόσον αὐτὰς ἡγούμην
καὶ καπνὸν εἶναι. 330

ΣΩ. οὐ γὰρ μὰ Δί' οἶσθ' ὁτιὴ πλείστους αὗται βόσκουσι σοφιστάς,
θουριομάντεις ἰατροτέχνας σφραγιδονυχαργοκο-
μήτας,

324. ἡσυχῇ αὐτάς Dind. Mein. al. ἥσυχος (vel -ως) αὐτὰς vel ἥσυχα ταύτας libri.
326. παρά· πρός nonnulli libri. οὕτως Herm. Dind. al. ὁρῶ libri.
329. ᾔδησθ' Cob. Mein. al. ᾔδεις vel ᾔδης libri.
330. καπνόν· σκιάν R al.
331. οἶσθ' ὁτιή· ἀλλ' ἴσθ' ὅτι Herm. Mein. al.

ΑΡΙΣΤΟΦΑΝΟΥΣ

κυκλίων τε χορῶν ἀσματοκάμπτας, ἄνδρας μετεωροφένακας,
οὐδὲν δρῶντας βόσκουσ᾽ ἀργούς, ὅτι ταύτας μουσοποιοῦσιν.
ΣΤ. ταῦτ᾽ ἄρ᾽ ἐποίουν ὑγρᾶν νεφελᾶν στρεπταίγλαν δάϊον ὁρμάν, 335
πλοκάμους θ᾽ ἑκατογκεφάλα Τυφῶ, πρημαινούσας τε θυέλλας,
εἶτ᾽ ἀερίας διερὰς, γαμψοὺς οἰωνοὺς ἀερονηχεῖς,
ὄμβρους θ᾽ ὑδάτων δροσερᾶν νεφελᾶν· εἶτ᾽ ἀντ᾽ αὐτῶν κατέπινον
κεστρᾶν τεμάχη μεγαλᾶν ἀγαθᾶν κρέα τ᾽ ὀρνίθεια κιχηλᾶν.
ΣΩ. διὰ μέντοι τάσδ᾽· οὐχὶ δικαίως; ΣΤ. λέξον δή μοι, τί παθοῦσαι, 340
εἴπερ νεφέλαι γ᾽ εἰσὶν ἀληθῶς, θνηταῖς εἴξασι γυναιξίν;
οὐ γὰρ ἐκεῖναί γ᾽ εἰσὶ τοιαῦται. ΣΩ. φέρε ποῖαι γάρ τινές εἰσιν;
ΣΤ. οὐκ οἶδα σαφῶς· εἴξασιν δ᾽ οὖν ἐρίοισιν πεπταμένοισιν,
κοὐχὶ γυναιξὶν μὰ Δί᾽ οὐδ᾽ ὁτιοῦν· αὗται δὲ ῥῖνας ἔχουσιν.
ΣΩ. ἀπόκριναί νυν ἅττ᾽ ἂν ἔρωμαι. ΣΤ. λέγε νυν ταχέως ὅ τι βούλει. 345
ΣΩ. ἤδη ποτ᾽ ἀναβλέψας εἶδες νεφέλην Κενταύρῳ ὁμοίαν

335. στρεπταίγλαν· στρεπταιγλᾶν Herm. Mein.
340. τάσδ᾽· οὐχί· τάσδ᾽ οὐχί vulgo.
343. δ᾽ οὖν R. γοῦν V al.

ΝΕΦΕΛΑΙ 23

  ἢ παρδάλει ἢ λύκῳ ἢ ταύρῳ; ΣΤ. νὴ Δί' ἔγωγ'.
  εἶτα τί τοῦτο;
ΣΩ. γίγνονται πάνθ' ὅ τι βούλονται· κᾆτ' ἢν μὲν
  ἴδωσι κομήτην
  ἄγριόν τινα τῶν λασίων τούτων, οἷόνπερ τὸν
  Ξενοφάντου,
  σκώπτουσαι τὴν μανίαν αὐτοῦ Κενταύροις ἤκα-
  σαν αὐτάς.   350
ΣΤ. τί γὰρ ἢν ἅρπαγα τῶν δημοσίων κατίδωσι
  Σίμωνα, τί δρῶσιν;
ΣΩ. ἀποφαίνουσαι τὴν φύσιν αὐτοῦ λύκοι ἐξαίφνης
  ἐγένοντο.
ΣΤ. ταῦτ' ἄρα ταῦτα Κλεώνυμον αὗται τὸν ῥίψασ-
  πιν χθὲς ἰδοῦσαι,
  ὅτι δειλότατον τοῦτον ἑώρων, ἔλαφοι διὰ τοῦτ'
  ἐγένοντο.
ΣΩ. καὶ νῦν γ' ὅτι Κλεισθένη εἶδον, ὁρᾷς, διὰ τοῦτ'
  ἐγένοντο γυναῖκες.   355
ΣΤ. χαίρετε τοίνυν, ὦ δέσποιναι· καὶ νῦν, εἴπερ τινὶ
  κἄλλῳ,
  οὐρανομήκη ῥήξατε κἀμοὶ φωνήν, ὦ παμβασί-
  λειαι.
ΧΟ. χαῖρ', ὦ πρεσβῦτα παλαιογενές, θηρατὰ λόγων
  φιλομούσων,
  σύ τε λεπτοτάτων λήρων ἱερεῦ, φράζε πρὸς ἡμᾶς
  ὅ τι χρῄζεις·
  οὐ γὰρ ἂν ἄλλῳ γ' ὑπακούσαιμεν τῶν νῦν μετεωροσοφιστῶν,   360

348. πάνθ' ὅ τι· πᾶν ὅ τι Mein. Cobet.   πάνθ' ἂν βούλωνται Dobr.
358. παλαιογενές AR al.   παλαιγενές SV al.

ΑΡΙΣΤΟΦΑΝΟΥΣ

πλὴν ἢ Προδίκῳ, τῷ μὲν σοφίας καὶ γνώμης
οὕνεκα, σοὶ δὲ
ὅτι βρενθύει τ᾽ ἐν ταῖσιν ὁδοῖς καὶ τὠφθαλμὼ
παραβάλλεις,
κἀνυπόδητος κακὰ πόλλ᾽ ἀνέχει, κἀφ᾽ ἡμῖν σεμ-
νοπροσωπεῖς.
ΣΤ. ὦ γῆ, τοῦ φθέγματος, ὡς ἱερὸν καὶ σεμνὸν καὶ
τερατῶδες.
ΣΩ. αὗται γάρ τοι μόναι εἰσὶ θεαί, τἄλλα δὲ πάντ᾽
ἐστὶ φλύαρος. 365
ΣΤ. ὁ Ζεὺς δ᾽ ὑμῖν, φέρε, πρὸς τῆς γῆς, οὑλύμπιος
οὐ θεός ἐστιν;
ΣΩ. ποῖος Ζεύς; οὐ μὴ ληρήσεις; οὐδ᾽ ἔστι Ζεύς.
ΣΤ. τί λέγεις σύ;
ἀλλὰ τίς ὕει; τουτὶ γὰρ ἔμοιγ᾽ ἀπόφηναι πρῶτον ἁπάντων.
ΣΩ. αὗται δή που· μεγάλοις δέ σ᾽ ἐγὼ σημείοις
αὐτὸ διδάξω.
φέρε, ποῦ γὰρ πώποτ᾽ ἄνευ νεφελῶν ὕοντ᾽ ἤδη
τεθέασαι; 370
καίτοιχρῆν αἰθρίας ὕειν αὐτόν,ταύτας δ᾽ ἀποδημεῖν.
ΣΤ. νὴ τὸν Ἀπόλλω τοῦτό γέ τοι δὴ τῷ νῦν λόγῳ
εὖ προσέφυσας.
ἀλλ᾽ ὅστις ὁ βροντῶν ἐστὶ φράσον, τοῦθ᾽ ὅ με
ποιεῖ τετρεμαίνειν.
ΣΩ. αὗται βροντῶσι κυλινδόμεναι. ΣΤ. τῷ τρόπῳ,
ὦ πάντα σὺ τολμῶν; 375

361. πλὴν ἤ· πλὴν εἰ Mein. Kock.
366. ὑμῖν Dind. Hold. ἡμῖν vulgo.
367. ληρήσεις· ληρήσῃς libri.
374. τοῦθ᾽ ὅ F al. Herm. Teuf. Blaydes. τοῦτό vulgo.

ΝΕΦΕΛΑΙ 25

ΣΩ. ὅταν ἐμπλησθῶσ᾽ ὕδατος πολλοῦ κἀναγκασθῶσι
 φέρεσθαι,
 κατακρημνάμεναι πλήρεις ὄμβρου δι᾽ ἀνάγκην
 εἶτα βαρεῖαι
 εἰς ἀλλήλας ἐμπίπτουσαι ῥήγνυνται καὶ πατα-
 γοῦσιν.
ΣΤ. ὁ δ᾽ ἀναγκάζων ἐστὶ τίς αὐτάς, οὐχ ὁ Ζεύς,
 ὥστε φέρεσθαι;
ΣΩ. ἥκιστ᾽, ἀλλ᾽ αἰθέριος δῖνος. ΣΤ. δῖνος; τουτί
 μ᾽ ἐλελήθειν, 380
 ὁ Ζεὺς οὐκ ὤν, ἀλλ᾽ ἀντ᾽ αὐτοῦ δῖνος νυνὶ
 βασιλεύων.
 ἀτὰρ οὐδέν πω περὶ τοῦ πατάγου καὶ τῆς
 βροντῆς μ᾽ ἐδίδαξας.
ΣΩ. οὐκ ἤκουσάς μου τὰς νεφέλας ὕδατος μεστὰς
 ὅτι φημὶ
 ἐμπιπτούσας εἰς ἀλλήλας παταγεῖν διὰ τὴν
 πυκνότητα;
ΣΤ. φέρε τουτὶ τῷ χρὴ πιστεύειν; ΣΩ. ἀπὸ σαυτοῦ
 'γώ σε διδάξω. 385
 ἤδη ζωμοῦ Παναθηναίοις ἐμπλησθεὶς εἶτ᾽ ἐταράχθης
 τὴν γαστέρα, καὶ κλόνος ἐξαίφνης αὐτὴν διεκορκορύγησεν;
ΣΤ. νὴ τὸν Ἀπόλλω καὶ δεινὰ ποιεῖ γ᾽ εὐθύς μοι,
 καὶ τετάρακται
 χὥσπερ βροντὴ τὸ ζωμίδιον παταγεῖ καὶ δεινὰ
 κέκραγεν·
 ἀτρέμας πρῶτον παππὰξ παππάξ, κἄπειτ᾽ ἐπάγει
 παπαπαππάξ. 390
ΣΩ. σκέψαι τοίνυν ἀπὸ γαστριδίου τυννουτουὶ οἷα
 κέκραγας·

τὸν δ' ἀέρα τόνδ' ὄντ' ἀπέραντον πῶς οὐκ εἰκὸς
μέγα βροντᾶν;
ΣΤ. ἀλλ' ὁ κεραυνὸς πόθεν αὖ φέρεται λάμπων πυρί,
τοῦτο δίδαξον, 395
καὶ καταφρύγει βάλλων ἡμᾶς, τοὺς δὲ ζῶντας
περιφλύει.
τοῦτον γὰρ δὴ φανερῶς ὁ Ζεὺς ἵησ' ἐπὶ τοὺς
ἐπιόρκους.
ΣΩ. καὶ πῶς, ὦ μῶρε σὺ καὶ Κρονίων ὄζων καὶ
βεκκεσέληνε,
εἴπερ βάλλει τοὺς ἐπιόρκους, δῆτ' οὐχὶ Σίμων'
ἐνέπρησεν
οὐδὲ Κλεώνυμον οὐδὲ Θέωρον· καίτοι σφόδρα γ'
εἴσ' ἐπίορκοι· 400
ἀλλὰ τὸν αὑτοῦ γε νεὼν βάλλει καὶ Σούνιον
ἄκρον Ἀθηνέων,
καὶ τὰς δρῦς τὰς μεγάλας; τί μαθών; οὐ γὰρ δὴ
δρῦς γ' ἐπιορκεῖ.
ΣΤ. οὐκ οἶδ'· ἀτὰρ εὖ σὺ λέγειν φαίνει. τί γάρ ἐστιν
δῆθ' ὁ κεραυνός;
ΣΩ. ὅταν ἐς ταύτας ἄνεμος ξηρὸς μετεωρισθεὶς κατα-
κλῃσθῇ,
ἔνδοθεν αὐτὰς ὥσπερ κύστιν φυσᾷ, κἄπειθ' ὑπ'
ἀνάγκης 405
ῥήξας αὐτὰς ἔξω φέρεται σοβαρὸς διὰ τὴν πυκνότητα,
ὑπὸ τοῦ ῥοίβδου καὶ τῆς ῥύμης αὐτὸς ἑαυτὸν
κατακάων.

399. δῆτ' V Teuf. al. πῶς A Dind. Mein. al. πῶς δῆτ' R.
401. Ἀθηνέων· Ἀθηναίων vel Ἀθηνῶν libri.
402. μαθών· παθών aliq. libri, plerique edd.

ΝΕΦΕΛΑΙ 27

ΣΤ. νὴ Δί', ἐγὼ γοῦν ἀτεχνῶς ἔπαθον τουτί ποτε
Διασίοισιν·
ὤπτων γαστέρα τοῖς ξυγγενέσιν, κᾆτ' οὐκ ἔσχων
ἀμελήσας·
ἡ δ' ἄρ' ἐφυσᾶτ', εἶτ' ἐξαίφνης διαλακήσασα πρὸς
αὐτὼ 410
τὠφθαλμώ μου προσετίλησεν καὶ κατέκαυσεν τὸ
πρόσωπον.

ΧΟ. ὦ τῆς μεγάλης ἐπιθυμήσας σοφίας ἄνθρωπε παρ'
ἡμῶν,
ὡς εὐδαίμων ἐν Ἀθηναίοις καὶ τοῖς Ἕλλησι
γενήσει,
εἰ μνήμων εἶ καὶ φροντιστὴς καὶ τὸ ταλαίπωρον
ἔνεστιν
ἐν τῇ ψυχῇ, καὶ μὴ κάμνεις μήθ' ἑστὼς μήτε
βαδίζων, 415
μηδὲ ῥιγῶν ἄχθει λίαν, μηδ' ἀριστᾶν ἐπιθυμεῖς,
οἴνου τ' ἀπέχει καὶ γυμνασίων καὶ τῶν ἄλλων
ἀνοήτων,
καὶ βέλτιστον τοῦτο νομίζεις, ὅπερ εἰκὸς δεξιὸν
ἄνδρα,
νικᾶν πράττων καὶ βουλεύων καὶ τῇ γλώττῃ
πολεμίζων.

ΣΤ. ἀλλ' οὕνεκά γε ψυχῆς στερρᾶς δυσκολοκοίτου τε
μερίμνης 420
καὶ φειδωλοῦ καὶ τρυσιβίου γαστρὸς καὶ θυμβρεπιδείπνου,
ἀμέλει θαρρῶν οὕνεκα τούτων ἐπιχαλκεύειν παρέχοιμ' ἄν.

416. μηδὲ...μηδέ Blaydes. μήτε...μήτε vulg.

ΑΡΙΣΤΟΦΑΝΟΥΣ

ΣΩ. ἄλλο τι δῆτ' οὐ νομιεῖς ἤδη θεὸν οὐδὲν πλὴν
ἅπερ ἡμεῖς,
τὸ χάος τουτὶ καὶ τὰς νεφέλας καὶ τὴν γλῶτταν,
τρία ταυτί;
ΣΤ. οὐδ' ἂν διαλεχθείην γ' ἀτεχνῶς τοῖς ἄλλοις, οὐδ'
ἂν ἀπαντῶν· 425
οὐδ' ἂν θύσαιμ', οὐδὲ σπείσαιμ', οὐδ' ἐπιθείην
λιβανωτόν.
ΧΟ. λέγε νυν ἡμῖν ὅ τι σοι δρῶμεν θαρρῶν, ὡς οὐκ
ἀτυχήσεις,
ἡμᾶς τιμῶν καὶ θαυμάζων καὶ ζητῶν δεξιὸς εἶναι.
ΣΤ. ὦ δέσποιναι, δέομαι τοίνυν ὑμῶν τουτὶ πάνυ
μικρόν,
τῶν Ἑλλήνων εἶναί με λέγειν ἑκατὸν σταδίοισιν
ἄριστον. 430
ΧΟ. ἀλλ' ἔσται σοι τοῦτο παρ' ἡμῶν· ὥστε τὸ λοιπόν
γ' ἀπὸ τουδὶ
ἐν τῷ δήμῳ γνώμας οὐδεὶς νικήσει πλείονας
ἢ σύ.
ΣΤ. μή μοί γε λέγειν γνώμας μεγάλας· οὐ γὰρ τούτων
ἐπιθυμῶ,
ἀλλ' ὅσ' ἐμαυτῷ στρεψοδικῆσαι καὶ τοὺς χρήστας διολισθεῖν.
ΧΟ. τεύξει τοίνυν ὧν ἱμείρεις· οὐ γὰρ μεγάλων ἐπιθυμεῖς. 435
ἀλλὰ σεαυτὸν παράδος θαρρῶν τοῖς ἡμετέροις
προπόλοισιν.
ΣΤ. δράσω ταῦθ' ὑμῖν πιστεύσας· ἡ γὰρ ἀνάγκη με
πιέζει

423. οὐ F Herm. al. Bl. οὖν V al. Bentl. Mein. Dind. οὐδέν edd.
οὐδένα pler. libri.

ΝΕΦΕΛΑΙ

διὰ τοὺς ἵππους τοὺς κοππατίας καὶ τὸν γάμον
ὅς μ' ἐπέτριψεν.
νῦν οὖν χρήσθων ὅ τι βούλονται·
τουτὶ τοὐμὸν σῶμ' αὐτοῖσιν 440
παρέχω τύπτειν, πεινῆν, διψῆν,
αὐχμεῖν, ῥιγῶν, ἀσκὸν δείρειν,
εἴπερ τὰ χρέα διαφευξοῦμαι,
τοῖς ἀνθρώποις τ' εἶναι δόξω
θρασύς, εὔγλωττος, τολμηρός, ἴτης, 445
βδελυρός, ψευδῶν ξυγκολλητής,
εὑρησιεπής, περίτριμμα δικῶν,
κύρβις, κρόταλον, κίναδος, τρύμη,
μάσθλης, εἴρων, γλοιός, ἀλαζών,
κέντρων, μιαρός, στρόφις, ἀργαλέος, 450
ματτυολοιχός.
ταῦτ' εἴ με καλοῦσ' ἀπαντῶντες,
δρώντων ἀτεχνῶς ὅ τι χρῄζουσιν,
κεἰ βούλονται,
νὴ τὴν Δήμητρ' ἔκ μου χορδὴν 455
τοῖς φροντισταῖς παραθέντων.
ΧΟ. λῆμα μὲν πάρεστι τῷδέ γ'
οὐκ ἄτολμον, ἀλλ' ἕτοιμον. ἴσθι δ' ὡς
ταῦτα μαθὼν παρ' ἐμοῦ κλέος οὐρανόμηκες
ἐν βροτοῖσιν ἕξεις. 460
ΣΤ. τί πείσομαι;
ΧΟ. τὸν πάντα χρόνον μετ' ἐμοῦ
ζηλωτότατον βίον ἀνθρώπων διάξεις.
ΣΤ. ἆρά γε τοῦτ' ἄρ' ἐγώ ποτ' 465

439. χρήσθων· χρήσθων ἀτεχνῶς libri. ἀτεχνῶς (om. χρήσθων)
Cob. Mein.

ΑΡΙΣΤΟΦΑΝΟΥΣ

ὄψομαι; ΧΟ. ὥστε γε σοῦ πολλοὺς ἐπὶ ταῖσι
θύραις ἀεὶ καθῆσθαι,
βουλομένους ἀνακοινοῦσθαί τε καὶ ἐς λόγον ἐλθεῖν
πράγματα κἀντιγραφὰς πολλῶν ταλάντων,
ἄξια σῇ φρενὶ συμβουλευσομένους μετὰ σοῦ. 475
ἀλλ' ἐγχείρει τὸν πρεσβύτην ὅ τι περ μέλλεις
προδιδάσκειν,
καὶ διακίνει τὸν νοῦν αὐτοῦ καὶ τῆς γνώμης
ἀποπειρῶ.

ΣΩ. ἄγε δὴ κάτειπέ μοι σὺ τὸν σαυτοῦ τρόπον,
ἵν' αὐτὸν εἰδὼς ὅστις ἐστὶ μηχανὰς
ἤδη 'πὶ τούτοις πρὸς σὲ καινὰς προσφέρω. 480
ΣΤ. τί δέ; τειχομαχεῖν μοι διανοεῖ πρὸς τῶν θεῶν;
ΣΩ. οὐκ ἀλλὰ βραχέα σου πυθέσθαι βούλομαι·
ἦ μνημονικὸς εἶ; ΣΤ. δύο τρόπω νὴ τὸν Δία·
ἢν μὲν γὰρ ὀφείληταί τί μοι, μνήμων πάνυ,
ἐὰν δ' ὀφείλω, σχέτλιος, ἐπιλήσμων πάνυ. 485
ΣΩ. ἔνεστι δῆτά σοι λέγειν ἐν τῇ φύσει;
ΣΤ. λέγειν μὲν οὐκ ἔνεστ', ἀποστερεῖν δ' ἔνι.
ΣΩ. πῶς οὖν δυνήσει μανθάνειν; ΣΤ. ἀμέλει καλῶς.
ΣΩ. ἄγε νυν ὅπως, ὅταν τι προβάλω σοι σοφὸν
περὶ τῶν μετεώρων, εὐθέως ὑφαρπάσει. 490
ΣΤ. τί δαί; κυνηδὸν τὴν σοφίαν σιτήσομαι;
ΣΩ. ἄνθρωπος ἀμαθὴς οὑτοσὶ καὶ βάρβαρος.
δέδοικά σ', ὦ πρεσβῦτα, μὴ πληγῶν δέῃ.
φέρ' ἴδω τί δρᾷς, ἤν τίς σε τύπτῃ; ΣΤ. τύπτομαι,

483. ἦ Dobr. Mein. al. εἰ vulg.
489. προβάλω σοι Hirsch. Bl. προβάλλω σοι Mein. Kock. προβάλωμαι vulg.
493. δέῃ V. δέει R al.

ΝΕΦΕΛΑΙ

ἔπειτ᾽ ἐπισχὼν ὀλίγον ἐπιμαρτύρομαι, 495
εἶτ᾽ αὖθις ἀκαρῆ διαλιπὼν δικάζομαι.
ΣΩ. ἴθι νῦν κατάθου θοἰμάτιον. ΣΤ. ἠδίκηκά τι;
ΣΩ. οὐκ ἀλλὰ γυμνοὺς εἰσιέναι νομίζεται.
ΣΤ. ἀλλ᾽ οὐχὶ φωράσων ἔγωγ᾽ εἰσέρχομαι.
ΣΩ. κατάθου. τί ληρεῖς; ΣΤ. εἰπὲ δή νύν μοι τοδί·
ἢν ἐπιμελὴς ὦ καὶ προθύμως μανθάνω, 501
τῷ τῶν μαθητῶν ἐμφερὴς γενήσομαι;
ΣΩ. οὐδὲν διοίσεις Χαιρεφῶντος τὴν φύσιν.
ΣΤ. οἴμοι κακοδαίμων ἡμιθνὴς γενήσομαι.
ΣΩ. οὐ μὴ λαλήσεις, ἀλλ᾽ ἀκολουθήσεις ἐμοὶ 505
ἀνύσας τι δευρὶ θᾶττον; ΣΤ. ἐς τὼ χεῖρέ νυν
δός μοι μελιτοῦτταν πρότερον· ὡς δέδοικ᾽ ἐγὼ
εἴσω καταβαίνων ὥσπερ ἐς Τροφωνίου.
ΣΩ. χώρει· τί κυπτάζεις ἔχων περὶ τὴν θύραν;
ΧΟ. ἀλλ᾽ ἴθι χαίρων τῆς ἀνδρείας 510
οὕνεκα ταύτης.
εὐτυχία γένοιτο τἀν-
θρώπῳ, ὅτι προήκων
ἐς βαθὺ τῆς ἡλικίας
νεωτέροις τὴν φύσιν αὑ- 515
τοῦ πράγμασιν χρωτίζεται,
καὶ σοφίαν ἐπασκεῖ.
ὦ θεώμενοι κατερῶ πρὸς ὑμᾶς ἐλευθέρως
τἀληθῆ νὴ τὸν Διόνυσον τὸν ἐκθρέψαντά με.
οὕτω νικήσαιμί τ᾽ ἐγὼ καὶ νομιζοίμην σοφός, 520
ὡς ὑμᾶς ἡγούμενος εἶναι θεατὰς δεξιούς,
καὶ ταύτην σοφώτατ᾽ ἔχειν τῶν ἐμῶν κωμῳδιῶν,
πρώτους ἠξίωσ᾽ ἀναγεῦσ᾽ ὑμᾶς, ἣ παρέσχε μοι

505. λαλήσεις R. λαλήσῃς V al.
523. πρώτους· πρώτην Mein. al.

ΑΡΙΣΤΟΦΑΝΟΥΣ

ἔργον πλεῖστον· εἶτ' ἀνεχώρουν ὑπ' ἀνδρῶν
   φορτικῶν 524
ἡττηθεὶς οὐκ ἄξιος ὤν· ταῦτ' οὖν ὑμῖν μέμφομαι
τοῖς σοφοῖς, ὧν οὕνεκ' ἐγὼ ταῦτ' ἐπραγματευόμην.
ἀλλ' οὐδ' ὡς ὑμῶν ποθ' ἑκὼν προδώσω τοὺς
   δεξιούς.
ἐξ ὅτου γὰρ ἐνθάδ' ὑπ' ἀνδρῶν, οἷς ἡδὺ καὶ λέγειν,
ὁ σώφρων τε χὡ καταπύγων ἄριστ' ἠκουσάτην,
κἀγώ, παρθένος γὰρ ἔτ' ἦ κοὐκ ἐξῆν πώ μοι
   τεκεῖν, 530
ἐξέθηκα, παῖς δ' ἑτέρα τις λαβοῦσ' ἀνείλετο,
ὑμεῖς δ' ἐξεθρέψατε γενναίως κἀπαιδεύσατε·
ἐκ τούτου μοι πιστὰ παρ' ὑμῖν γνώμης ἔσθ' ὅρκια.
νῦν οὖν Ἠλέκτραν κατ' ἐκείνην ἥδ' ἡ κωμῳδία
ζητοῦσ' ἦλθ', ἤν που 'πιτύχῃ θεαταῖς οὕτω
   σοφοῖς· 535
γνώσεται γάρ, ἤνπερ ἴδῃ, τἀδελφοῦ τὸν βόσ-
   τρυχον.
ὡς δὲ σώφρων ἐστὶ φύσει σκέψασθ'· ἥτις πρῶτα
   μὲν
οὐκ ἔσκωψε τοὺς φαλακρούς, οὐδὲ κόρδαχ' εἵλκυσεν, 540
οὐδὲ πρεσβύτης ὁ λέγων τἄπη τῇ βακτηρίᾳ
τύπτει τὸν παρόντ' ἀφανίζων πονηρὰ σκώμματα,
οὐδ' εἰσῇξε δᾷδας ἔχουσ', οὐδ' ἰοὺ ἰοὺ βοᾷ,
ἀλλ' αὑτῇ καὶ τοῖς ἔπεσιν πιστεύουσ' ἐλήλυθεν.
κἀγὼ μὲν τοιοῦτος ἀνὴρ ὢν ποιητὴς οὐ κομῶ, 545
οὐδ' ὑμᾶς ζητῶ 'ξαπατᾶν δὶς καὶ τρὶς ταῦτ'
   εἰσάγων,

530. ἦ· ἦν libri et vulg.
533. ὑμῖν· ὑμῶν Mein. al.

ΝΕΦΕΛΑΙ

ἀλλ' ἀεὶ καινὰς ἰδέας ἐσφέρων σοφίζομαι,
οὐδὲν ἀλλήλαισιν ὁμοίας καὶ πάσας δεξιάς·
ὃς μέγιστον ὄντα Κλέων' ἔπαισ' ἐς τὴν γαστέρα,
κοὐκ ἐτόλμησ' αὖθις ἐπεμπηδῆσ' αὐτῷ κειμένῳ.
οὗτοι δ', ὡς ἅπαξ παρέδωκεν λαβὴν Ὑπέρβολος,
τοῦτον δείλαιον κολετρῶσ' ἀεὶ καὶ τὴν μητέρα. 552
Εὔπολις μὲν τὸν Μαρικᾶν πρώτιστον παρείλκυσεν
ἐκστρέψας τοὺς ἡμετέρους Ἱππέας κακὸς κακῶς,
προσθεὶς αὐτῷ γραῦν μεθύσην τοῦ κόρδακος
οὕνεχ', ἣν   555
Φρύνιχος πάλαι πεποίηχ', ἣν τὸ κῆτος ἤσθιεν.
εἶθ' Ἕρμιππος αὖθις ἐποίησεν εἰς Ὑπέρβολον,
ἄλλοι τ' ἤδη πάντες ἐρείδουσιν εἰς Ὑπέρβολον,
τὰς εἰκοὺς τῶν ἐγχέλεων τὰς ἐμὰς μιμούμενοι.
ὅστις οὖν τούτοισι γελᾷ, τοῖς ἐμοῖς μὴ χαιρέτω·
ἢν δ' ἐμοὶ καὶ τοῖσιν ἐμοῖς εὐφραίνησθ' εὑρήμασιν,
ἐς τὰς ὥρας τὰς ἑτέρας εὖ φρονεῖν δοκήσετε. 562

Strophe (563—574)

ὑψιμέδοντα μὲν θεῶν
Ζῆνα τύραννον ἐς χορὸν
πρῶτα μέγαν κικλήσκω·   565
τόν τε μεγασθενῆ τριαίνης ταμίαν,
γῆς τε καὶ ἁλμυρᾶς θαλάσσης ἄγριον μοχλευτήν·
καὶ μεγαλώνυμον ἡμέτερον πατέρ'
αἰθέρα σεμνότατον βιοθρέμμονα πάντων·   570
τόν θ' ἱππονώμαν, ὃς ὑπερ-
λάμπροις ἀκτῖσιν κατέχει
γῆς πέδον μέγας ἐν θεοῖς

553. πρώτιστον· πρώτιστος Cob. Mein. al.
571. ἱππονώμαν· ἱππονόμαν RV.

ΑΡΙΣΤΟΦΑΝΟΥΣ

ἐν θνητοῖσί τε δαίμων.
ὦ σοφώτατοι θεαταί, δεῦρο τὸν νοῦν πρόσσχετε.
ἠδικημέναι γὰρ ὑμῖν μεμφόμεσθ' ἐναντίον·   576
πλεῖστα γὰρ θεῶν ἁπάντων ὠφελούσαις τὴν πόλιν
δαιμόνων ἡμῖν μόναις οὐ θύετ' οὐδὲ σπένδετε,
αἵτινες τηροῦμεν ὑμᾶς. ἢν γὰρ ᾖ τις ἔξοδος
μηδενὶ ξὺν νῷ, τότ' ἢ βροντῶμεν ἢ ψακάζομεν.
εἶτα τὸν θεοῖσιν ἐχθρὸν βυρσοδέψην Παφλαγόνα
ἡνίχ' ᾑρεῖσθε στρατηγόν, τὰς ὀφρῦς συνήγομεν
κἀποιοῦμεν δεινά· βροντὴ δ' ἐρράγη δι' ἀστραπῆς·
ἡ σελήνη δ' ἐξέλειπε τὰς ὁδούς· ὁ δ' ἥλιος
τὴν θρυαλλίδ' εἰς ἑαυτὸν εὐθέως ξυνελκύσας   585
οὐ φανεῖν ἔφασκεν ὑμῖν, εἰ στρατηγήσει Κλέων.
ἀλλ' ὅμως εἵλεσθε τοῦτον. φασὶ γὰρ δυσβουλίαν
τῇδε τῇ πόλει προσεῖναι, ταῦτα μέντοι τοὺς θεοὺς
ἅττ' ἂν ὑμεῖς ἐξαμάρτητ' ἐπὶ τὸ βέλτιον τρέπειν.
ὡς δὲ καὶ τοῦτο ξυνοίσει ῥᾳδίως διδάξομεν.   590
ἢν Κλέωνα τὸν λάρον δώρων ἑλόντες καὶ κλοπῆς,
εἶτα φιμώσητε τούτου 'ν τῷ ξύλῳ τὸν αὐχένα,
αὖθις ἐς τἀρχαῖον ὑμῖν, εἴ τι κἀξημάρτετε,
ἐπὶ τὸ βέλτιον τὸ πρᾶγμα τῇ πόλει ξυνοίσεται.

Antistrophe (595—606)

ἀμφί μοι αὖτε, Φοῖβ' ἄναξ   595
Δήλιε, Κυνθίαν ἔχων
ὑψικέρατα πέτραν·
ἥ τ' Ἐφέσου μάκαιρα πάγχρυσον ἔχεις
οἶκον, ἐν ᾧ κόραι σε Λυδῶν μεγάλως σέβουσιν·

575. πρόσσχετε· προσέχετε libri. πρόσχετε plur. edd.
577. ὠφελούσαις· ὠφελοῦσαι R.
586. στρατηγήσει· -σοι Blaydes.

ΝΕΦΕΛΑΙ   35

ἥ τ' ἐπιχώριος ἡμετέρα θεὸς   601
αἰγίδος ἡνίοχος πολιοῦχος Ἀθάνα·
Παρνασσίαν θ' ὃς κατέχων
πέτραν σὺν πεύκαις σελαγεῖ
Βάκχαις Δελφίσιν ἐμπρέπων,   605
κωμαστὴς Διόνυσος.
ἡνίχ' ἡμεῖς δεῦρ' ἀφορμᾶσθαι παρεσκευάσμεθα,
ἡ σελήνη συντυχοῦσ' ἡμῖν ἐπέστειλεν φράσαι,
πρῶτα μὲν χαίρειν Ἀθηναίοισι καὶ τοῖς ξυμ-
   μάχοις·
εἶτα θυμαίνειν ἔφασκε· δεινὰ γὰρ πεπονθέναι 610
ὠφελοῦσ' ὑμᾶς ἅπαντας οὐ λόγοις ἀλλ' ἐμφανῶς.
πρῶτα μὲν τοῦ μηνὸς ἐς δᾷδ' οὐκ ἔλαττον ἢ
   δραχμήν·
ὥστε καὶ λέγειν ἅπαντας ἐξιόντας ἑσπέρας,
μὴ πρίῃ παῖ δᾷδ', ἐπειδὴ φῶς σεληναίας καλόν.
ἄλλα τ' εὖ δρᾶν φησιν, ὑμᾶς δ' οὐκ ἄγειν τὰς
   ἡμέρας   615
οὐδὲν ὀρθῶς, ἀλλ' ἄνω τε καὶ κάτω κυδοιδοπᾶν·
ὥστ' ἀπειλεῖν φησιν αὐτῇ τοὺς θεοὺς ἑκάστοτε
ἡνίκ' ἂν ψευσθῶσι δείπνου, κἀπίωσιν οἴκαδε
τῆς ἑορτῆς μὴ τυχόντες κατὰ λόγον τῶν ἡμερῶν.
κᾆθ' ὅταν θύειν δέῃ, στρεβλοῦτε καὶ δικάζετε· 620
πολλάκις δ' ἡμῶν ἀγόντων τῶν θεῶν ἀπαστίαν,
ἡνίκ' ἂν πενθῶμεν ἢ τὸν Μέμνον' ἢ Σαρπηδόνα,
σπένδεθ' ὑμεῖς καὶ γελᾶτ'· ἀνθ' ὧν λαχὼν
   Ὑπέρβολος
τῆτες ἱερομνημονεῖν, κἄπειθ' ὑφ' ἡμῶν τῶν θεῶν
τὸν στέφανον ἀφῃρέθη· μᾶλλον γὰρ οὕτως εἴσεται
κατὰ σελήνην ὡς ἄγειν χρὴ τοῦ βίου τὰς ἡμέρας.

   622. ἢ τὸν· ἤτοι Mein. Blaydes.

ΑΡΙΣΤΟΦΑΝΟΥΣ

ΣΩΚΡΑΤΗΣ. ΣΤΡΕΨΙΑΔΗΣ. ΧΟΡΟΣ

ΣΩ. μὰ τὴν ἀναπνοήν, μὰ τὸ χάος, μὰ τὸν ἀέρα,
οὐκ εἶδον οὕτως ἄνδρ' ἄγροικον οὐδένα,
οὐδ' ἄπορον οὐδὲ σκαιὸν οὐδ' ἐπιλήσμονα·
ὅστις σκαλαθυρμάτι' ἄττα μικρὰ μανθάνων 630
ταῦτ' ἐπιλέλησται πρὶν μαθεῖν· ὅμως γε μὴν
αὐτὸν καλῶ θύραζε δευρὶ πρὸς τὸ φῶς.
ποῦ Στρεψιάδης; ἕξει τὸν ἀσκάντην λαβών.
ΣΤ. ἀλλ' οὐκ ἐῶσί μ' ἐξενεγκεῖν οἱ κόρεις.
ΣΩ. ἀνύσας τι κατάθου καὶ πρόσεχε τὸν νοῦν.
ΣΤ. ἰδού. 635
ΣΩ. ἄγε δή, τί βούλει πρῶτα νυνὶ μανθάνειν
ὧν οὐκ ἐδιδάχθης πώποτ' οὐδέν; εἰπέ μοι.
πότερον περὶ μέτρων ἢ ῥυθμῶν ἢ περὶ ἐπῶν;
ΣΤ. περὶ τῶν μέτρων ἔγωγ'· ἔναγχος γάρ ποτε
ὑπ' ἀλφιταμοιβοῦ παρεκόπην διχοινίκῳ. 640
ΣΩ. οὐ τοῦτ' ἐρωτῶ σ', ἀλλ' ὅ τι κάλλιστον μέτρον
ἡγεῖ· πότερον τὸ τρίμετρον ἢ τὸ τετράμετρον;
ΣΤ. ἐγὼ μὲν οὐδὲν πρότερον ἡμιεκτέου.
ΣΩ. οὐδὲν λέγεις, ὤνθρωπε. ΣΤ. περίδου νυν ἐμοί,
εἰ μὴ τετράμετρόν ἐστιν ἡμιεκτέον. 645
ΣΩ. ἐς κόρακας, ὡς ἄγροικος εἶ καὶ δυσμαθής.
ταχύ γ' ἂν δύναιο μανθάνειν περὶ ῥυθμῶν.
ΣΤ. τί δέ μ' ὠφελήσουσ' οἱ ῥυθμοὶ πρὸς τἄλφιτα;
ΣΩ. πρῶτον μὲν εἶναι κομψὸν ἐν συνουσίᾳ,
ἐπαΐονθ' ὁποῖός ἐστι τῶν ῥυθμῶν 650
κατ' ἐνόπλιον, χὠποῖος αὖ κατὰ δάκτυλον.

633. λαβών· λαβών; Dobr. Blaydes.
647. ταχύ γ' ἂν libri. τάχα δ' ἂν Reisk. Dind. Mein. al.
650. ἐπαΐονθ'· ἐπαΐοντ' R. εἶτ' ἐπαΐειν cet. ἐπαΐειν θ' Bl.

ΣΤ. κατὰ δάκτυλον; νὴ τὸν Δί' ἀλλ' οἶδ'. ΣΩ. εἰπὲ
 δή.
ΣΤ. τίς ἄλλος ἀντὶ τουτουὶ τοῦ δακτύλου;
 πρὸ τοῦ μέν, ἔτ' ἐμοῦ παιδὸς ὄντος, οὑτοσί.
ΣΩ. ἀγρεῖος εἶ καὶ σκαιός. ΣΤ. οὐ γάρ, ᾠζυρέ, 655
 τούτων ἐπιθυμῶ μανθάνειν οὐδέν. ΣΩ. τί δαί;
ΣΤ. ἐκεῖν' ἐκεῖνο, τὸν ἀδικώτατον λόγον.
ΣΩ. ἀλλ' ἕτερα δεῖ σε πρότερα τούτων μανθάνειν,
 τῶν τετραπόδων ἅττ' ἐστὶν ὀρθῶς ἄρρενα.
ΣΤ. ἀλλ' οἶδ' ἔγωγε τἄρρεν', εἰ μὴ μαίνομαι· 660
 κριός, τράγος, ταῦρος, κύων, ἀλεκτρυών.
ΣΩ. ὁρᾷς ὃ πάσχεις; τήν τε θήλειαν καλεῖς
 ἀλεκτρυόνα κατὰ ταὐτὸ καὶ τὸν ἄρρενα.
ΣΤ. πῶς δή; φέρ'. ΣΩ. ὅπως; ἀλεκτρυὼν κἀλεκ-
 τρυών.
ΣΤ. νὴ τὸν Ποσειδῶ. νῦν δὲ πῶς με χρὴ καλεῖν;
ΣΩ. ἀλεκτρύαιναν, τὸν δ' ἕτερον ἀλέκτορα. 666
ΣΤ. ἀλεκτρύαιναν; εὖ γε νὴ τὸν ἀέρα·
 ὥστ' ἀντὶ τούτου τοῦ διδάγματος μόνου
 διαλφιτώσω σου κύκλῳ τὴν κάρδοπον.
ΣΩ. ἰδοὺ μάλ' αὖθις τοῦθ' ἕτερον. τὴν κάρδοπον 670
 ἄρρενα καλεῖς θήλειαν οὖσαν. ΣΤ. τῷ τρόπῳ
 ἄρρενα καλῶ 'γὼ κάρδοπον; ΣΩ. μάλιστά γε,
 ὥσπερ γε καὶ Κλεώνυμον. ΣΤ. πῶς δή; φράσον
ΣΩ. ταὐτὸν δύναταί σοι κάρδοπος Κλεωνύμῳ.
ΣΤ. ἀλλ', ὦγάθ', οὐδ' ἦν κάρδοπος Κλεωνύμῳ, 675
 ἀλλ' ἐν θυείᾳ στρογγύλῃ 'νεμάττετο.
 ἀτὰρ τὸ λοιπὸν πῶς με χρὴ καλεῖν; ΣΩ. ὅπως;
 τὴν καρδόπην, ὥσπερ καλεῖς τὴν Σωστράτην.

652. νὴ τὸν Δί' Socrati dant Hirschig, Teuf. Mein. al.
676. 'νεμάττετο· Dobr. Dind. Mein. γ' ἀνεμάττετο libri.

ΣΤ. τὴν καρδόπην θήλειαν; ΣΩ. ὀρθῶς γὰρ λέγεις.
ΣΤ. ἐκεῖνο δ' ἦν ἂν καρδόπη, Κλεωνύμη. 680
ΣΩ. ἔτι δέ γε περὶ τῶν ὀνομάτων μαθεῖν σε δεῖ,
ἅττ' ἄρρεν' ἐστίν, ἅττα δ' αὐτῶν θήλεα.
ΣΤ. ἀλλ' οἶδ' ἔγωγ' ἃ θήλε' ἐστίν. ΣΩ. εἰπὲ δή.
ΣΤ. Λύσιλλα Φίλιννα Κλειταγόρα Δημητρία.
ΣΩ. ἄρρενα δὲ ποῖα τῶν ὀνομάτων; ΣΤ. μυρία. 685
Φιλόξενος Μελησίας Ἀμυνίας.
ΣΩ. ἀλλ', ὦ πονηρέ, ταῦτά γ' οὔκ ἐστ' ἄρρενα.
ΣΤ. οὐκ ἄρρεν' ὑμῖν ἐστιν; ΣΩ. οὐδαμῶς γ', ἐπεὶ
πῶς ἂν καλέσειας ἐντυχὼν Ἀμυνίᾳ;
ΣΤ. ὅπως ἄν; ὡδί, δεῦρο δεῦρ', Ἀμυνία. 690
ΣΩ. ὁρᾷς; γυναῖκα τὴν Ἀμυνίαν καλεῖς.
ΣΤ. οὔκουν δικαίως ἥτις οὐ στρατεύεται;
ἀτὰρ τί ταῦθ' ἃ πάντες ἴσμεν μανθάνω;
ΣΩ. οὐδὲν μὰ Δί', ἀλλὰ κατακλινεὶς δευρὶ ΣΤ. τί
δρῶ;
ΣΩ. ἐκφρόντισόν τι τῶν σεαυτοῦ πραγμάτων. 695
ΣΤ. μὴ δῆθ', ἱκετεύω σ', ἐνθάδ'· ἀλλ' εἴπερ γε χρή,
χαμαί μ' ἔασον αὐτὰ ταῦτ' ἐκφροντίσαι.
ΣΩ. οὐκ ἔστι παρὰ ταῦτ' ἄλλα. ΣΤ. κακοδαίμων
ἐγώ,
οἵαν δίκην τοῖς κόρεσι δώσω τήμερον.

Strophe (700—5)

ΧΟ. φρόντιζε δὴ καὶ διάθρει, πάντα τρόπον τε σαυτὸν
στρόβει πυκνώσας. 701
ταχὺς δ', ὅταν εἰς ἄπορον πέσῃς,

681. ἔτι δέ γε Kock Mein. ἔτι γε RSV. ἔτι δή γε (δέ) vel ἀλλ'
ἔτι γε vel ἔθ' ἔν τι edd. 687. οὔκ ἐστ'· Kock Mein. ἔστ' οὐκ libri.
688. ὑμῖν· ἡμῖν plur. libri. 696. ἐνθάδ'· ἐνταῦθα RV al. unde
μὴ δῆθ', ἱκετεύω, ἐνταῦθά γ' Dobr. Mein.

ΝΕΦΕΛΑΙ 39

ἐπ᾽ ἄλλο πήδα
νόημα φρενός· ὕπνος δ᾽ ἀπέστω γλυκύθυμος
ὀμμάτων.
ΣΤ. ἀτταταῖ ἀτταταῖ.
ΧΟ. τί πάσχεις; τί κάμνεις;
ΣΤ. ἀπόλλυμαι δείλαιος· ἐκ τοῦ σκίμποδος
δάκνουσί μ᾽ ἐξέρποντες οἱ Κορίνθιοι, 710
καὶ τὰς πλευρὰς δαρδάπτουσιν
καὶ τὴν ψυχὴν ἐκπίνουσιν
καί μ᾽ ἀπολοῦσιν. 715
ΧΟ. μή νυν βαρέως ἄλγει λίαν.
ΣΤ. καὶ πῶς, ὅτε μου
φροῦδα τὰ χρήματα, φρούδη χροιά,
φρούδη ψυχή, φρούδη δ᾽ ἐμβάς·
καὶ πρὸς τούτοις ἔτι τοῖσι κακοῖς 720
φρουρᾶς ᾄδων
ὀλίγου φροῦδος γεγένημαι;
ΣΩ. οὗτος τί ποιεῖς; οὐχὶ φροντίζεις; ΣΤ. ἐγώ;
νὴ τὸν Ποσειδῶ. ΣΩ. καὶ τί δῆτ᾽ ἐφρόντισας;
ΣΤ. ὑπὸ τῶν κόρεων εἴ μού τι περιλειφθήσεται. 725
ΣΩ. ἀπολεῖ κάκιστ᾽. ΣΤ. ἀλλ᾽ ὠγάθ᾽, ἀπόλωλ᾽
ἀρτίως.
ΣΩ. οὐ μαλθακιστέ, ἀλλὰ περικαλυπτέα.
ἐξευρετέος γὰρ νοῦς ἀποστερητικὸς
κἀπαιόλημ᾽. ΣΤ. οἴμοι τίς ἂν δῆτ᾽ ἐπιβάλοι
ἐξ ἀρνακίδων γνώμην ἀποστερητρίδα; 730
ΣΩ. φέρε νυν ἀθρήσω πρῶτον ὅ τι δρᾷ τουτονί.
οὗτος καθεύδεις; ΣΤ. μὰ τὸν Ἀπόλλω 'γὼ
μὲν οὔ.
ΣΩ. ἔχεις τι; ΣΤ. μὰ Δί᾽ οὐ δῆτ᾽ ἔγωγ᾽. ΣΩ. οὐδὲν
πάνυ;

ΑΡΙΣΤΟΦΑΝΟΥΣ

   οὐκ ἐγκαλυψάμενος ταχέως τι φροντιεῖς; 735
ΣΤ. περὶ τοῦ; σὺ γάρ μοι τοῦτο φράσον, ὦ Σώκρατες.
ΣΩ. αὐτὸς ὅ τι βούλει πρῶτον ἐξευρεῖν λέγε.
ΣΤ. ἀκήκοας μυριάκις ἁγὼ βούλομαι,
  περὶ τῶν τόκων, ὅπως ἀποδώσω μηδενί.
ΣΩ. ἴθ' ἐγκαλύπτου καὶ σχάσας τὴν φροντίδα 740
  λεπτὴν κατὰ μικρὸν περιφρόνει τὰ πράγματα,
  ὀρθῶς διαιρῶν καὶ σκοπῶν. ΣΤ. οἴμοι τάλας.
ΣΩ. ἔχ' ἀτρέμα· κἂν ἀπορῇς τι τῶν νοημάτων,
  ἀφεὶς ἄπελθε· κᾆτα τὴν γνώμην πάλιν
  κίνησον αὖθις αὐτὸ καὶ ζυγώθρισον. 745
ΣΤ. ὦ Σωκρατίδιον φίλτατον. ΣΩ. τί ὦ γέρον;
ΣΤ. ἔχω τόκου γνώμην ἀποστερητικήν.
ΣΩ. ἐπίδειξον αὐτήν. ΣΤ. εἰπὲ δή νύν μοι ΣΩ. τὸ
  τί;
ΣΤ. γυναῖκα φαρμακίδ' εἰ πριάμενος Θετταλὴν
  καθέλοιμι νύκτωρ τὴν σελήνην, εἶτα δὲ 750
  αὐτὴν καθείρξαιμ' ἐς λοφεῖον στρογγύλον,
  ὥσπερ κάτοπτρον, κᾆτα τηροίην ἔχων,
ΣΩ. τί δῆτα τοῦτ' ἂν ὠφελήσειέν σ'; ΣΤ. ὅ τι;
  εἰ μηκέτ' ἀνατέλλοι σελήνη μηδαμοῦ,
  οὐκ ἂν ἀποδοίην τοὺς τόκους. ΣΩ. ὁτιὴ τί δή; 755
ΣΤ. ὁτιὴ κατὰ μῆνα τἀργύριον δανείζεται.
ΣΩ. εὖ γ'· ἀλλ' ἕτερον αὖ σοι προβαλῶ τι δεξιόν·
  εἴ σοι γράφοιτο πεντετάλαντός τις δίκη,
  ὅπως ἂν αὐτὴν ἀφανίσειας εἰπέ μοι.
ΣΤ. ὅπως; ὅπως; οὐκ οἶδ'· ἀτὰρ ζητητέον. 760

  737. πρῶτον ἐξευρεῖν· πρῶτος ἐξευρὼν vulg.
  739. ὅπως ἀποδώσω· ὅπως ἂν ἀποδῶ vulg.
  745. αὐτὸ καὶ· αὖ σὺ καὶ Kust. αὐτό τε Bl.
  748. τὸ τί; τοδί (cont. Str.) C Dind. Bl.

ΣΩ. μή νυν περὶ σαυτὸν εἷλλε τὴν γνώμην ἀεί,
ἀλλ' ἀποχάλα τὴν φροντίδ' ἐς τὸν ἀέρα
λινόδετον ὥσπερ μηλολόνθην τοῦ ποδός.
ΣΤ. εὕρηκ' ἀφάνισιν τῆς δίκης σοφωτάτην,
ὥστ' αὐτὸν ὁμολογεῖν σ' ἐμοί. ΣΩ. ποίαν τινά;
ΣΤ. ἤδη παρὰ τοῖσι φαρμακοπώλαις τὴν λίθον 766
ταύτην ἑόρακας τὴν καλὴν τὴν διαφανῆ,
ἀφ' ἧς τὸ πῦρ ἅπτουσι; ΣΩ. τὴν ὕαλον λέγεις;
ΣΤ. ἔγωγε. φέρε τί δῆτ' ἄν, εἰ ταύτην λαβών,
ὁπότε γράφοιτο τὴν δίκην ὁ γραμματεύς, 770
ἀπωτέρω στὰς ὧδε πρὸς τὸν ἥλιον
τὰ γράμματ' ἐκτήξαιμι τῆς ἐμῆς δίκης;
ΣΩ. σοφῶς γε νὴ τὰς Χάριτας. ΣΤ. οἴμ' ὡς ἥδομαι
ὅτι πεντετάλαντος διαγέγραπταί μοι δίκη.
ΣΩ. ἄγε δὴ ταχέως τουτὶ ξυνάρπασον. ΣΤ. τὸ τί;
ΣΩ. ὅπως ἂν ἀποτρέψειας ἀντιδικῶν δίκην, 776
μέλλων ὀφλήσειν μὴ παρόντων μαρτύρων.
ΣΤ. φαυλότατα καὶ ῥᾷστ'. ΣΩ. εἰπὲ δή. ΣΤ. καὶ
   δὴ λέγω.
εἰ πρόσθεν ἔτι μιᾶς ἐνεστώσης δίκης,
πρὶν τὴν ἐμὴν καλεῖσθ', ἀπαγξαίμην τρέχων. 780
ΣΩ. οὐδὲν λέγεις. ΣΤ. νὴ τοὺς θεοὺς ἔγωγ', ἐπεὶ
οὐδεὶς κατ' ἐμοῦ τεθνεῶτος εἰσάξει δίκην.
ΣΩ. ὑθλεῖς· ἄπερρ', οὐκ ἂν διδάξαιμ' ἄν σ' ἔτι.
ΣΤ. ὁτιὴ τί; ναὶ πρὸς τῶν θεῶν, ὦ Σώκρατες.
ΣΩ. ἀλλ' εὐθὺς ἐπιλήθει σύ γ' ἅττ' ἂν καὶ μάθῃς·
ἐπεὶ τί νυνὶ πρῶτον ἐδιδάχθης; λέγε. 786

776. ὅπως ἂν ἀποτρέψειας Bl. ὅπως ἀπο(σ)τρέψαις ἂν libri edd.
ὅπως ἀποστρέψαι ἂν Mein. Kock. ἀντιδικῶν· ἀντιδίκων Reisig.
783. διδάξαιμ' ἂν cor. Emsl. διδαξαίμην libri.
786. νυνὶ RSV. νῦν, δή γε, δῆτα al. libri. νῦν δή, ἢν ὅ vel δὴ τό
edd. ἐδιδάχθης vel ἐδιδάσκου libri.

ΣΤ. φέρ' ἴδω τί μέντοι πρῶτον ἦν; τί πρῶτον ἦν;
τίς ἦν ἐν ᾗ ματτόμεθα μέντοι τἄλφιτα;
οἴμοι τίς ἦν; ΣΩ. οὐκ ἐς κόρακας ἀποφθερεῖ
ἐπιλησμότατον καὶ σκαιότατον γερόντιον; 790
ΣΤ. οἴμοι τί οὖν δῆθ' ὁ κακοδαίμων πείσομαι;
ἀπὸ γὰρ ὀλοῦμαι μὴ μαθὼν γλωττοστροφεῖν.
ἀλλ', ὦ νεφέλαι, χρηστόν τι συμβουλεύσατε.
ΧΟ. ἡμεῖς μέν, ὦ πρεσβῦτα, συμβουλεύομεν,
εἴ σοί τις υἱός ἐστιν ἐκτεθραμμένος, 795
πέμπειν ἐκεῖνον ἀντὶ σαυτοῦ μανθάνειν.
ΣΤ. ἀλλ' ἔστ' ἔμοιγ' υἱὸς καλός τε κἀγαθός·
ἀλλ' οὐκ ἐθέλει γὰρ μανθάνειν· τί ἐγὼ πάθω;
ΧΟ. σὺ δ' ἐπιτρέπεις; ΣΤ. εὐσωματεῖ γὰρ καὶ
σφριγᾷ,
κἄστ' ἐκ γυναικῶν εὐπτέρων τῶν Κοισύρας. 800
ἀτὰρ μέτειμί γ' αὐτόν· ἢν δὲ μὴ θέλῃ,
οὐκ ἔσθ' ὅπως οὐκ ἐξελῶ 'κ τῆς οἰκίας.
ἀλλ' ἐπανάμεινόν μ' ὀλίγον εἰσελθὼν χρόνον.

Antistrophe (805—812)

ΧΟ. ἆρ' αἰσθάνει πλεῖστα δι' ἡμᾶς ἀγάθ' αὐτίχ'
ἕξων 805
μόνας θεῶν; ὡς
ἕτοιμος ὅδ' ἐστὶν ἅπαντα δρᾶν
ὅσ' ἂν κελεύῃς.
σὺ δ' ἀνδρὸς ἐκπεπληγμένου καὶ φανερῶς ἐπηρ-
μένου 810
γνοὺς ἀπολάψεις ὅ τι πλεῖστον δύνασαι,
ταχέως· φιλεῖ γάρ πως τὰ τοιαῦθ' ἑτέρᾳ τρέ-
πεσθαι.

795. ἐκτεθραμμένος· εὖ τεθρ. Mein.
811. ἀπολάψεις· ἀπολαύσαι:s Herm.

ΝΕΦΕΛΑΙ 43

ΣΤΡΕΨΙΑΔΗΣ. ΦΕΙΔΙΠΠΙΔΗΣ. ΣΩΚΡΑΤΗΣ. ΧΟΡΟΣ

ΣΤ. οὗτοι μὰ τὴν Ὁμίχλην ἔτ' ἐνταυθὶ μενεῖς·
ἀλλ' ἔσθι' ἐλθὼν τοὺς Μεγακλέους κίονας. 815
ΦΕ. ὦ δαιμόνιε, τί χρῆμα πάσχεις, ὦ πάτερ;
οὐκ εὖ φρονεῖς μὰ τὸν Δία τὸν Ὀλύμπιον.
ΣΤ. ἰδού γ' ἰδού, Δί' Ὀλύμπιον· τῆς μωρίας,
τὸ Δία νομίζειν ὄντα τηλικουτονί. 819
ΦΕ. τί δὲ τοῦτ' ἐγέλασας ἐτεόν; ΣΤ. ἐνθυμούμενος
ὅτι παιδάριον εἶ καὶ φρονεῖς ἀρχαιικά.
ὅμως γε μὴν πρόσελθ', ἵν' εἰδῇς πλείονα,
καί σοι φράσω τι πρᾶγμ' ὃ μαθὼν ἀνὴρ ἔσει.
ὅπως δὲ τοῦτο μὴ διδάξεις μηδένα.
ΦΕ. ἰδού· τί ἔστιν; ΣΤ. ὤμοσας νυνὶ Δία. 825
ΦΕ. ἔγωγ'. ΣΤ. ὁρᾷς οὖν ὡς ἀγαθὸν τὸ μανθάνειν;
οὐκ ἔστιν, ὦ Φειδιππίδη, Ζεύς. ΦΕ. ἀλλὰ τίς;
ΣΤ. δῖνος βασιλεύει τὸν Δί' ἐξεληλακώς.
ΦΕ. αἰβοῖ, τί ληρεῖς; ΣΤ. ἴσθι τοῦθ' οὕτως ἔχον.
ΦΕ. τίς φησι ταῦτα; ΣΤ. Σωκράτης ὁ Μήλιος 830
καὶ Χαιρεφῶν, ὃς οἶδε τὰ ψυλλῶν ἴχνη.
ΦΕ. σὺ δ' ἐς τοσοῦτον τῶν μανιῶν ἐλήλυθας
ὥστ' ἀνδράσιν πείθει χολῶσιν; ΣΤ. εὐστόμει
καὶ μηδὲν εἴπῃς φλαῦρον ἄνδρας δεξιοὺς
καὶ νοῦν ἔχοντας· ὧν ὑπὸ τῆς φειδωλίας 835
ἀπεκείρατ' οὐδεὶς πώποτ' οὐδ' ἠλείψατο,
οὐδ' εἰς βαλανεῖον ἦλθε λουσόμενος· σὺ δὲ
ὥσπερ τεθνεῶτος καταλόει μου τὸν βίον.
ἀλλ' ὡς τάχιστ' ἐλθὼν ὑπὲρ ἐμοῦ μάνθανε.

815. ἐνταυθὶ· ἐνταυθοῖ libri vulg.
825. νυνὶ· νῦν νὴ plur. libr. νῦν δὴ Reisig. νυνδὴ Cobet.
827. οὐκ ἔστιν· οὐκ ἔνεστιν R. οὐκ ἔστ' ἔτ' Mein. Kock.

ΦΕ. τί δ' ἂν παρ' ἐκείνων καὶ μάθοι χρηστόν τις ἄν;
ΣΤ. ἄληθες; ὅσαπερ ἔστ' ἐν ἀνθρώποις σοφά· 841
γνώσει δὲ σαυτὸν ὡς ἀμαθὴς εἶ καὶ παχύς.
ἀλλ' ἐπανάμεινόν μ' ὀλίγον ἐνταυθὶ χρόνον.
ΦΕ. οἴμοι τί δράσω παραφρονοῦντος τοῦ πατρός;
πότερον παρανοίας αὐτὸν εἰσαγαγὼν ἕλω, 845
ἢ τοῖς σοροπηγοῖς τὴν μανίαν αὐτοῦ φράσω;
ΣΤ. φέρ' ἴδω, σὺ τουτονὶ τί νομίζεις; εἰπέ μοι.
ΦΕ. ἀλεκτρυόνα. ΣΤ. καλῶς γε. ταυτηνὶ δὲ τί;
ΦΕ. ἀλεκτρυόν'. ΣΤ. ἄμφω ταὐτό; καταγέλαστος εἶ.
μή νυν τὸ λοιπόν, ἀλλὰ τήνδε μὲν καλεῖν 850
ἀλεκτρύαιναν, τουτονὶ δ' ἀλέκτορα.
ΦΕ. ἀλεκτρύαιναν; ταῦτ' ἔμαθες τὰ δεξιὰ
εἴσω παρελθὼν ἄρτι παρὰ τοὺς γηγενεῖς;
ΣΤ. χἄτερά γε πόλλ'· ἀλλ' ὅ τι μάθοιμ' ἑκάστοτε,
ἐπελανθανόμην ἂν εὐθὺς ὑπὸ πλήθους ἐτῶν. 855
ΦΕ. διὰ ταῦτα δὴ καὶ θοἰμάτιον ἀπώλεσας;
ΣΤ. ἀλλ' οὐκ ἀπολώλεκ', ἀλλὰ καταπεφρόντικα.
ΦΕ. τὰς δ' ἐμβάδας ποῖ τέτροφας, ὦνόητε σύ;
ΣΤ. ὥσπερ Περικλέης ἐς τὸ δέον ἀπώλεσα.
ἀλλ' ἴθι βάδιζ', ἴωμεν· εἶτα τῷ πατρὶ 860
πιθόμενος ἐξάμαρτε· κἀγώ τοί ποτε,
οἶδ' ἐξέτει σοι τραυλίσαντι πιθόμενος·
ὃν πρῶτον ὀβολὸν ἔλαβον ἡλιαστικόν,
τούτου 'πριάμην σοι Διασίοις ἁμαξίδα.
ΦΕ. ἦ μὴν σὺ τούτοις τῷ χρόνῳ ποτ' ἀχθέσει. 865
ΣΤ. εὖ γ' ὅτι ἐπείσθης. δεῦρο δεῦρ', ὦ Σώκρατες,
ἔξελθ'· ἄγω γάρ σοι τὸν υἱὸν τουτονὶ

845. πότερον· πότερ' ἂν RSV. πότερα Dind.
847. τουτονὶ τί νομίζεις; τοῦτον(ὶ) τίνα libri. τοῦτον τί ὀνομάζεις; Mein.
861. πιθόμενος· πειθ. libri (exc. Δ).

ΝΕΦΕΛΑΙ 45

ἄκοντ᾽ ἀναπείσας. ΣΩ. νηπύτιος γάρ ἐστ᾽ ἔτι,
καὶ τῶν κρεμαθρῶν οὐ τρίβων τῶν ἐνθάδε.
ΦΕ. αὐτὸς τρίβων εἴης ἄν, εἰ κρέμαιό γε. 870
ΣΤ. οὐκ ἐς κόρακας; καταρᾷ σὺ τῷ διδασκάλῳ;
ΣΩ. ἰδοὺ κρέμαι᾽, ὡς ἠλίθιον ἐφθέγξατο
καὶ τοῖσι χείλεσιν διερρυηκόσιν.
πῶς ἂν μάθοι ποθ᾽ οὗτος ἀπόφευξιν δίκης
ἢ κλῆσιν ἢ χαύνωσιν ἀναπειστηρίαν; 875
καίτοι ταλάντου τοῦτ᾽ ἔμαθεν Ὑπέρβολος.
ΣΤ. ἀμέλει δίδασκε· θυμόσοφός ἐστιν φύσει·
εὐθύς γέ τοι παιδάριον ὂν τυννουτονὶ
ἔπλαττεν ἔνδον οἰκίας ναῦς τ᾽ ἔγλυφεν,
ἁμαξίδας τε συκίνας εἰργάζετο, 880
κἀκ τῶν σιδίων βατράχους ἐποίει πῶς δοκεῖς.
ὅπως δ᾽ ἐκείνω τὼ λόγω μαθήσεται,
τὸν κρείττον᾽ ὅστις ἐστὶ καὶ τὸν ἥττονα,
ὃς τἄδικα λέγων ἀνατρέπει τὸν κρείττονα·
ἐὰν δὲ μή, τὸν γοῦν ἄδικον πάσῃ τέχνῃ. 885
ΣΩ. αὐτὸς μαθήσεται παρ᾽ αὐτοῖν τοῖν λόγοιν.
ἐγὼ δ᾽ ἀπέσομαι. ΣΤ. τοῦτό νυν μέμνησ᾽, ὅπως
πρὸς πάντα τὰ δίκαι᾽ ἀντιλέγειν δυνήσεται.

ΧΟΡΟΣ

* * * * *

ΔΙΚΑΙΟΣ ΛΟΓΟΣ. ΑΔΙΚΟΣ ΛΟΓΟΣ. ΧΟΡΟΣ
ΔΙ. χώρει δευρί, δεῖξον σαυτὸν
τοῖσι θεαταῖς, καίπερ θρασὺς ὤν. 890

869. κρεμαθρῶν οὐ· κρεμαθρῶν οὔπω Mein. al. κρεμαστρῶν οὐ Bentl.
872. κρέμαι᾽· κρέμαιο γ᾽ libri.
880. συκίνας Naber. σκυτίνας libri ac vulg.

ΑΡΙΣΤΟΦΑΝΟΥΣ

ΛΔ. ἴθ' ὅποι χρῄζεις. πολὺ γὰρ μᾶλλόν σ'
ἐν τοῖς πολλοῖσι λέγων ἀπολῶ.
ΔΙ. ἀπολεῖς σύ; τίς ὤν; ΛΔ. λόγος. ΔΙ. ἥττων
γ' ὤν.
ΛΔ. ἀλλά σε νικῶ τὸν ἐμοῦ κρείττω
φάσκοντ' εἶναι. ΔΙ. τί σοφὸν ποιῶν; 895
ΛΔ. γνώμας καινὰς ἐξευρίσκων.
ΔΙ. ταῦτα γὰρ ἀνθεῖ διὰ τουτουσὶ
τοὺς ἀνοήτους.
ΛΔ. οὔκ, ἀλλὰ σοφούς. ΔΙ. ἀπολῶ σε κακῶς.
ΛΔ. εἰπέ, τί ποιῶν; ΔΙ. τὰ δίκαια λέγων. 900
ΛΔ. ἀλλ' ἀνατρέψω 'γὼ αὔτ' ἀντιλέγων·
οὐδὲ γὰρ εἶναι πάνυ φημὶ δίκην.
ΔΙ. οὐκ εἶναι φῄς; ΛΔ. φέρε γὰρ ποῦ 'στιν;
ΔΙ. παρὰ τοῖσι θεοῖς.
ΛΔ. πῶς δῆτα δίκης οὔσης ὁ Ζεὺς
οὐκ ἀπόλωλεν τὸν πατέρ' αὐτοῦ 905
δήσας; ΔΙ. αἰβοῖ τουτὶ καὶ δὴ
χωρεῖ τὸ κακόν· δότε μοι λεκάνην.
ΛΔ. τυφογέρων εἶ κἀνάρμοστος.
ΔΙ. καταπύγων εἶ κἀναίσχυντος.
ΛΔ. ῥόδα μ' εἴρηκας. ΔΙ. καὶ βωμολόχος. 910
ΛΔ. κρίνεσι στεφανοῖς. ΔΙ. καὶ πατραλοίας.
ΛΔ. χρυσῷ πάττων μ' οὐ γιγνώσκεις.
ΔΙ. οὐ δῆτα πρὸ τοῦ γ', ἀλλὰ μολύβδῳ.
ΛΔ. νῦν δέ γε κόσμος τοῦτ' ἐστὶν ἐμοί.
ΔΙ. θρασὺς εἶ πολλοῦ. ΛΔ. σὺ δέ γ' ἀρχαῖος. 915
ΔΙ. διὰ σ' οὐ φοιτᾶν
οὐδεὶς ἐθέλει τῶν μειρακίων·
γνωσθήσει τοι ποτ' Ἀθηναίοις

901. ἀνατρέψω· ἀναστρέψω RV.

ΝΕΦΕΛΑΙ 47

  οἷα διδάσκεις τοὺς ἀνοήτους.
ΑΔ. αὐχμεῖς αἰσχρῶς. ΔΙ. σὺ δέ γ' εὖ πράττεις.
  καίτοι πρότερόν γ' ἐπτώχευες,   921
  Τήλεφος εἶναι Μυσὸς φάσκων,
  ἐκ πηριδίου
  γνώμας τρώγων Πανδελετείους.
ΑΔ. ὤμοι σοφίας ΔΙ. ὤμοι μανίας   925
ΑΔ. ἧς ἐμνήσθης
ΔΙ. τῆς σῆς, πόλεώς θ' ἥτις σε τρέφει
  λυμαινόμενον τοῖς μειρακίοις.
ΑΔ. οὐχὶ διδάξεις τοῦτον Κρόνος ὤν.
ΔΙ. εἴπερ γ' αὐτὸν σωθῆναι χρὴ   930
  καὶ μὴ λαλιὰν μόνον ἀσκῆσαι.
ΑΔ. δεῦρ' ἴθι, τοῦτον δ' ἔα μαίνεσθαι.
ΔΙ. κλαύσει, τὴν χεῖρ' ἢν ἐπιβάλλῃς.
ΧΟ. παύσασθε μάχης καὶ λοιδορίας.
  ἀλλ' ἐπίδειξαι σύ τε τοὺς προτέρους 935
  ἅττ' ἐδίδασκες, σύ τε τὴν καινὴν
  παίδευσιν, ὅπως ἂν ἀκούσας σφῶν
  ἀντιλεγόντοιν κρίνας φοιτᾷ.
ΔΙ. δρᾶν ταῦτ' ἐθέλω. ΑΔ. κἄγωγ' ἐθέλω.
ΧΟ. φέρε δὴ πότερος λέξει πρότερος;   940
ΑΔ. τούτῳ δώσω·
  κᾆτ' ἐκ τούτων ὧν ἂν λέξῃ
  ῥηματίοισιν καινοῖς αὐτὸν
  καὶ διανοίαις κατατοξεύσω.
  τὸ τελευταῖον δ', ἢν ἀναγρύξῃ,   945
  τὸ πρόσωπον ἅπαν καὶ τὠφθαλμὼ
  κεντούμενος ὥσπερ ὑπ' ἀνθρηνῶν

940. δὴ πότερος λέξει Herm. Dind. al. (δὴ) τίς λέξει πρότερος (ν) libri.

ὑπὸ τῶν γνωμῶν ἀπολεῖται.

ΧΟ. νῦν δείξετον τὼ πισύνω τοῖς περιδεξίοισι 949
λόγοισι καὶ φροντίσι καὶ γνωμοτύποις μερίμναις,
ὁπότερος αὐτοῖν λέγων ἀμείνων φανήσεται.
νῦν γὰρ ἅπας ἐνθάδε κίνδυνος ἀνεῖται σοφίας,
ἧς πέρι τοῖς ἐμοῖς φίλοις ἔστιν ἀγὼν μέγιστος.
ἀλλ', ὦ πολλοῖς τοὺς πρεσβυτέρους ἤθεσι χρηστοῖς στεφανώσας,
ῥῆξον φωνὴν ᾗτινι χαίρεις, καὶ τὴν σαυτοῦ φύσιν εἰπέ. 960

ΔΙ. λέξω τοίνυν τὴν ἀρχαίαν παιδείαν ὡς διέκειτο,
ὅτ' ἐγὼ τὰ δίκαια λέγων ἤνθουν καὶ σωφροσύνη
'νενόμιστο.
πρῶτον μὲν ἔδει παιδὸς φωνὴν γρύξαντος μηδέν'
ἀκοῦσαι·
εἶτα βαδίζειν ἐν ταῖσιν ὁδοῖς εὐτάκτως ἐς
κιθαριστοῦ
τοὺς κωμήτας γυμνοὺς ἁθρόους, κεἰ κριμνώδη
κατανίφοι. 965
εἶτ' αὖ προμαθεῖν ᾆσμ' ἐδίδασκεν τὼ μηρὼ μὴ
ξυνέχοντας,
ἢ Παλλάδα περσέπολιν δεινὰν ἢ Τηλέπορόν τι
βόαμα,
ἐντειναμένους τὴν ἁρμονίαν, ἣν οἱ πατέρες παρέδωκαν.
εἰ δέ τις αὐτῶν βωμολοχεύσαιτ' ἢ κάμψειέν τινα
καμπήν, 970

948. ὑπὸ τῶν γνωμῶν· τῶν γνωμιδίων vel τῶν γνωμῶν ἔξαπ. Mein.
960. σαυτοῦ· αὐτοῦ RV.
966. ἐδίδασκεν· an ἐδίδασκον Büch. cf. 935.
969. ἐντειναμένους· -νος Bergk. ἐντυναμένης R.

ΝΕΦΕΛΑΙ 49

οἵας οἱ νῦν τὰς κατὰ Φρῦνιν ταύτας τὰς δυσκολοκάμπτους,
ἐπετρίβετο τυπτόμενος πολλὰς ὡς τὰς Μούσας
ἀφανίζων.
οὐδ᾽ ἀνελέσθαι δειπνοῦντ᾽ ἐξῆν κεφάλαιον τῆς
ῥαφανῖδος, 981
οὐδ᾽ ἄννηθον τῶν πρεσβυτέρων ἁρπάζειν οὐδὲ
σέλινον,
οὐδ᾽ ὀψοφαγεῖν οὐδὲ κιχλίζειν οὐδ᾽ ἴσχειν τὼ
πόδ᾽ ἐναλλάξ.

ΑΔ. ἀρχαῖά γε καὶ Διπολιώδη καὶ τεττίγων ἀνά-
μεστα
καὶ Κηκείδου καὶ Βουφονίων. ΔΙ. ἀλλ᾽ οὖν
ταῦτ᾽ ἐστὶν ἐκεῖνα, 985
ἐξ ὧν ἄνδρας Μαραθωνομάχους ἡμὴ παίδευσις
ἔθρεψεν.
σὺ δὲ τοὺς νῦν εὐθὺς ἐν ἱματίοισι διδάσκεις
ἐντετυλίχθαι.
πρὸς ταῦτ᾽, ὦ μειράκιον, θαρρῶν ἐμὲ τὸν κρείττω
λόγον αἱροῦ· 990
κἀπιστήσει μισεῖν ἀγορὰν καὶ βαλανείων ἀπέχεσθαι,
καὶ τοῖς αἰσχροῖς αἰσχύνεσθαι, κἂν σκώπτῃ τίς
σε φλέγεσθαι·
καὶ τῶν θάκων τοῖς πρεσβυτέροις ὑπανίστασθαι
προσιοῦσιν,

981. ἀνελέσθαι· ἂν ἐλέσθαι plur. libri vulg. κεφάλαιον τῆς· καὶ
φυλλεῖον Blaydes.
982. ἄννηθον· ἄνηθον RV. ἂν ἄνηθον plur. libri vulg.
987. ἱματίοισι διδ— libri. ἱματίοις προδιδάσκεις Brunck. edd. (metri grat.).

G. C. 4

ΑΡΙΣΤΟΦΑΝΟΥΣ

καὶ μὴ περὶ τοὺς σαυτοῦ γονέας σκαιουργεῖν,
ἄλλο τε μηδὲν
αἰσχρὸν ποιεῖν, ὅτι τῆς αἰδοῦς μέλλεις τἄγαλμ'
ἀναπλάττειν· 995
μηδ' ἀντειπεῖν τῷ πατρὶ μηδέν, μηδ' Ἰαπετὸν
καλέσαντα
μνησικακῆσαι τὴν ἡλικίαν, ἐξ ἧς ἐνεοττοτροφήθης.

ΛΔ. εἰ ταῦτ', ὦ μειράκιον, πείσει τούτῳ, νὴ τὸν
Διόνυσον 1000
τοῖς Ἱπποκράτους υἱέσιν εἴξεις, καί σε καλοῦσι
βλιτομάμμαν.

ΔΙ. ἀλλ' οὖν λιπαρός γε καὶ εὐανθὴς ἐν γυμνασίοις
διατρίψεις,
οὐ στωμύλλων κατὰ τὴν ἀγορὰν τριβολεκτράπελ'
οἷάπερ οἱ νῦν,
οὐδ' ἑλκόμενος περὶ πραγματίου γλισχραντιλογ-
εξεπιτρίπτου·
ἀλλ' εἰς Ἀκαδήμειαν κατιὼν ὑπὸ ταῖς μορίαις
ἀποθρέξει 1005
στεφανωσάμενος καλάμῳ λευκῷ μετὰ σώφρονος
ἡλικιώτου,
μίλακος ὄζων καὶ ἀπραγμοσύνης καὶ λεύκης
φυλλοβολούσης,
ἦρος ἐν ὥρᾳ χαίρων, ὁπόταν πλάτανος πτελέᾳ
ψιθυρίζῃ.

994. περί· παρά RSV Reisig Herm. σκαιουργεῖν R Herm. al.
κακουργεῖν plur. libri. κακοεργεῖν G V Blaydes.
995. ἀναπλάττειν R. ἀναπλήσειν V al. vid. com.
1005. ἀποθρέξει R edd. ἀποθρέξεις plur. libri. καταθρέξεις SV
Blaydes.

ἢν ταῦτα ποιῇς ἁγὼ φράζω,
καὶ πρὸς τούτοις προσέχῃς τὸν νοῦν,   1010
ἕξεις ἀεὶ
στῆθος λιπαρόν, χροιὰν λαμπράν,
ὤμους μεγάλους, γλῶτταν βαιάν.
ἢν δ' ἅπερ οἱ νῦν ἐπιτηδεύῃς,   1015
πρῶτα μὲν ἕξεις
χροιὰν ὠχράν, ὤμους μικρούς,
στῆθος λεπτόν, γλῶτταν μεγάλην,
ψήφισμα μακρόν· καί σ' ἀναπείσει
τὸ μὲν αἰσχρὸν ἅπαν καλὸν ἡγεῖσθαι,   1020
τὸ καλὸν δ' αἰσχρόν·
καὶ πρὸς τούτοις τῆς Ἀντιμάχου
καταπυγοσύνης ἀναπλήσει.

Antistrophe (1024—1035)

ΧΟ. ὦ καλλίπυργον σοφίαν κλεινοτάτην ἐπασκῶν
ὡς ἡδύ σου τοῖσι λόγοις σῶφρον ἔπεστιν ἄνθος.
εὐδαίμονες δ' ἦσαν ἄρ' οἱ ζῶντες τότ' ἐπὶ τῶν
προτέρων.
πρὸς οὖν τάδ', ὦ κομψοπρεπῆ μοῦσαν ἔχων,   1030
δεῖ σε λέγειν τι καινόν, ὡς ηὐδοκίμηκεν ἀνήρ.
δεινῶν δέ σοι βουλευμάτων ἔοικε δεῖν πρὸς αὐτόν,
εἴπερ τὸν ἄνδρ' ὑπερβαλεῖ καὶ μὴ γέλωτ'
ὀφλήσεις.   1035
ΑΔ. καὶ μὴν πάλαι γ' ἐπνιγόμην τὰ σπλάγχνα
κἀπεθύμουν
ἅπαντα ταῦτ' ἐναντίαις γνώμαισι συνταράξαι.

1012. λαμπράν A etc. Blaydes.   λευκήν RS Dind. Mein. al.
1023. ἀναπλήσει· σ' ἀναπλήσει Teuf. Blaydes.
1031. ηὐδοκίμηκεν· εὐδοκίμηκ(σ)εν libri.
1036. πάλαι γ'· aliquot libri edd.   πάλαί γ' ἔγωγ' G al. ἔγωγ' RSV.

4—2

ἐγὼ γὰρ ἥττων μὲν λόγος δι' αὐτὸ τοῦτ' ἐκλήθην
ἐν τοῖσι φροντισταῖσιν, ὅτι πρώτιστος ἐπενόησα
καὶ τοῖς νόμοις καὶ ταῖς δίκαις τἀναντί' ἀντιλέξαι. 1040
καὶ τοῦτο πλεῖν ἢ μυρίων ἔστ' ἄξιον στα-
τήρων,
αἱρούμενον τοὺς ἥττονας λόγους ἔπειτα νικᾶν.
σκέψαι δὲ τὴν παίδευσιν ᾗ πέποιθεν ὡς ἐλέγξω,
ὅστις σε θερμῷ φησι λοῦσθαι πρῶτον οὐκ
ἐάσειν.
καίτοι τίνα γνώμην ἔχων ψέγεις τὰ θερμὰ
λουτρά; 1045
ΔΙ. ὁτιὴ κάκιστόν ἐστι καὶ δειλὸν ποιεῖ τὸν ἄνδρα.
ΑΔ. ἐπίσχες· εὐθὺς γάρ σ' ἔχω μέσον λαβὼν ἄφυκτον.
καί μοι φράσον, τῶν τοῦ Διὸς παίδων τίν' ἄνδρ'
ἄριστον
ψυχὴν νομίζεις, εἰπέ, καὶ πλείστους πόνους
πονῆσαι; 1049
ΔΙ. ἐγὼ μὲν οὐδέν' Ἡρακλέους βελτίον' ἄνδρα κρίνω.
ΑΔ. ποῦ ψυχρὰ δῆτα πώποτ' εἶδες Ἡράκλεια λουτρά;
καίτοι τίς ἀνδρειότερος ἦν; ΔΙ. ταῦτ' ἐστὶ
ταῦτ' ἐκεῖνα,
ἃ τῶν νεανίσκων ἀεὶ δι' ἡμέρας λαλούντων
πλῆρες τὸ βαλανεῖον ποιεῖ, κενὰς δὲ τὰς
παλαίστρας.
ΑΔ. εἶτ' ἐν ἀγορᾷ τὴν διατριβὴν ψέγεις· ἐγὼ δ'
ἐπαινῶ. 1055
εἰ γὰρ πονηρὸν ἦν, Ὅμηρος οὐδέποτ' ἂν ἐποίει
τὸν Νέστορ' ἀγορητὴν ἂν οὐδὲ τοὺς σοφοὺς
ἅπαντας.
ἄνειμι δῆτ' ἐντεῦθεν ἐς τὴν γλῶτταν, ἣν ὁδὶ μὲν
οὔ φησι χρῆναι τοὺς νέους ἀσκεῖν, ἐγὼ δὲ φημί.

ΝΕΦΕΛΑΙ

    καὶ σωφρονεῖν αὖ φησὶ χρῆναι· δύο κακὼ
    μεγίστω.   1060
    ἐπεὶ σὺ διὰ τὸ σωφρονεῖν τῷ πώποτ' εἶδες ἤδη
    ἀγαθόν τι γενόμενον, φράσον, καί μ' ἐξέλεγξον
    εἰπών.
ΔΙ. πολλοῖς. ὁ γοῦν Πηλεὺς ἔλαβε δι' αὐτὸ τὴν
    μάχαιραν.
ΛΔ. μάχαιραν; ἀστεῖόν γε κέρδος ἔλαβεν ὁ κακο-
    δαίμων.
    Ὑπέρβολος δ' οὐκ τῶν λύχνων πλεῖν ἢ τάλαντα
    πολλὰ   1065
    εἴληφε διὰ πονηρίαν, ἀλλ' οὐ μὰ Δία μά-
    χαιραν.
ΔΙ. καὶ τὴν Θέτιν γ' ἔγημε διὰ τὸ σωφρονεῖν ὁ
    Πηλεύς.
ΛΔ. κᾆτ' ἀπολιποῦσά γ' αὐτὸν ᾤχετ'· οὐ γὰρ ἦν
    ὑβριστής.   1068
    σκέψαι γάρ, ὦ μειράκιον, ἐν τῷ σωφρονεῖν
    ἅπαντα
    ἄνεστιν, ἡδονῶν θ' ὅσων μέλλεις ἀποστερεῖσθαι.
    παίδων, γυναικῶν, κοττάβων, ὄψων, πότων, κι-
    χλισμῶν.
    καίτοι τί σοι ζῆν ἄξιον, τούτων ἐὰν στερηθῇς;
    εἶεν. πάρειμ' ἐντεῦθεν ἐς τὰς τῆς φύσεως ἀνάγ-
    κας.   1075
    ἥμαρτες, ἠράσθης, ἐμοίχευσάς τι κᾆτ' ἐλήφθης·
    ἀπόλωλας· ἀδύνατος γὰρ εἶ λέγειν. ἐμοὶ δ'
    ὁμιλῶν

1062. εἰπών· εὑρών Mein.
1063. δι' αὐτὸ Pors. (metri grat.). διὰ τοῦτο libri.
1076. κᾆτ' ἐλήφθης· κατελήφθης libri. κἀπελήφθης Mein.

χρῶ τῇ φύσει, σκίρτα, γέλα, νόμιζε μηδὲν
αἰσχρόν.
μοιχὸς γὰρ ἦν τύχης ἁλούς, τάδ' ἀντερεῖς πρὸς
αὐτόν, 1079
ὡς οὐδὲν ἠδίκηκας· εἶτ' ἐς τὸν Δί' ἐπανενεγκεῖν,
κἀκεῖνος ὡς ἥττων ἔρωτός ἐστι καὶ γυναικῶν·
καίτοι σὺ θνητὸς ὢν θεοῦ πῶς μεῖζον ἂν δύναιο;
τί δῆτ' ἐρεῖς; ΔΙ. ἡττήμεθα· 1102
πρὸς τῶν θεῶν δέξασθέ μου
θοἰμάτιον, ὡς
ἐξαυτομολῶ πρὸς ὑμᾶς.

ΣΩΚΡΑΤΗΣ.   ΣΤΡΕΨΙΑΔΗΣ.   ΦΕΙΔΙΠΠΙΔΗΣ

ΣΩ. τί δῆτα; πότερα τοῦτον ἀπάγεσθαι λαβὼν 1105
βούλει τὸν υἱόν, ἢ διδάσκω σοι λέγειν;
ΣΤ. δίδασκε καὶ κόλαζε καὶ μέμνησ' ὅπως
εὖ μοι στομώσεις αὐτόν, ἐπὶ μὲν θάτερα
οἷον δικιδίοις, τὴν δ' ἑτέραν αὐτοῦ γνάθον
στόμωσον οἵαν ἐς τὰ μείζω πράγματα. 1110
ΣΩ. ἀμέλει κομιεῖ τοῦτον σοφιστὴν δεξιόν.
ΦΕ. ὠχρὸν μὲν οὖν, οἶμαί γε, καὶ κακοδαίμονα.

ΧΟΡΟΣ

χωρεῖτέ νυν. οἶμαι δέ σοι ταῦτα μεταμελήσειν.
τοὺς κριτὰς ἃ κερδανοῦσιν, ἢν τι τόνδε τὸν
χορὸν 1115
ὠφελῶσ' ἐκ τῶν δικαίων, βουλόμεσθ' ἡμεῖς
φράσαι.

1109. οἷον · οἵαν (e prox. vers.) libri.
1115. τοὺς κριτὰς · qu. τοῖς κριταῖς Blaydes.

πρῶτα μὲν γάρ, ἢν νεᾶν βούλησθ' ἐν ὥρᾳ τοὺς
  ἀγρούς,
ὕσομεν πρώτοισιν ὑμῖν τοῖσι δ' ἄλλοις ὕστερον.
εἶτα τὸν καρπόν τε καὶ τὰς ἀμπέλους φυλάξομεν,
ὥστε μήτ' αὐχμὸν πιέζειν μήτ' ἄγαν ἐπομβρίαν.
ἢν δ' ἀτιμάσῃ τις ἡμᾶς θνητὸς ὢν οὔσας θεάς, 1121
προσεχέτω τὸν νοῦν, πρὸς ἡμῶν οἷα πείσεται
  κακά,
λαμβάνων οὔτ' οἶνον οὔτ' ἄλλ' οὐδὲν ἐκ τοῦ
  χωρίου.
ἡνίκ' ἂν γὰρ αἵ τ' ἐλᾶαι βλαστάνωσ' αἵ τ'
  ἄμπελοι, 1124
ἀποκεκόψονται· τοιαύταις σφενδόναις παιήσομεν.
ἢν δὲ πλινθεύοιτ' ἴδωμεν, ὕσομεν καὶ τοῦ τέγους
τὸν κέραμον αὐτοῦ χαλάζαις στρογγύλαις συντρί-
  ψομεν.
κἂν γαμῇ ποτ' αὐτὸς ἢ τῶν ξυγγενῶν τις ἢ
  φίλων,
ὕσομεν τὴν νύκτα πᾶσαν· ὥστ' ἴσως βουλήσεται
κἂν ἐν Αἰγύπτῳ τυχεῖν ὢν μᾶλλον ἢ κρῖναι
  κακῶς. 1130

ΣΤΡΕΨΙΑΔΗΣ.   ΣΩΚΡΑΤΗΣ.   ΦΕΙΔΙΠΠΙΔΗΣ

ΣΤ. πέμπτη, τετράς, τρίτη, μετὰ ταύτην δευτέρα,
εἶθ', ἣν ἐγὼ μάλιστα πασῶν ἡμερῶν
δέδοικα καὶ πέφρικα καὶ βδελύττομαι,
εὐθὺς μετὰ ταύτην ἔσθ' ἕνη τε καὶ νέα.
πᾶς γάρ τις ὀμνύς, οἷς ὀφείλων τυγχάνω, 1135

1119. καρπόν τε καὶ τὰς Cornes.   καρπὸν τεκούσας libri.
1128. τις ἢ Bl.   ἢ τῶν vulg.
1135. ὀμνύς· ὄμνυσ' plur. libri

ΑΡΙΣΤΟΦΑΝΟΥΣ

θείς μοι πρυτανεί' ἀπολεῖν μέ φησι κἀξολεῖν·
κἀμοῦ μέτρι' ἄττα καὶ δίκαι' αἰτουμένου,
'ὦ δαιμόνιε, τὸ μέν τι νυνὶ μὲν λαβέ,
τὸ δ' ἀναβαλοῦ μοι, τὸ δ' ἄφες,' οὔ φασίν ποτε
οὕτως ἀπολήψεσθ', ἀλλὰ λοιδοροῦσί με   1140
ὡς ἄδικός εἰμι, καὶ δικάσεσθαί φασί μοι.
νῦν οὖν δικαζέσθων· ὀλίγον γάρ μοι μέλει,
εἴπερ μεμάθηκέ γ' εὖ λέγειν Φειδιππίδης.
τάχα δ' εἴσομαι κόψας τὸ φροντιστήριον.
παῖ, ἠμί, παῖ παῖ.   ΣΩ. Στρεψιάδην ἀσπάζομαι.
ΣΤ. κἄγωγέ σ'· ἀλλὰ τουτονὶ πρῶτον λαβέ·   1146
χρὴ γὰρ ἐπιθαυμάζειν τι τὸν διδάσκαλον.
καί μοι τὸν υἱὸν εἰ μεμάθηκε τὸν λόγον
ἐκεῖνον εἴφ' ὃν ἀρτίως εἰσήγαγες.
ΣΩ. μεμάθηκεν.   ΣΤ. εὖ γ', ὦ παμβασίλει' Ἀπαιόλη.
ΣΩ. ὥστ' ἀποφύγοις ἂν ἥντιν' ἂν βούλῃ δίκην.   1151
ΣΤ. κεἰ μάρτυρες παρῆσαν, ὅτ' ἐδανειζόμην;
ΣΩ. πολλῷ γε μᾶλλον, κἂν παρῶσι χίλιοι.
ΣΤ. βοάσομαί τἄρα τὰν ὑπέρτονον
βοάν. ἰώ, κλάετ', ὠβολοστάται,   1155
αὐτοί τε καὶ τἀρχαῖα καὶ τόκοι τόκων·
οὐδὲν γὰρ ἄν με φλαῦρον ἐργάσαισθ' ἔτι·
οἷος ἐμοὶ τρέφεται
τοῖσδ' ἐνὶ δώμασι παῖς,
ἀμφήκει γλώττῃ λάμπων,   1160
πρόβολος ἐμός, σωτὴρ δόμοις, ἐχθροῖς βλάβη,
λυσανίας πατρῴων μεγάλων κακῶν·

1137. κἀμοῦ· ἐμοῦ vulg.   μέτρι' ἄττα· μέτρια τε libri.
1138. μὲν λαβέ Blaydes.   μὴ λάβῃς vulg.
1141. δικάσεσθαι· -σασθαι plur. libri.
1153. κἂν παρῶσι· κεἰ παρῆσαν Blaydes.

ΝΕΦΕΛΑΙ 57

   ὃν κάλεσον τρέχων ἔνδοθεν ὡς ἐμέ.
ΣΩ. ὦ τέκνον, ὦ παῖ, ἔξελθ' οἴκων,   1165
   ἄϊε σοῦ πατρός.
   ὅδ' ἐκεῖνος ἀνήρ.
ΣΤ. ὦ φίλος, ὦ φίλος.
ΣΩ. ἄπιθι λαβὼν τὸν υἱόν.
ΣΤ. ἰὼ ἰὼ τέκνον, ἰὼ ἰοῦ ἰοῦ,   1170
   ὡς ἥδομαί σου πρῶτα τὴν χροιὰν ἰδών.
   νῦν μέν γ' ἰδεῖν εἶ πρῶτον ἐξαρνητικὸς
   κἀντιλογικός, καὶ τοῦτο τοὐπιχώριον
   ἀτεχνῶς ἐπανθεῖ, τὸ τί λέγεις σύ; καὶ δοκεῖν
   ἀδικοῦντ' ἀδικεῖσθαι καὶ κακουργοῦντ' οἶδ' ὅτι.
   ἐπὶ τοῦ προσώπου τ' ἐστὶν Ἀττικὸν βλέπος. 1176
   νῦν οὖν ὅπως σώσεις μ', ἐπεὶ κἀπώλεσας.
ΦΕ. φοβεῖ δὲ δὴ τί; ΣΤ. τὴν ἕνην τε καὶ νέαν.
ΦΕ. ἕνη γάρ ἐστι καὶ νέα τις ἡμέρα;
ΣΤ. εἰς ἥν γε θήσειν τὰ πρυτανεῖά φασί μοι.   1180
ΦΕ. ἀπολοῦσ' ἄρ' αὔθ' οἱ θέντες· οὐ γὰρ ἔσθ' ὅπως
   μἴ ἡμέρα γένοιτ' ἂν ἡμέρα δύο.
ΣΤ. οὐκ ἂν γένοιτο; ΦΕ. πῶς γάρ; εἰ μή πέρ γ'
   ἅμα
   αὐτὴ γένοιτ' ἂν γραῦς τε καὶ νέα γυνή.
ΣΤ. καὶ μὴν νενόμισταί γ'. ΦΕ. οὐ γάρ, οἶμαι, τὸν
   νόμον   1185
   ἴσασιν ὀρθῶς ὅ τι νοεῖ. ΣΤ. νοεῖ δὲ τί;
ΦΕ. ὁ Σόλων ὁ παλαιὸς ἦν φιλόδημος τὴν φύσιν.
ΣΤ. τουτὶ μὲν οὐδέν πω πρὸς ἕνην τε καὶ νέαν.
ΦΕ. ἐκεῖνος οὖν τὴν κλῆσιν ἐς δύ' ἡμέρας
   ἔθηκεν, ἔς γε τὴν ἕνην τε καὶ νέαν,   1190
   ἵν' αἱ θέσεις γίγνοιντο τῇ νουμηνίᾳ.

  1175. οἶδ' ὅτι· εὖ ποιεῖν Bentl. Blaydes.

ΣΤ. ἵνα δὴ τί τὴν ἕνην προσέθηχ'; ΦΕ. ἵν', ὦ μέλε,
παρόντες οἱ φεύγοντες ἡμέρᾳ μιᾷ
πρότερον ἀπαλλάττοινθ' ἑκόντες, εἰ δὲ μή,
ἕωθεν ὑπανιῷντο τῇ νουμηνίᾳ. 1195
ΣΤ. πῶς οὐ δέχονται δῆτα τῇ νουμηνίᾳ
ἀρχαὶ τὰ πρυτανεῖ', ἀλλ' ἕνῃ τε καὶ νέᾳ;
ΦΕ. ὅπερ οἱ προτένθαι γὰρ δοκοῦσί μοι ποιεῖν·
ἵν' ὡς τάχιστα τὰ πρυτανεῖ' ὑφελοίατο,
διὰ τοῦτο προὐτένθευσαν ἡμέρᾳ μιᾷ. 1200
ΣΤ. εὖ γ'· ὦ κακοδαίμονες, τί κάθησθ' ἀβέλτεροι,
ἡμέτερα κέρδη τῶν σοφῶν ὄντες, λίθοι,
ἀριθμός, πρόβατ' ἄλλως, ἀμφορῆς νενημένοι;
ὥστ' εἰς ἐμαυτὸν καὶ τὸν υἱὸν τουτονὶ
ἐπ' εὐτυχίαισιν ᾀστέον μοὐγκώμιον. 1205
'μάκαρ ὦ Στρεψίαδες,
αὐτός τ' ἔφυς ὡς σοφός,
χοῖον τὸν υἱὸν τρέφεις,'
φήσουσι δή μ' οἱ φίλοι
χοἰ δημόται 1210
ζηλοῦντες ἡνίκ' ἂν σὺ νικᾷς λέγων τὰς δίκας.
ἀλλ' εἰσάγων σε βούλομαι πρῶτον ἑστιᾶσαι.

ΠΑΣΙΑΣ

εἶτ' ἄνδρα τῶν αὑτοῦ τι χρὴ προϊέναι;
οὐδέποτέ γ', ἀλλὰ κρεῖττον εὐθὺς ἦν τότε 1215
ἀπερυθριᾶσαι μᾶλλον ἢ σχεῖν πράγματα,
ὅτε τῶν ἐμαυτοῦ γ' ἕνεκα νυνὶ χρημάτων

1197. ἀρχαί· ἀρχαί libri.
1198. ποιεῖν· παθεῖν plur. libri.
1199. ἵν' ὡς aliquot libri Dind. Bl. ὅπως RV al. Herm. Kock al.
1203. νενημένοι· νενησμένοι plur. libri.

ΝΕΦΕΛΑΙ

ἕλκω σε κλητεύσοντα, καὶ γενήσομαι
ἐχθρὸς ἔτι πρὸς τούτοισιν ἀνδρὶ δημότῃ.
ἀτὰρ οὐδέποτέ γε τὴν πατρίδα καταισχυνῶ 1220
ζῶν, ἀλλὰ καλοῦμαι Στρεψιάδην ΣΤ. τίς οὑτοσί;
ΠΑ. ἐς τὴν ἕνην τε καὶ νέαν. ΣΤ. μαρτύρομαι,
ὅτι ἐς δύ᾽ εἶπεν ἡμέρας. τοῦ χρήματος;
ΠΑ. τῶν δώδεκα μνῶν, ἃς ἔλαβες ὠνούμενος
τὸν ψαρὸν ἵππον. ΣΤ. ἵππον; οὐκ ἀκούετε,
ὃν πάντες ὑμεῖς ἴστε μισοῦνθ᾽ ἱππικήν. 1226
ΠΑ. καὶ νὴ Δί᾽ ἀποδώσειν γ᾽ ἐπώμνυς τοὺς θεούς.
ΣΤ. μὰ τὸν Δί᾽ οὐ γάρ πω τότ᾽ ἐξηπίστατο
Φειδιππίδης μοι τὸν ἀκατάβλητον λόγον.
ΠΑ. νῦν δὲ διὰ τοῦτ᾽ ἔξαρνος εἶναι διανοεῖ; 1230
ΣΤ. τί γὰρ ἄλλ᾽ ἂν ἀπολαύσαιμι τοῦ μαθήματος;
ΠΑ. καὶ ταῦτ᾽ ἐθελήσεις ἀπομόσαι μοι τοὺς θεούς;
ΣΤ. ποίους θεούς;
ΠΑ. τὸν Δία, τὸν Ἑρμῆν, τὸν Ποσειδῶ. ΣΤ. νὴ
 Δία,
κἂν προσκαταθείην γ᾽ ὥστ᾽ ὀμόσαι τριώβολον.
ΠΑ. ἀπόλοιο τοίνυν ἕνεκ᾽ ἀναιδείας ἔτι. 1236
ΣΤ. ἁλσὶν διασμηχθεὶς ὄναιτ᾽ ἂν οὑτοσί.
ΠΑ. οἴμ᾽ ὡς καταγελᾷς. ΣΤ. ἒξ χόας χωρήσεται.
ΠΑ. οὔ τοι μὰ τὸν Δία τὸν μέγαν καὶ τοὺς θεοὺς
ἐμοῦ καταπροίξει. ΣΤ. θαυμασίως ἥσθην θεοῖς,
καὶ Ζεὺς γέλοιος ὀμνύμενος τοῖς εἰδόσιν. 1241
ΠΑ. ἦ μὴν σὺ τούτων τῷ χρόνῳ δώσεις δίκην.
ἀλλ᾽ εἴτ᾽ ἀποδώσεις μοι τὰ χρήματ᾽ εἴτε μὴ
ἀπόπεμψον ἀποκρινάμενος. ΣΤ. ἔχε νυν ἥσυχος.
ἐγὼ γὰρ αὐτίκ᾽ ἀποκρινοῦμαί σοι σαφῶς. 1245

1228. μὰ τὸν Δί᾽ οὐ γάρ· μὰ τὸν Δί᾽· οὐ γάρ Dind. Mein.

ΑΡΙΣΤΟΦΑΝΟΥΣ

ΠΑ. τί σοι δοκεῖ δράσειν; ἀποδώσειν σοι δοκεῖ;
ΣΤ. ποῦ 'σθ' οὗτος ἀπαιτῶν με τἀργύριον; λέγε,
τουτὶ τί ἔστι; ΠΑ. τοῦθ' ὅ τι ἐστί; κάρδοπος.
ΣΤ. ἔπειτ' ἀπαιτεῖς τἀργύριον τοιοῦτος ὤν;
οὐκ ἂν ἀποδοίην οὐδ' ἂν ὀβολὸν οὐδενί, 1250
ὅστις καλέσειε κάρδοπον τὴν καρδόπην.
ΠΛ. οὐκ ἄρ' ἀποδώσεις; ΣΤ. οὐχ ὅσον γέ μ' εἰδέναι.
οὔκουν ἀνύσας τι θᾶττον ἀπολιταργιεῖς
ἀπὸ τῆς θύρας; ΠΑ. ἄπειμι, καὶ τοῦτ' ἴσθ' ὅτι
θήσω πρυτανεῖ' ἢ μηκέτι ζῴην ἐγώ. 1255
ΣΤ. προσαποβαλεῖς ἄρ' αὐτὰ πρὸς ταῖς δώδεκα.
καίτοι σε τοῦτό γ' οὐχὶ βούλομαι παθεῖν,
ὁτιὴ 'κάλεσας εὐηθικῶς τὴν κάρδοπον.

ΑΜΥΝΙΑΣ
ἰώ μοί μοι.
ΣΤ. ἔα.
τίς οὑτοσί ποτ' ἔσθ' ὁ θρηνῶν; οὔ τί που 1260
τῶν Καρκίνου τις δαιμόνων ἐφθέγξατο;
ΑΜ. τί δ' ὅστις εἰμὶ τοῦτο βούλεσθ' εἰδέναι;
ἀνὴρ κακοδαίμων. ΣΤ. κατὰ σεαυτόν νυν τρέπου.
ΑΜ. ὦ σκληρὲ δαῖμον, ὦ τύχαι θραυσάντυγες
ἵππων ἐμῶν, ὦ Παλλάς, ὥς μ' ἀπώλεσας. 1265
ΣΤ. τί δαί σε Τληπόλεμός ποτ' εἴργασται κακόν;
ΑΜ. μὴ σκῶπτέ μ', ὦ τᾶν, ἀλλά μοι τὰ χρήματα
τὸν υἱὸν ἀποδοῦναι κέλευσον ἅλαβεν,
ἄλλως τε μέντοι καὶ κακῶς πεπραγότι.

1246. ἀποδώσειν σοι δοκεῖ; ΜΑΡ. ἀποδώσειν μοι δοκεῖ· Herm. Dind.
1254. καὶ τοῦτ'· καὶ τοί γ' C al. καὶ σοί γ' Reisig. Bl.
1262. τί δ' ὅστις· τί δ'; ὅστις Mein. Kock.

ΝΕΦΕΛΑΙ

ΣΤ. τὰ ποῖα ταῦτα χρήμαθ'; ΑΜ. ἀδανείσατο. 1270
ΣΤ. κακῶς ἄρ' ὄντως εἶχες, ὥς γ' ἐμοὶ δοκεῖς.
ΑΜ. ἵππους ἐλαύνων ἐξέπεσον νὴ τοὺς θεούς.
ΣΤ. τί δῆτα ληρεῖς ὥσπερ ἀπ' ὄνου καταπεσών;
ΑΜ. ληρῶ, τὰ χρήματ' ἀπολαβεῖν εἰ βούλομαι;
ΣΤ. οὐκ ἔσθ' ὅπως σύ γ' αὐτὸς ὑγιαίνεις. ΑΜ. τί δαί;
ΣΤ. τὸν ἐγκέφαλον ὥσπερ σεσεῖσθαί μοι δοκεῖς. 1276
ΑΜ. σὺ δὲ νὴ τὸν Ἑρμῆν προσκεκλήσεσθαί γ' ἐμοί,
εἰ μὴ 'ποδώσεις τἀργύριον. ΣΤ. κάτειπέ νυν,
πότερα νομίζεις καινὸν ἀεὶ τὸν Δία
ὕειν ὕδωρ ἑκάστοτ', ἢ τὸν ἥλιον   1280
ἕλκειν κάτωθεν ταὐτὸ τοῦθ' ὕδωρ πάλιν;
ΑΜ. οὐκ οἶδ' ἔγωγ' ὁπότερον, οὐδέ μοι μέλει.
ΣΤ. πῶς οὖν ἀπολαβεῖν τἀργύριον δίκαιος εἶ,
εἰ μηδὲν οἶσθα τῶν μετεώρων πραγμάτων;
ΑΜ. ἀλλ' εἰ σπανίζεις ἀργυρίου, τὸν γοῦν τόκον 1285
ἀπόδοτε. ΣΤ. τοῦτο δ' ἔσθ' ὁ τόκος τί θηρίον;
ΑΜ. τί δ' ἄλλο γ' ἢ κατὰ μῆνα καὶ καθ' ἡμέραν
πλέον πλέον τἀργύριον ἀεὶ γίγνεται
ὑπορρέοντος τοῦ χρόνου; ΣΤ. καλῶς λέγεις.
τί δῆτα; τὴν θάλατταν ἔσθ' ὅτι πλείονα 1290
νυνὶ νομίζεις ἢ πρὸ τοῦ; ΑΜ. μὰ Δί' ἀλλ' ἴσην.
οὐ γὰρ δίκαιον πλείον' εἶναι. ΣΤ. κᾆτα πῶς
αὕτη μέν, ὦ κακόδαιμον, οὐδὲν γίγνεται
ἐπιρρεόντων τῶν ποταμῶν πλείων, σὺ δὲ
ζητεῖς ποιῆσαι τἀργύριον πλεῖον τὸ σόν; 1295
οὐκ ἀποδιώξει σαυτὸν ἀπὸ τῆς οἰκίας;

1276. ὥσπερ· ὦνερ Mein.
1277. προσκεκλήσεσθαί γ' ἐμοί· προσκεκλῆσθαί μοι δοκεῖς RSV Herm. Teuf.
1285. ἀργυρίου· τἀργυρίου libri vulg.
1296. ἀποδιώξει· ἀποδιώξεις plur. libri.

φέρε μοι τὸ κέντρον. ΑΜ. ταῦτ' ἐγὼ μαρτύρομαι.
ΣΤ. ὕπαγε, τί μέλλεις; οὐκ ἐλᾷς, ὦ σαμφόρα;
ΑΜ. ταῦτ' οὐχ ὕβρις δῆτ' ἐστίν; ΣΤ. ἄξεις; ἐπιαλῶ
κεντῶν ὑπὸ τὸν πρωκτόν σε τὸν σειραφόρον. 1300
φεύγεις; ἔμελλον ἄρα σε κινήσειν ἐγὼ
αὐτοῖς τροχοῖς τοῖς σοῖσι καὶ ξυνωρίσιν.
ΧΟ. οἷον τὸ πραγμάτων ἐρᾶν φλαύρων· ὁ γὰρ   στρ.
γέρων ὅδ' ἐξαρθεὶς
ἀποστερῆσαι βούλεται   1305
τὰ χρήμαθ' ἁδανείσατο·
κοὐκ ἔσθ' ὅπως οὐ τήμερον
λήψεταί τι πρᾶγμ', ὃ τοῦ-
τον ποιήσει τὸν σοφιστὴν ἴσως,
ἀνθ' ὧν πανουργεῖν ἤρξατ', ἐξαίφνης λαβεῖν
κακόν τι.   1310
οἶμαι γὰρ αὐτὸν αὐτίχ' εὑρήσειν ὅπερ   ἀντ.
πάλαι ποτ' ἐζήτει,
εἶναι τὸν υἱὸν δεινόν οἱ
γνώμας ἐναντίας λέγειν
τοῖσιν δικαίοις, ὥστε νι-   1315
κᾶν ἅπαντας οἷσπερ ἂν
ξυγγένηται, κἂν λέγῃ παμπόνηρ'.
ἴσως δ' ἴσως βουλήσεται κἄφωνον αὐτὸν εἶναι.

ΣΤΡΕΨΙΑΔΗΣ. ΦΕΙΔΙΠΠΙΔΗΣ. ΧΟΡΟΣ

ΣΤ. ἰοὺ ἰού.   1321
ὦ γείτονες καὶ ξυγγενεῖς καὶ δημόται,
ἀμυνάθετέ μοι τυπτομένῳ πάσῃ τέχνῃ.

1301. ἄρα σε F al. Herm. Cobet.   σ' ἄρα libri.   σ' ἄρα edd.
1304. ἐξαρθεὶς Reisig edd.   ἐρασθείς libri.

ΝΕΦΕΛΑΙ 63

  οἴμοι κακοδαίμων τῆς κεφαλῆς καὶ τῆς γνάθου.
  ὦ μιαρέ, τύπτεις τὸν πατέρα; ΦΕ. φήμ', ὦ
  πάτερ.   1325
ΣΤ. ὁρᾶθ' ὁμολογοῦνθ' ὅτι με τύπτει; ΦΕ. καὶ
  μάλα.
ΣΤ. ὦ μιαρὲ καὶ πατραλοῖα καὶ τοιχωρύχε.
ΦΕ. αὖθίς με ταὐτὰ ταῦτα καὶ πλείω λέγε.
  ἆρ' οἶσθ' ὅτι χαίρω πόλλ' ἀκούων καὶ κακά; 1329
ΣΤ. τὸν πατέρα τύπτεις; ΦΕ. κἀποφανῶ γε νὴ Δία
  ὡς ἐν δίκῃ σ' ἔτυπτον. ΣΤ. ὦ μιαρώτατε,
  καὶ πῶς γένοιτ' ἂν πατέρα τύπτειν ἐν δίκῃ;
ΦΕ. ἔγωγ' ἀποδείξω καί σε νικήσω λέγων.
ΣΤ. τουτὶ σὺ νικήσεις; ΦΕ. πολύ γε καὶ ῥᾳδίως. 1335
  ἑλοῦ δ' ὁπότερον τοῖν λόγοιν βούλει λέγειν.
ΣΤ. ποίοιν λόγοιν; ΦΕ. τὸν κρείττον' ἢ τὸν ἥττονα.
ΣΤ. ἐδιδαξάμην μέντοι σε νὴ Δί', ὦ μέλε,
  τοῖσιν δικαίοις ἀντιλέγειν, εἰ ταῦτά γε
  μέλλεις ἀναπείσειν, ὡς δίκαιον καὶ καλὸν 1340
  τὸν πατέρα τύπτεσθ' ἐστὶν ὑπὸ τῶν υἱέων.
ΦΕ. ἀλλ' οἴομαι μέντοι σ' ἀναπείσειν, ὥστε γε
  οὐδ' αὐτὸς ἀκροασάμενος οὐδὲν ἀντερεῖς.
ΣΤ. καὶ μὴν ὅ τι καὶ λέξεις ἀκοῦσαι βούλομαι.
ΧΟ. σὸν ἔργον, ὦ πρεσβῦτα, φροντίζειν ὅπῃ στρ. 1345
  τὸν ἄνδρα κρατήσεις,
  ὡς οὗτος, εἰ μή τῳ 'πεποίθειν, οὐκ ἂν ἦν
  οὕτως ἀκόλαστος.
  ἀλλ' ἔσθ' ὅτῳ θρασύνεται· δῆλόν γε τἀν-
  θρώπου 'στι τὸ λῆμα.   1350
  ἀλλ' ἐξ ὅτου τὸ πρῶτον ἤρξαθ' ἡ μάχη γενέσθαι,

1347. 'πεποίθειν· πέποιθεν plur. libri. πεποίθει R.

χρὴ δὴ λέγειν πρὸς τὸν χορόν· πάντως δὲ τοῦτο
δράσεις.
ΣΤ. καὶ μὴν ὅθεν γε πρῶτον ἠρξάμεσθα λοιδορεῖσθαι
ἐγὼ φράσω· 'πειδὴ γὰρ εἰστιώμεθ', ὥσπερ ἴστε,
πρῶτον μὲν αὐτὸν τὴν λύραν λαβόντ' ἐγὼ 'κέ-
λευσα   1355
ᾆσαι Σιμωνίδου μέλος, τὸν κριὸν ὡς ἐπέχθη.
ὁ δ' εὐθέως ἀρχαῖον εἶν' ἔφασκε τὸ κιθαρίζειν
ᾄδειν τε πίνονθ' ὡσπερεὶ κάχρυς γυναῖκ' ἀλοῦσαν.
ΦΕ. οὐ γὰρ τότ' εὐθὺς χρῆν σε τύπτεσθαί τε καὶ
πατεῖσθαι,
ᾄδειν κελεύονθ' ὡσπερεὶ τέττιγας ἑστιῶντα; 1360
ΣΤ. τοιαῦτα μέντοι καὶ τότ' ἔλεγεν ἔνδον οἷάπερ νῦν,
καὶ τὸν Σιμωνίδην ἔφασκ' εἶναι κακὸν ποιητήν.
κἀγὼ μόλις μὲν ἀλλ' ὅμως ἠνεσχόμην τὸ πρῶτον·
ἔπειτα δ' ἐκέλευσ' αὐτὸν ἀλλὰ μυρρίνην λαβόντα
τῶν Αἰσχύλου λέξαι τί μοι· κᾆθ' οὗτος εὐθὺς
εἶπεν,   1365
'ἐγὼ γὰρ Αἰσχύλον νομίζω πρῶτον ἐν ποιηταῖς,
ψόφου πλέων, ἀξύστατον, στόμφακα, κρημνοποιόν;'
κἀνταῦθα πῶς οἴεσθέ μου τὴν καρδίαν ὀρεχθεῖν;
ὅμως δὲ τὸν θυμὸν δακὼν ἔφην· 'σὺ δ' ἀλλὰ τούτων
λέξον τι τῶν νεωτέρων, ἅττ' ἐστὶ τὰ σοφὰ ταῦτα.'
ὁ δ' εὐθὺς ᾖσ' Εὐριπίδου ῥῆσίν τιν', ὡς ἐκίνει 1371
ἀδελφός, ὠλεξίκακε, τὴν ὁμομητρίαν ἀδελφήν.

1352. χρὴ δὴ...τὸν χορόν· ἤδη λέγειν χρὴ πρὸς χορόν libri vulg.
ἡμῖν λέγειν χρὴ πρὸς χάριν Dobr.
1356. κριόν· Κριόν Dind. Teuf.
1359. χρῆν σε τύπτεσθαι Bentl. Pors. Dind. χρῆν σ' ἄρα τύπτεσθαι
libri. unde χρῆν σ' ἀράττεσθαι Mein. Kock.
1366. ante 1365 Schutz. post 1368 Herm.

ΝΕΦΕΛΑΙ

κἀγὼ οὐκέτ' ἐξηνεσχόμην, ἀλλ' εὐθὺς ἐξαράττω
πολλοῖς κακοῖς καἰσχροῖσι· κᾆτ' ἐντεῦθεν, οἷον
εἰκός, 1374
ἔπος πρὸς ἔπος ἠρειδόμεσθ'· εἶθ' οὗτος ἐπαναπηδᾷ,
κἄπειτ' ἔφλα με κἀσπόδει κἄπνιγε κἀπέτριβεν.
ΦΕ. οὔκουν δικαίως, ὅστις οὐκ Εὐριπίδην ἐπαινεῖς
σοφώτατον; ΣΤ. σοφώτατόν γ' ἐκεῖνον· ὦ τί
σ' εἴπω; 1378
ἀλλ' αὖθις αὖ τυπήσομαι. ΦΕ. νὴ τὸν Δί' ἐν
δίκῃ γ' ἄν.
ΣΤ. καὶ πῶς δικαίως; ὅστις, ὠναίσχυντέ, σ' ἐξέθρεψα,
αἰσθανόμενός σου πάντα τραυλίζοντος ὅ τι νοοίης.
εἰ μέν γε βρῦν εἴποις, ἐγὼ γνοὺς ἂν πιεῖν ἐπέσχον·
μαμμᾶν δ' ἂν αἰτήσαντος ἧκόν σοι φέρων ἂν ἄρτον.
ΧΟ. οἶμαί γε τῶν νεωτέρων τὰς καρδίας   ἀντ. 1391
πηδᾶν ὅ τι λέξει.
εἰ γὰρ τοιαῦτά γ' οὗτος ἐξειργασμένος
λαλῶν ἀναπείσει,
τὸ δέρμα τῶν γεραιτέρων λάβοιμεν ἂν 1395
ἀλλ' οὐδ' ἐρεβίνθου.
σὸν ἔργον, ὦ καινῶν ἐπῶν κινητὰ καὶ μοχλευτά,
πειθώ τινα ζητεῖν, ὅπως δόξεις λέγειν δίκαια.
ΦΕ. ὡς ἡδὺ καινοῖς πράγμασιν καὶ δεξιοῖς ὁμιλεῖν,
καὶ τῶν καθεστώτων νόμων ὑπερφρονεῖν δύνασθαι.
ἐγὼ γάρ, ὅτε μὲν ἱππικῇ τὸν νοῦν μόνον προσ-
εῖχον, 1401

1373. κἀγώ· κᾆτ' Mein.
1375. ἐπαναπηδᾷ· ἐπενεπήδα Blaydes.
1376. κἀπέτριβεν· κἀπέθλιβε RS.
1379. τυπήσομαι Dind. Kock Mein. τυπτήσομαι libri vulg.
1401. μόνον R. μόνῃ Bentl. Dind. Mein. al.

G. C. 5

ΑΡΙΣΤΟΦΑΝΟΥΣ

οὐδ' ἂν τρί' εἰπεῖν ῥήμαθ' οἷός τ' ἦ πρὶν ἐξα-
μαρτεῖν·
νυνὶ δ' ἐπειδή μ' οὑτοσὶ τούτων ἔπαυσεν αὐτός,
γνώμαις δὲ λεπταῖς καὶ λόγοις ξύνειμι καὶ
μερίμναις,
οἶμαι διδάξειν ὡς δίκαιον τὸν πατέρα κολάζειν.
ΣΤ. ἵππευε τοίνυν νὴ Δί', ὡς ἔμοιγε κρεῖττόν ἐστιν
ἵππων τρέφειν τέθριππον ἢ τυπτόμενον ἐπι-
τριβῆναι. 1407
ΦΕ. ἐκεῖσε δ' ὅθεν ἀπέσχισάς με τοῦ λόγου μέτειμι,
καὶ πρῶτ' ἐρήσομαί σε τουτί· παῖδά μ' ὄντ'
ἔτυπτες;
ΣΤ. ἔγωγέ σ' εὐνοῶν γε καὶ κηδόμενος. ΦΕ. εἰπὲ
δή μοι, 1410
οὐ κἀμὲ σοὶ δίκαιόν ἐστιν εὐνοεῖν ὁμοίως
τύπτειν τ', ἐπειδήπερ γε τοῦτ' ἔστ' εὐνοεῖν, τὸ
τύπτειν;
πῶς γὰρ τὸ μὲν σὸν σῶμα χρὴ πληγῶν ἀθῷον
εἶναι,
τοὐμὸν δὲ μή; καὶ μὴν ἔφυν ἐλεύθερός γε κἀγώ.
κλάουσι παῖδες, πατέρα δ' οὐ κλάειν δοκεῖς;
φήσεις νομίζεσθαι σὺ παιδὸς τοῦτο τοὔργον εἶναι·
ἐγὼ δέ γ' ἀντείποιμ' ἂν ὡς δὶς παῖδες οἱ γέροντες,
εἰκός τε μᾶλλον τοὺς γέροντας ἢ νέους τι κλάειν,
ὅσῳπερ ἐξαμαρτάνειν ἧττον δίκαιον αὐτούς.
ΣΤ. ἀλλ' οὐδαμοῦ νομίζεται τὸν πατέρα τοῦτο πάσ-
χειν. 1420

1402. ἦ· ἦν vulg.
1411. ἐστιν εὐνοεῖν· ἔστ' ἀντευνοεῖν Cob.
1412. τύπτειν τ' AF al. Teuf. Dind. τυπτόντ' E Herm. Mein.
1418. ἢ νέους edd. ἢ τοὺς νέους vel τοὺς νεωτέρους libri.

ΝΕΦΕΛΑΙ 67

ΦΕ. οὔκουν ἀνὴρ ὁ τὸν νόμον θεὶς τοῦτον ἦν τὸ
πρῶτον
ὥσπερ σὺ κἀγώ, καὶ λέγων ἔπειθε τοὺς παλαιούς;
ἧττον τί δῆτ' ἔξεστι κἀμοὶ καινὸν αὖ τὸ λοιπὸν
θεῖναι νόμον τοῖς υἱέσιν, τοὺς πατέρας ἀντι-
τύπτειν; 1424
ὅσας δὲ πληγὰς εἴχομεν πρὶν τὸν νόμον τεθῆναι,
ἀφίεμεν, καὶ δίδομεν αὐτοῖς προῖκα συγκεκόφθαι.
σκέψαι δὲ τοὺς ἀλεκτρυόνας καὶ τἄλλα τὰ βοτὰ
ταυτί,
ὡς τοὺς πατέρας ἀμύνεται· καίτοι τί διαφέρουσιν
ἡμῶν ἐκεῖνοι, πλήν γ' ὅτι ψηφίσματ' οὐ γρά-
φουσιν; 1429
ΣΤ. τί δῆτ', ἐπειδὴ τοὺς ἀλεκτρυόνας ἅπαντα μιμεῖ,
οὐκ ἐσθίεις καὶ τὴν κόπρον κἀπὶ ξύλου καθεύδεις;
ΦΕ. οὐ ταὐτόν, ὦ τᾶν, ἐστίν, οὐδ' ἂν Σωκράτει δοκοίη.
ΣΤ. πρὸς ταῦτα μὴ τύπτ'· εἰ δὲ μή, σαυτόν ποτ'
αἰτιάσει.
ΦΕ. καὶ πῶς; ΣΤ. ἐπεὶ σὲ μὲν δίκαιός εἰμ' ἐγὼ
κολάζειν,
σὺ δ', ἢν γένηταί σοι, τὸν υἱόν. ΦΕ. ἢν δὲ μὴ
γένηται, 1435
μάτην ἐμοὶ κεκλαύσεται, σὺ δ' ἐγχανὼν τεθνήξεις.
ΣΤ. ἐμοὶ μέν, ὦνδρες ἥλικες, δοκεῖ λέγειν δίκαια·
κἄμοιγε συγχωρεῖν δοκεῖ τούτοισι τἀπιεική.
κλάειν γὰρ ἡμᾶς εἰκός ἐστ', ἢν μὴ δίκαια δρῶμεν.

1421. θεὶς τοῦτον A al. Dind. Bl. τοῦτον τιθεὶς Herm. Teuf. θεὶς τουτονὶ Mein.
1423. ἧττον τί· ἧττόν τι Kock Teuf. Bl.
1427. ἀλεκτρυόνας· ἀλέκτορας Beck. Both. Mein.
1436. τεθνήξεις edd. τεθνήξει libri.

ΦΕ. σκέψαι δὲ χἀτέραν ἔτι γνώμην. ΣΤ. ἀπὸ γὰρ
    ὀλοῦμαι.   1440
ΦΕ. καὶ μὴν ἴσως γ' οὐκ ἀχθέσει παθὼν ἃ νῦν
    πέπονθας.
ΣΤ. πῶς δή; δίδαξον γὰρ τί μ' ἐκ τούτων ἐπω-
    φελήσεις.
ΦΕ. τὴν μητέρ' ὥσπερ καὶ σὲ τυπτήσω. ΣΤ. τί
    φής, τί φὴς σύ;
    τοῦθ' ἕτερον αὖ μεῖζον κακόν. ΦΕ. τί δ', ἢν
    ἔχων τὸν ἥττω
    λόγον σὲ νικήσω λέγων   1445
    τὴν μητέρ' ὡς τύπτειν χρεών;
ΣΤ. τί δ' ἄλλο γ' ἤ, ταῦτ' ἢν ποιῇς,
    οὐδέν σε κωλύσει σεαυ-
    τὸν ἐμβαλεῖν ἐς τὸ βάραθρον
    μετὰ Σωκράτους   1450
    καὶ τὸν λόγον τὸν ἥττω.
    ταυτὶ δι' ὑμᾶς, ὦ νεφέλαι, πέπονθ' ἐγώ,
    ὑμῖν ἀναθεὶς ἅπαντα τἀμὰ πράγματα.
ΧΟ. αὐτὸς μὲν οὖν σαυτῷ σὺ τούτων αἴτιος,
    στρέψας σεαυτὸν ἐς πονηρὰ πράγματα.   1455
ΣΤ. τί δῆτα ταῦτ' οὔ μοι τότ' ἠγορεύετε,
    ἀλλ' ἄνδρ' ἄγροικον καὶ γέροντ' ἐπήρετε;
ΧΟ. ἡμεῖς ποιοῦμεν ταῦθ' ἑκάστοθ' ὅντιν' ἂν
    γνῶμεν πονηρῶν ὄντ' ἐραστὴν πραγμάτων,
    ἕως ἂν αὐτὸν ἐμβάλωμεν ἐς κακόν,   1460
    ὅπως ἂν εἰδῇ τοὺς θεοὺς δεδοικέναι.

1444. τί δ', ἢν ἔχων κ.τ.λ. τί δῆτ' ἂν ἢν τὸν ἥττω ἔχων Fritzsch.
Mein.
   1458. ἡμεῖς RSV edd. ἀεί plur. libri. ὅντιν' ἂν Pors. edd. ὅταν
τινὰ libri.

ΝΕΦΕΛΑΙ

ΣΤ. οἴμοι, πονηρά γ', ὦ νεφέλαι, δίκαια δέ.
οὐ γάρ μ' ἐχρῆν τὰ χρήμαθ' ἀδανεισάμην
ἀποστερεῖν. νῦν οὖν ὅπως, ὦ φίλτατε,
τὸν Χαιρεφῶντα τὸν μιαρὸν καὶ Σωκράτη 1465
ἀπολεῖς μετ' ἐμοῦ 'λθὼν οἳ σὲ κἄμ' ἐξηπάτων.
ΦΕ. ἀλλ' οὐκ ἂν ἀδικήσαιμι τοὺς διδασκάλους.
ΣΤ. ναὶ ναὶ καταιδέσθητι πατρῷον Δία.
ΦΕ. ἰδού γε Δία πατρῷον· ὡς ἀρχαῖος εἶ.
Ζεὺς γάρ τις ἔστιν; ΣΤ. ἔστιν. ΦΕ. οὐκ
  ἔστ', οὔκ, ἐπεὶ 1470
δῖνος βασιλεύει τὸν Δί' ἐξεληλακώς.
ΣΤ. οὐκ ἐξελήλακ', ἀλλ' ἐγὼ τοῦτ' ᾠόμην
διὰ τουτονὶ τὸν δῖνον. οἴμοι δείλαιος,
ὅτε καὶ σὲ χυτρεοῦν ὄντα θεὸν ἡγησάμην.
ΦΕ. ἐνταῦθα σαυτῷ παραφρόνει καὶ φληνάφα. 1475
ΣΤ. οἴμοι παρανοίας· ὡς ἐμαινόμην ἄρα,
ὅτ' ἐξέβαλλον τοὺς θεοὺς διὰ Σωκράτη.
ἀλλ', ὦ φίλ' Ἑρμῆ, μηδαμῶς θύμαινέ μοι
μηδέ μ' ἐπιτρίψῃς, ἀλλὰ συγγνώμην ἔχε
ἐμοῦ παρανοήσαντος ἀδολεσχίᾳ· 1480
καί μοι γενοῦ ξύμβουλος, εἴτ' αὐτοὺς γραφὴν
διωκάθω γραψάμενος εἴθ' ὅ τι σοι δοκεῖ.
ὀρθῶς παραινεῖς οὐκ ἐῶν δικορραφεῖν,
ἀλλ' ὡς τάχιστ' ἐμπιμπράναι τὴν οἰκίαν
τῶν ἀδολεσχῶν. δεῦρο δεῦρ', ὦ Ξανθία, 1485
κλίμακα λαβὼν ἔξελθε καὶ σμινύην φέρων,
κἄπειτ' ἐπαναβὰς ἐπὶ τὸ φροντιστήριον
τὸ τέγος κατάσκαπτ', εἰ φιλεῖς τὸν δεσπότην,
ἕως ἂν αὐτοῖς ἐμβάλῃς τὴν οἰκίαν·

1465. Σωκράτη· Σωκράτην vulg.
1466. μετ' ἐμοῦ 'λθών· μετελθών Herm. Mein. al.

ἐμοὶ δὲ δᾷδ' ἐνεγκάτω τις ἡμμένην,   1490
κἀγώ τιν' αὐτῶν τήμερον δοῦναι δίκην
ἐμοὶ ποιήσω, κεἰ σφόδρ' εἴσ' ἀλαζόνες.

ΜΑΘΗΤΗΣ

ἰοὺ ἰού.
ΣΤ. σὸν ἔργον, ὦ δᾴς, ἰέναι πολλὴν φλόγα.
ΜΑΘ. ἄνθρωπε, τί ποιεῖς; ΣΤ. ὅ τι ποιῶ; τί δ'
 ἄλλο γ' ἢ   1495
διαλεπτολογοῦμαι ταῖς δοκοῖς τῆς οἰκίας;
ΜΑΘ. οἴμοι τίς ἡμῶν πυρπολεῖ τὴν οἰκίαν;
ΣΤ. ἐκεῖνος οὗπερ θοἰμάτιον εἰλήφατε.
ΜΑΘ. ἀπολεῖς ἀπολεῖς. ΣΤ. τοῦτ' αὐτὸ γὰρ καὶ
 βούλομαι,
ἢν ἡ σμινύη μοι μὴ προδῷ τὰς ἐλπίδας,   1500
ἢ 'γὼ πρότερόν πως ἐκτραχηλισθῶ πεσών.

ΣΩΚΡΑΤΗΣ

οὗτος τί ποιεῖς ἐτεὸν οὑπὶ τοῦ τέγους;
ΣΤ. ἀεροβατῶ καὶ περιφρονῶ τὸν ἥλιον.
ΣΩ. οἴμοι τάλας, δείλαιος ἀποπνιγήσομαι.
ΜΑΘ. ἐγὼ δὲ κακοδαίμων γε κατακαυθήσομαι.   1505
ΣΤ. τί γὰρ μαθόντες τοὺς θεοὺς ὑβρίζετε,
καὶ τῆς σελήνης ἐσκοπεῖσθε τὴν ἕδραν;
δίωκε βάλλε παῖε, πολλῶν οὕνεκα,
μάλιστα δ' εἰδὼς τοὺς θεοὺς ὡς ἠδίκουν.
ΧΟ. ἡγεῖσθ' ἔξω· κεχόρευται γὰρ μετρίως τό γε
 τήμερον ἡμῖν.   1510

1505. ΜΑΘ. R Bergk. ΧΑΙΡ. vulg. Dind.
1506. μαθόντες· μαθόντ' εἰς al. vid. com.

NOTES ON THE ARGUMENTS

I

1. τὸ δρᾶμα κ.τ.λ.—the play is an express attack on Socrates for corrupting the youth of Athens by his teaching; no love being lost between the comic writers and the professors.

4. οὐχ, ὥς τινες—sc. λέγουσι. It was not inspired by private pique. We may note that Archelaus, the great patron of Euripides, did not become king of Macedonia till 413.

ὁ χορός—for the composition and arrangement of the Chorus, of which a description is here given, see Dict. Ant. *chorus*.

II

1. φασί κ.τ.λ.—an idle tradition, that the men who accused Socrates more than twenty years after got Aristophanes to put forth this play as a feeler of the public inclination.

3. ηὐλαβοῦντο γάρ—because Alcibiades and his friends were warm partizans of Socrates; and indeed brought about the failure of the *Clouds*.

6. ὁ δὲ πρόλογος—i.e. the opening scene, 1—125.

9. ἡ γάρ...οἰκία—see note on line 14.

III

A complete syllabus of the play in the form in which we have it.

7. ἐκ(κυκλη)θείσης δὲ τῆς διατριβῆς—'the school being thrown open,' by the stage contrivance called the *eccyclema*.

IV

A traditional account of the recasting of the *Clouds*.

1. φησί—see lines 522 sq.
8. ἐπὶ 'Αμεινίου ἄρχοντος—in 422. The statement is most improbable, as Aristophanes exhibited the *Wasps* and probably the *Rehearsal* in 422. Moreover the *Maricas* of Eupolis, which is mentioned in the *parabasis* (553), did not appear till 421.
9. τοῦτο κ.τ.λ.—the second edition is a reproduction of the former, but re-modelled in part, as if the poet had meant to reproduce the play, but had not done so for some reason. The re-writing is extensive, and the arrangement of the scenes is altered. The *parabasis* is new; so is the contest between the two Arguments, and the final burning of the philosophers' school.

V

1. Ἄνυτος κ.τ.λ.—see Argument II, and VI 19 sq.

NOTES

Prologue, lines 1—275

The Prologue is all that part of the play which comes before the entrance of the Chorus.

1—125. The scene shows the interior of the house of Strepsiades. Father, son and slaves are lying on their mats, Strepsiades trying in vain to sleep. Time (as in the *Wasps*) a little before daybreak.

2. ὦ Ζεῦ βασιλεῦ—cf. *Ran.* 1278, ὦ Ζεῦ βασιλεῦ, τὸ χρῆμα τῶν κόπων ὅσον. For τὸ χρῆμα cf. *Ach.* 150, ὅσον τὸ χρῆμα παρνόπων: also with sing. *Eq.* 1219. Such phrases, emphasizing size or strangeness, are especially common in Herodotus.

τῶν νυκτῶν—the plural here suggests other uneasy nights which Strepsiades had spent. Blaydes however says '*noctis*, ex usu Atticorum.' No doubt μέσαι νύκτες is a regular term for midnight, while in such phrases as Plat. *Protag.* 310 C, λίαν πόρρω ἔδοξε τῶν νυκτῶν εἶναι, the plural means the hours or watches of the night.

It is best to take ὅσον as exclamatory, with a stop at the end of the line. This agrees with the quotation from the *Frogs*; and the short jerky sentences suit a man trying to sleep.

Otherwise, if ὅσον be taken with ἀπέραντον, the phrase must be explained either (1) as equivalent to ἀπέραντον ὅσον, like ὑπερφυὴς ὅσος, *mirum quantum*, and the like; or (2) as a relative construction, (τοσοῦτον) ὅσον ἀπέραντον. The view that ὅσον is used like ὡς, 'how endless,' is not supported by Attic usage.

5. οἱ δ' οἰκέται ῥέγκουσι—the house-slaves had an easy time of it during the war. If harshly treated they might desert, nor could they be sent to work in the country as in time of peace: cf. *Eq.* 26: also

Pac. 451, where a δοῦλος αὐτομολεῖν παρεσκευασμένος is a likely opponent of peace. When the Lacedaemonians occupied Decelea more than 20,000 slaves deserted from Athens, Thuc. vii. 27, 5.

οὐκ ἄν—sc. ἔ(ρ)ρεγκον (Eur. *Rhes.* 785): *Ach.* 137, μὰ Δί' οὐκ ἄν: *Pac.* 907, ἀλλ' οὐκ ἄν. For **πρὸ τοῦ** cf. *Vesp.* 231 and 268: so ἐν τῷ πρὸ τοῦ, Thuc. i. 32, 4 and iv. 72, 3.

6. **ἀπόλοιο—πόλεμος** is more or less personified, as in *Ach.* 981, ὅτι παροίνιος ἀνὴρ ἔφυ. The repeated πολ-jingle in this line is intentional. **πολλῶν οὕνεκα**—Blaydes here and elsewhere follows Kock and Teuffel in reading εἵνεκα.

7. **ὅτ'**—τὸ δ' ὅτε ποτὲ μὲν μόνον χρόνον δηλοῖ, ποτὲ δὲ καὶ χρόνον καὶ αἰτίαν, ὥς ἐστι κἀνταῦθα (schol.); so *cum, quando,* and our *when*: cf. 34, 717 etc.: *Ach.* 401,

ὦ τρισμακάρι' Εὐριπίδη
ὅθ' ὁ δοῦλος οὑτωσὶ σοφῶς ἀπ(ὑπ)οκρίνεται.

κολάσ' ἔξεστι—Blaydes cites numerous instances of this elision, as in line 42, and adds, 'eliditur semper diphthongus αι ante vocalem in thesi; contra in arsi servatur aut crasis fit'; as in *Ach.* 62, ἄχθομαι'γώ. Green points out that ἐπιδιδόναι (ἐπιδοῦναι) 'μαντόν is read by Mein. in *Thesm.* 217, which seems inconsistent with this rule.

8. **χρηστός**—'worthy,' ironical, as often in Demosthenes. **οὑτοσί**—the son is sleeping near the father, who points to him; cf. 14: *Vesp.* 67, ἔστιν γὰρ ἡμῖν δεσπότης ἐκεινοσί, 'over yonder.'

9. **τῆς νυκτός**—genitive of time 'within which'; see note on *Vesp.* 91,

ὕπνου δ' ὁρᾷ τῆς νυκτὸς οὐδὲ πασπάλην·

also Monro's *Homeric Gr.* § 150: Krüger § 47. 1—4.

10. **ἐγκεκορδυλημένος**—'rolled up,' in a shapeless lump, as the scholiast explains, ὥστε μηδὲ ἀνθρώπου σχῆμα δηλοῦν. κορδύλη is a lump or swelling on the head from a blow, and also some sort of headgear (πρὸς κεφαλῇ προσείλημα, which suggests a turban).

11. **ἀλλ' εἰ δοκεῖ**—'well, if you like.' He turns over, wrapping himself up, and tries to sleep, but presently starts up again.

12. **δακνόμενος**—'tormented'; the literal meaning too is of course suggested, as in 37 and 710. Note the alliteration in this line and the next.

13. **τῆς**—'all this,' i.e. the expense I incur.

14. **διὰ...τὸν υἱόν**—cf. Dem. *c. Phaenip.* 1046 § 24, ἱπποτρόφος ἀγαθός ἐστι καὶ φιλότιμος ἅτε νέος καὶ πλούσιος ὤν. The extravagant young Pheidippides, as Dr Merry says, 'was intended to remind the

audience of Alcibiades, who sought θαυμάζεσθαι ἀπὸ τῆς ἱπποτροφίας (Thuc. vi. 12, 2). Pheidippides belonged on his mother's side (46) to the family of the Alcmaeonidae, and Alcmaeon himself τεθριπποτροφήσας Ὀλυμπιάδα ἀναιρέεται, Hdt. vi. 125.'
κόμην ἔχων—the fashion of conceited youth: *Vesp.* 1069, πολλῶν κικίννους νεανιῶν: cf. κομᾶν. Alcibiades himself, it was said, κάλλιστος ὢν τὴν μορφὴν κόμην ἔτρεφεν ἐπὶ πολὺ τῆς ἡλικίας, Athen. xii. 534 c (§ 47).

15. ἱππάζεται κ.τ.λ.—riding and driving are meant; νῦν μὲν ἐπὶ κέλητος, νῦν δὲ ἐπὶ ξυνωρίδος ἅρματος ὀχούμενος ἄνω καὶ κάτω βακχεύει (schol.). ἱππάζομαι, as Mr Green points out, is used in Homer of driving; as ἱππεύς and ἱππότης denote the charioteer or the hero driven.

16. ὀνειροπολεῖ—so line 27: *Eq.* 809, with περί. Blaydes gives several instances with the direct accusative from Lucian, Plutarch etc. In Dem. *Phil.* i. 54 § 49, we have the cognate construction πολλὰ τοιαῦτα ὀνειροπολεῖν.

17. εἰκάδας—the twentieth, twenty-first etc. The 'twenties,' as we speak of the 'teens' (Green). The interest would be due at the end of the month, and this would be drawing unpleasantly near; cf. 1131. For the counting εἰκάς, πρώτη ἐπὶ εἰκάδι κ.τ.λ. see Dict. Ant. i. 338, *calendarium*: also note on 1131.

18. χωροῦσιν—'are coming on' or 'going on': *Vesp.* 1483, τουτὶ καὶ δὴ χωρεῖ τὸ κακόν. ἅπτε—Strepsiades now gives up the idea of sleep. He calls for a light, and begins to examine his accounts.

21. Πασίᾳ—see 1213 sq. Pasias sounds like a banker's name. Thus Pasion the banker, who appears in Demosthenes' speech *for Phormion*, had a son named Pasicles.

22. τοῦ—for the genitive of price and the like, cf. 31, 864 etc.
τί ἐχρησάμην—'what was that loan?' i.e. what was it for? τί is generally explained as equivalent to εἰς τί; but the construction is more strictly cognate: cf. 202, τί ἐστι χρήσιμον;

23. κοππατίαν—so 438: *Koppa* was the first letter of Κόρινθος in old inscriptions, and the *koppa* stamp (Ϙ) was said to mark a Corinthian breed of horses, of fabled descent from Pegasus. σαμφόρας (122) was another brand. In the *Anagyrus* of Aristophanes (Fr. 235) βουκέφαλος and κοππατίας are coupled together, whence it is supposed that βουκέφαλος too denoted a brand, and was not a name derived from the shape of the horse's head.

24. ἐξεκόπην—most editors read ἐξεκόπη, for if the horse's eye had

been knocked out Pheidippides would not have made his father buy him. But ἐξεκόπην is found in all the manuscripts, and as the third person is the more obvious, why should it have been altered to the first? The meaning is, I would sooner have lost an eye, than lost all this money in horse-dealing (Rogers); and, as Mr Green says, 'We may suppose the expression colloquial and common, and chosen here chiefly for the sake of the alliterative pun.' The jingle on κοπ, 'I wish I'd had my eye copped out,' suggests a pun on the horse's brand *I* and *eye* to Walsh, and a better, 'hack' and 'hacked out,' to Rogers.

25. Φίλων, ἀδικεῖς—Pheidippides is dreaming of a race. ἀδικεῖν is used of unfair conduct in any sport. ἔλαυνε...δρόμον—'keep your own course': cf. ἐκ δρόμου, ἔξω δρόμου.

26. τοῦτ' ἔστι τουτί—cf. 1052: *Pac.* 64, τοῦτ' ἔστι τουτὶ τὸ κακόν.

27. ἱππικήν—'sine articulo, ut saepe alibi' (Blaydes): so μουσική, γυμναστική etc.

28. πόσους δρόμους κ.τ.λ.—'how many courses (rounds) are the chariots to drive?' This is the simplest view of the line. Kock however would make Φίλων the subject of ἐλᾷ: and Blaydes approves of ἐλᾷς, 'will you drive?' τὰ πολεμιστήρια—sc. ἅρματα: a contest of chariots driven by men in warlike armour. We have πολεμιστήριος ἵππος, Dem. *c. Phaenip.* 1046 § 24: so θώραξ, *Ach.* 1132.

29. ἐμὲ μέν—'me in truth': a common usage with pronouns; cf. 1038, 1050.

30. τί χρέος ἔβα—a choric fragment, as the Doric dialect shows. The scholiast cites τί χρέος ἔβα δῶμα; from Euripides. τί χρέος in the tragedy would mean 'what harsh necessity?' as in *Herc. Fur.* 530, τί καινὸν ἦλθε δώμασιν χρέος; Strepsiades however means 'what debt?' χρέως is the Attic form. The scholiast explains ἔβα by κατέλαβε. For the accusative which follows cf. Eur. *Hipp.* 840, θανάσιμος τύχα σὰν ἔβα καρδίαν: ib. 1371, καὶ νῦν ὀδύνα μ' ὀδύνα βαίνει. For τὸν Πασίαν Blaydes suggests τὸ Πασίου or Πασία.

31. τρεῖς μναῖ—the nominative continues the construction of the line before (see 21); or Strepsiades simply reads the entry, sc. ὀφείλονται.

διφρίσκου—the diminutive expresses contempt, or is used διὰ τὸ μικροὺς εἶναι καὶ κούφους τοῖς ἀγωνιζομένοις. τροχοῖν—'a pair of wheels.' The old man seems to mean a racing chariot, made up of 'a couple of wheels and a bit of board.' Ἀμυνίᾳ—a friend and fellow enthusiast seems meant, not a money-lender; though he did oblige Pheidippides with a loan, 1270 sq. Amynias is therefore probably the person mentioned in 686, who is satirized in the *Wasps* as a gambler (74) and a fop (466, 1267). One scholiast fancies that a cut is intended at Ameinias the archon of 422 B.C.

32. **ἐξαλίσας**—cf. Xen. *Oec.* xi. 18, ὁ παῖς τὸν ἵππον ἐξαλίσας οἴκαδε ἀπάγει. 'After giving him a roll,' is the accepted explanation; cf. ἀλινδέω, ἀλινδήθρα. Mr Green however, following Paley, prefers 'taking him out of his harness' i.e. stripping him of girths, saddle etc., which agrees better with the compound ἐξαλῖσαι 'to roll out of.'

33. **ἐξήλικας**—'you have rolled me out of,' or 'stripped me bare enough of my substance,' as Mr Green renders it.

34. **ὅτε καί**—see line 7. **τόκου**—'for interest,' as we say to distrain for rent; see line 22: so the genitive is used with ὑποτίθημι, 'to pledge,' e.g. ταλάντου.

35. **ἐνεχυράσεσθαι**—sc. τὰ χρήματα. The middle, as in *Eccl.* 567, implies taking security for one's own debt. The active is used in a law cited Dem. *Meid.* 518, § 4: so *Androt.* 762 § 197, ταύτην ἐνεχυράζειν, 'to take her (a slave) in pledge,' for money due to the state. For the passive, see infr. line 241.

As regards the reading, there is some slight manuscript authority for the future (see critical note), and it is certainly right. The aorist infinitive is indeed used, in reference to future time, with verbs of *promising*, *hoping*, and the like; but such instances with verbs of *saying* or *thinking*, though found in the text of various authors, are anomalous, or according to some critics totally inadmissible; see Goodwin §§ 127 and 136.

ἐτεόν is always interrogative in Aristophanes; line 93: *Vesp.* 836, τί δ' ἔστιν ἐτεόν; Pheidippides now wakes up and complains of his father's restlessness.

37. **δήμαρχος**—see Dict. Ant. for the various duties of these officials. Here the allusion is to their right of distraint. For the joke cf. 710. As the scholiast explains, παίζει ὡς εἰ ἔλεγε κόρις ἢ ψύλλα.

39. **σὺ δ' οὖν κάθευδε**—'well sleep away.' So *Vesp.* 6, σὺ δ' οὖν παρακινδύνευ': ib. 754, 1154: Soph. *El.* 891, σὺ δ' οὖν λέγ': *Trach.* 1157. In these phrases the stress is on the verb more than on the personal pronoun. This is somewhat different from the common use of δ' οὖν in the sense of 'however,' or like *ceterum* after a parenthesis or digression.

40. **ἐς τὴν κεφαλήν**—*Pac.* 1063, ἐς κεφαλὴν σοί: so Dem. *de Cor.* 322 § 290: cf. Verg. *Aen.* viii. 484, di *capiti* ipsius generique reservent: 2 *Sam.* iii. 29, 'Let it rest on the head of Joab, and on all his father's house.'

41. **εἴθ' ὤφελ'**—'versus tragici et epici coloris' (Blaydes). The scholiast compares the first line of the *Medea*, εἴθ' ὤφελ' Ἀργοῦς κ.τ.λ. **ἡ προμνήστρια**—see Dict. Ant. ii. 135, *matrimonium*. 'There were professional matchmakers called προμνηστρίδες or προμνήστριαι (Plat. *Theaet.* 149 D: Xen. *Mem.* ii. 6, 36: Pollux iii. 31), who however did not stand high in public esteem' owing to ignorant and dishonest practitioners (Plat. *Theaet.* 150 B). But others are called πάσσοφοι and ἀγαθαί.

42. **ἥτις**—i.e. 'because she,' like *quae* with the subjunctive. ὅστις, 'the relative of a class,' speaks of a person as possessing the characteristics of that class. **γῆμ'**—see note on line 7. **ἐπῆρε** so 1457: κυρίως ἀντὶ τοῦ ἐχαύνωσεν καὶ ἀνεκούφισεν, elated him with hopes of a great dowry, according to the scholiast's explanation. But it was rather the brilliancy of the match that dazzled him.

44. **εὐρωτῶν** properly 'mouldy,' from εὐρώς. Here however it seems to be simply dirty and rough, as opposed to the spick and span tidiness of city life. **ἀκόρητος**—from κορέω 'to sweep': elsewhere the same form is derived from κορέννυμι. **εἰκῇ κείμενος**—'lying at random.' The meaning is either that farm and household things in the country are left 'lying about anyhow,' or that the life of the farmer itself is one of careless ease and comfort. The scholiast takes the first view and applies it to the whole line; as things which are left about grow mouldy and rusty.

45. **βρύων μελίτταις** βρύω is constructed with the dative in Aeschylus, Euripides etc.: with the genitive, *Ran.* 329: Aesch. *Choeph.* 67: Soph. *O. C.* 16 etc.

στεμφύλοις—from στίμβω, to press, crush: κυρίως λέγεται τὰ ἀποπιέσματα τῶν ἐλαῶν (schol.), cakes of dried olives. The word is also used of raisins.

46. **Μεγακλέους τοῦ Μεγακλέους** the τοῦ, as Blaydes points out, agrees with the first genitive: *Eq.* 449, τῶν Βυρσίνης τῆς Ἱππίου. Megacles was a common name in the illustrious family of the Alcmaeonidae (Hdt. vi. 125).

47. **ἄγροικος ὢν ἐξ ἄστεως**—note the antithesis; '*rusticus urbanum*, ut loquitur Horatius, *Sat.* ii. 6, 80' (Blaydes). ἄστεως is rightly read for ἄστεος, which is only used 'apud scenicos' when required by the metre.

48. **σεμνήν**—here probably in a bad sense, 'haughty': *Plut.* 275, ὡς σεμνὸς οὑπίτριπτος, 'what airs the rogue gives himself': σεμνὴ γυνή might however simply mean a lady of dignity and position.

ἐγκεκοισυρωμένην—'Coesyrified': cf. 800. Coesyra was the daughter of Megacles and married to Peisistratus, Hdt. i. 60. περισσῶς κεκοσμημένη is the scholiast's explanation of the word, but it suggests pride of birth as well as costly dress.

49. ὅτ' ἐγάμουν—'nuptiarum tempore,' as Blaydes explains; while the aorist ἔγημα (46) simply states a past fact. ξυγκατεκλινόμην— Blaydes understands this of the marriage feast, comparing *Ach.* 980, γὰρ ἐμοὶ ξυγκατακλινεῖς, where the word certainly means reclining at table.

52. Κωλιάδος—Aphrodite Κωλιάς had a temple at Colias near Phalerum: Hdt. viii. 96, ἔφερε τῆς Ἀττικῆς ἐπὶ τὴν ἠϊόνα τὴν καλεομένην Κωλιάδα. Γενετυλλίδος—a title of Aphrodite, or, according to the scholiast on *Lys.* 2 (ἢ 'πὶ Κωλιάδ' ἢ 's Γενετυλλίδος), of an attendant goddess, ἀπὸ τῆς γενέσεως τῶν παίδων ὠνομασμένη. From these passages Bentley suggested *Genetyllis*, Hor. *Carm. Sec.* 16, sive tu Lucina probas vocari, seu Genitalis.

53. ἐσπάθα—σπαθᾶν in weaving, as Dr Merry explains, means 'to make the web upon the loom close and thick by beating the threads of the woof together with a wooden blade (σπάθη)': cf. Aesch. *Choeph.* 232, ἰδοῦ δ' ὕφασμα τοῦτο...σπάθης τε πληγάς. Metaphorically it is used for wasting: σπαθᾶν δὲ τὸ ἀφειδῶς ἀναλίσκειν, παρὰ δὲ τοῖς ῥήτορσιν εἴρηται πολλάκις (schol.): e.g. Dem. *Fals. leg.* 354 § 43, διὰ ταῦτ' ἐσπάθᾶτο ταῦτα (which Heslop however thinks may be literal). Mr Green suggests the rendering, 'And yet I will not say she was no spinster, she made my money spin.'

54. ἐγὼ δ' ἄν—for this *iterative* use of ἄν with the imperfect indicative see note on *Vesp.* 269: also Goodwin § 162. What one 'would do' (on due occasion) one does often or habitually. In Aristophanes this construction has a tendency to occur in groups, e.g. *Av.* 505.

55. πρόφασιν—'by way of pretext'; the accusative is adverbially used in apposition to the sentence: *Eq.* 466, πρόφασιν μὲν Ἀργείους φίλους ἡμῖν ποιεῖ. Strepsiades pretended that the coat he had now (τοδί) was too closely woven, and so brought in the double meaning of λίαν σπαθᾷς, 'you lay it on too thick' (Merry). Green's view is that Strepsiades would take his coat (threadbare, unmended and buttonless probably) as the text (πρόφασιν) of his preaching and ironically commend his wife's housewifery.' But this gives too mean an idea of the old man's circumstances. He was not a poor yeoman but rather a prosperous country gentleman.

56. ἔλαιον κ.τ.λ.—a slave interrupts, complaining that there is no oil in his lamp. The household was apparently getting up. The old man's testiness reminds us of the scene in the *Wasps* (251) where the father reproaches the son for wasting oil.

57. τί...ἦπτες—'why must you light?' We might expect the aorist; but the imperfect, like ἐνετίθεις below, gives a 'side-view' of the action taking place, instead of an 'end-view' regarding it as completed. μοι is ethical dative, here = for my annoyance, 'why must I have you lighting?' πότην—'bibulous,' because it had a thick wick.

58. δεῦρ' ἔλθ' ἵνα κλάῃς—i.e. come and be cuffed. διὰ τί δῆτα;—Blaydes reads διὰ δὲ δὴ τί; but δῆτα is common enough in questions, e.g. line 87.

59. τῶν...θρυαλλίδων—partitive genitive, sc. 'one of.'

60. ὅπως—'when'; a sense common in Sophocles and Euripides, e.g. *Ant.* 253, ὅπως δ' ὁ πρῶτος ἡμῖν ἡμεροσκόπος δείκνυσι. υἱὸς οὑτοσί—'a son, this fellow here,' not = ὁ υἱὸς οὗτος : see line 8.

61. τἀγαθῇ—partly ironical, like χρηστός in line 8.

62. δὴ 'νταῦθ'—'thereupon,' an almost certain correction for δὴ ταῦτ'. ἐνταῦθα δή is common, e.g. *Ran.* 796, ἐνταῦθα δὴ τὰ δεινὰ κινηθήσεται. Blaydes says of δὴ 'ντεῦθεν, 'tolerari non potest propter caesuram pravam anapaesti.' Otherwise one would adopt it, as nearest to the readings of R and V. ἐλοιδορούμεθα—'we began to quarrel': so the following imperfects denote the name which each 'was for giving,' 'wished to give,' while the aorists in line 67 give the final decision.

63. ἡ μὲν γὰρ ἵππον—'she wished to put a horse in the name.' Many illustrious Greek names were thus compounded, Hippias, Hipparchus, Philippus, Chrysippus.

64. Ξάνθιππον—a name among the Alcmaeonidae. Both the father and the son of Pericles were so called. Χαίριππον—see critical note. All three names there given are found in good writers.

65. τὸ τοῦ πάππου—sc. ὄνομα. Either this or ἀπὸ τοῦ πάππου must be read, according to Meineke, and Blaydes says 'vulgata certe defendi nequit.' Mr Green indeed urges that the genitive is used with καλεῖν of the person *after* whom another is named; and suggests that ἐτιθέμην is substituted for ἐκάλουν, 'I, after his grandfather, was for making him Phidonides.' But surely ὄνομα must be implied, as it is two lines below, while τίθεσθαι ὄνομα is perpetually occurring. Besides, the instances cited in Liddell and Scott, which are all passive, do not shew

that καλεῖν τινά τινος means to call a person after another: e.g. Pind. *Pyth.* iii. 67 (119), ἥ τινα Λατοΐδα κεκλημένον ἢ πατέρος is not 'called after Apollo,' i.e. by his name, but 'called (being) the son of Apollo.'

66. τέως μέν...εἶτα—cf. Thuc. v. 7, 1, ὁ Κλέων τέως μὲν ἡσύχαζεν, ἔπειτα κ.τ.λ. So πρῶτον μέν...ἔπειτα without δέ is common. ἐκρινόμεθα—'we disputed': Hdt. iii. 120, κρινομένων περὶ ἀρετῆς. τῷ χρόνῳ occurs 865 and 1242.

67. κοινῇ ξυνέβημεν—'we came to terms,' compromised the matter. καθέμεθα Φειδιππίδην—sc. ὄνομα: *Av.* 815, Σπάρτην γὰρ ἂν θείμην ἐγὼ τήμῇ πόλει; The old gentleman wished to call the boy 'Spareson' after his own father (134), as children often had their grandfather's name. The compromise comes out as it were 'Sparehorson.' The name Pheidippus is found in Homer and elsewhere.

68. ἐκορίζετο—the compound verb occurs *Plut.* 1011, νηττάριον ἂν καὶ φάττιον ὑπεκορίζετο.

69. ὅταν σύ—i.e. 'that will be delightful,' or the like. πρὸς πόλιν—to the acropolis (Thuc. ii. 15 fin.), probably after a victory in the Panathenaea, as the commentators explain.

70. Μεγακλέης—Pindar, *Pyth.* vii., celebrates a Pythian chariot victory of Megacles; and speaks of other triumphs of his family.

ξυστίδα—a purple or saffron robe worn by charioteers in triumphal processions.

71. ὅταν μὲν οὖν—'nay rather, when': cf. 221. φελλέως— explained by the scholiast as τόπος τῆς Ἀττικῆς ἐπιτήδειος εἰς βόσιν αἰγῶν τραχύς: but, according to Harpocration, not a proper name but a general term for such districts; τὰ πετρώδη καὶ αἰγίβοτα χωρία φελλέας ἐκάλουν.

72. διφθέραν ἐνημμένος—like a herdsman; so *Eccl.* 80, *Ran.* 430, λεοντῆν ἐνημμένον.

74. ἵππερον—Meineke and Dindorf read ἱππέρων, following Photius, ἱππέρων· τὸν ἐφ' ἵπποις ἔρωτα. Blaydes however urges that the accusative ought to be either ἱππέρωτα or ἵππερον, 'ut ἔρον pro ἔρωτα legitur Eur. *Iph. T.* 1172.' There is also an allusion to ἵκτερος, a disease of the eyes, which makes κατέχεεν appropriate, χρημάτων following instead of ὀμμάτων. μου from its position has somewhat the same force as an ethical dative 'incommodi.' In construction it either follows χρημάτων, or is governed directly by κατέχεεν, τῶν χρημάτων being a genitive of further definition: cf. *Vesp.* 6,

καὐτοῦ γ' ἐμοῦ
κατὰ τοῖν κόραιν ὕπνου τι καταχεῖται γλυκύ.

κατέχεεν—cf. *Eq.* 1090,
καὶ μοὐδόκει ἡ θεὸς αὐτὴ
τοῦ δήμου καταχεῖν ἀρυταίνῃ πλουθυγίειαν.
ἔχεε(ν) uncontracted is aorist, the imperfect is ἔχει. For the contraction of such verbs see *New Phryn.* p. 300.

75. **φροντίζων ὁδοῦ**—'thinking of a road': so Blaydes, Meineke, etc. Green and others put a comma after φροντίζων, making ὁδοῦ depend on ἀτραπόν, 'a path to go by.' Both rhythm and sense are in favour of the former view, if only the use of φροντίζων can be supported. φροντίζω is generally used in a negative sense of 'not thinking much of' somebody or something (125), or else absolutely in the sense of 'pondering.' Blaydes indeed cites Xen. *Mem.* iv. 8, 5, φροντίσαι τῆς πρὸς τοὺς δικαστὰς ἀπολογίας, and a passage from Pollux, but no other authorities. He adds 'sed scripserat, ni fallor, comicus φροντίζων μόλις etc.,' μόλις being written over μίαν in one manuscript. This however would lose the antithesis between ὁδοῦ and ἀτραπόν.

76. **ἀτραπόν**—cf. *Av.* 21,
οὐ γάρ ἐστ' ἐνταῦθά τις
ὁδός. ΠΕ. οὐδὲ μὰ Δί' ἐνταῦθά γ' ἀτραπὸς οὐδαμοῦ.
The distinction is found in many proverbial expressions, e.g. ὁδοῦ παρούσης τὴν ἀτραπὸν μὴ ζήτει, quoted by Blaydes from the *Proverbs* of Appian: so Ennius ap. Cic. *Divin.* i. 58, 132, qui sibi semitam non sapiunt alteri monstrant viam.

77. **ἦν...τουτονί—πείθω** often takes a double accusative, one of the person, the other a neuter cognate with the verb, e.g. Aesch. *Ag.* 1212, ἔπειθον οὐδέν' οὐδέν. But πείθειν τινὰ ἀτραπόν is quite different: though it may be justified by Thuc. ii. 21, 1, δόξαντι χρήμασι πεισθῆναι τὴν ἀναχώρησιν, if the reading be genuine (which is questioned). The explanation, I think, is to be found by understanding βαδίζειν or the like, 'which if I can persuade him to take': cf. *Av.* 1,
ὀρθὴν κελεύεις ᾗ τὸ δένδρον φαίνεται;
The accusative of 'the road by which' is not uncommon; e.g. Thuc. v. 10, 6, ἔθει τὴν ὁδὸν ταύτην.

80. **Φειδιππίδιον**—a coaxing diminutive of endearment (ἥδιστα); cf. 222: *Ach.* 404, Εὐριπίδη, Εὐριπίδιον.

81. **κύσον με κ.τ.λ.**—Teuffel compares Soph. *Trach.* 1181, where the dying Heracles says to his son, on whom he is laying his last commands,
ἔμβαλλε χεῖρα δεξιὰν πρώτιστά μοι·
and Hyllus responds
ἰδοὺ προτείνω κ.τ.λ.

82. ἰδού—'there,' giving his hand; cf. 255, ἰδοὺ κάθημαι, 635 etc.

83. τουτονί—pointing to an image of Poseidon, or, according to the scholiast, to his own chariot or harness. The Athenians swore by Apollo ἀγυιεύς, whose statue stood by their doors, and the son naturally appeals to his own tutelary god, whose image he had placed near at hand. Dindorf indeed urges that οὗτος and οὑτοσί do not necessarily imply actual presence, but are often used emphatically where we say 'that,' e.g. Plat. *Gorg.* 470 D, ὁρᾷς Ἀρχέλαον τοῦτον τὸν Περδίκκου; Dem. *Fals. leg.* 447 § 331, Ξενοκλείδην τουτονὶ τὸν ποιητὴν ἐξεκήρυξεν. See the question which arises on line 1473.

84. μή μοί γε—cf. 433: *Vesp.* 1179, μή μοί γε μύθους.

87. τί οὖν πίθωμαι—'what am I to obey you in?' cf. *Vesp.* 760, ἴθ', ὦ πάτερ, ἐμοὶ πιθοῦ. ΦΙ. τί σοι πίθωμαι; For this interrogative subjunctive see Goodwin § 287.

88. ἔκστρεψον—according to the scholiast, this is a metaphor from turning a dirty garment inside out, τὸ ἀλλάξαι τὸ πρὸς τὸ σῶμα μέρος ἔξω. Any way it suggests a complete change.

90. καί τι πείσει;—there is something deprecatory and insinuating about τι, and no alteration is needed.

91. νὴ τὸν Διόνυσον—forbidden to swear by Poseidon (83) the son appeals to the presiding deity of the theatre.

92. τῳκίδιον—another coaxing diminutive. οἰκίδιον, i.e. οἰκι-ίδιον from οἰκία: so καλῴδιον, σηπίδιον etc. from words in -ία (Blaydes): δικαστηριδιον (*Vesp.* 803), ἀργυρίδιον (*Plut.* 147), from words in -ιον.

93. ἐτεόν—cf. 35.

94. φροντιστήριον—a word apparently coined by Aristophanes, on the analogy of βουλευτήριον, δικαστήριον etc. 'Contemplatory' (cf. refectory) is approved by Mr Green as a translation; and it certainly represents both sound and sense. Dr Merry's 'Reflectory' is better still.

The scholiast says that Socrates and his school were called φροντισταί, διὰ τὸ φροντίζειν περὶ ἀλλήλων καὶ διὰ τὸ μηδέποτε παύεσθαι τῆς φροντίδος, meaning, I suppose, that they spent their lives in thinking, and that their thinking never came to any practical good.

95. οἳ τὸν οὐρανόν—for the construction cf. ψύλλαν, 145: αὐτόν, 479 etc.

96. πνιγεύς—so *Av.* 1001, where Meton says

αὐτίκα γὰρ ἀήρ ἐστι τὴν ἰδέαν ὅλος
κατὰ πνιγέα μάλιστα.

'An oven' or furnace is the received translation; but, as Mr Green points out, something of the nature of a round cover seems certainly implied. This piece of natural science, according to the scholiast, was attributed by Cratinus in his *Panoptae* to the philosopher Hippo.

97. ἄνθρακες—διὰ τὸ ὑπὸ ἡλίου θερμαίνεσθαι (schol.). There may be some sort of etymological joke on ἄνθρωποι, which would not sound very unlike if pronounced by accent (Green). Socrates, as we often find in Plato, was given to such fanciful analogies.

98. ἀργύριον ἦν τις διδῷ—a transparent calumny in the case of Socrates, who notoriously never taught for gain; see note on 245.

99. λέγοντα νικᾶν—cf. 115, 1210 etc. The accusative depends on either word, or rather on the compound idea of both. For the use of νικᾶν cf. *Vesp.* 594, γνώμην ἐνίκησεν.

101. μεριμνοφροντισταί—i.e. μεριμνηταί and φροντισταί. Both words are applied to students and philosophers: cf. 951, and 1404. Eur., *Med.* 1228, derides μεριμνητὰς λόγων and τοὺς σοφοὺς δοκοῦντας εἶναι. καλοί τε κἀγαθοί—'right worthy gentlemen'; a favourite phrase, says Blaydes, with the Socratic school.

102. αἰβοῖ—an expression of disgust, e.g. at a bad smell; here at the distasteful recollection of the men whom Pheidippides already knew by sight. πονηροί γ', οἶδα—'a scrubby lot, I know': or perhaps with a pause, 'I know them.' τοὺς ἀλαζόνας—'those humbugs': 'proprium et constans sophistarum epithetum' (Blaydes).

103. τοὺς ὠχριῶντας—'the pale student' has always been a stock figure in comedy, and the Smike-like Chaerephon was an unusually obnoxious specimen: cf. 504: *Vesp.* 1412. ἀνυποδήτους—a peculiarity of philosophers and others who affected hardiness and simplicity of life, and a characteristic habit of Socrates. Thus Phaedrus says when Socrates proposes to walk along the Ilissus, 'It is lucky I came without my shoes; you never wear them' (Plat. *Phaedr.* 229 A).

104. ὧν—sc. εἰσί: cf. 107. Χαιρεφῶν—a friend of Socrates from his youth; cf. Plat. *Apol.* 21 A, where the scholiast says he was lean and pale, a sycophant and parasite, dishonest and dirty. He was called the bat from his dark looks and thin voice.

105. ἢ ἤ—*Ran.* 271, ἢ Ξανθίας. The sound corresponds to our *eh!*

106. ἀλλ', εἴ τι κήδει—a line of mock-tragic ring: *Ach.* 1028, ἀλλ' εἴ τι κήδει Δερκέτου Φυλασίου. ἀλφίτων—ἀντὶ τοῦ χρημάτων, ὡς ἄγροικος, τουτέστι τῆς πατρῴας οὐσίας (schol.).

107. τούτων γενοῦ—partitive genitive with εἶναι, γίγνομαι and the like; cf. ὧν (104): Dem. *Meid.* 579 § 202, τῶν συγχαιρόντων ἐξητάσθη τῷ δήμῳ. For μοι cf. 116: so σοι 111. σχασάμενος—'dropping,'

or 'cutting': so Plat. Com. ii. 628, καὶ τὰς ὀφρῦς σχάσασθε καὶ τὰς ὄμφακας, i.e. have done with your ill-temper. These are metaphorical and apparently slang uses of the word; derived, according to the scholiast, from rowing: Pind. *Pyth.* x. 51, κώπαν σχάσον. The primary meaning of σχάζω, as is shown in Mr Green's note, is to cut or slit open: 'then what has been tightly done up is, by slitting, loosed or opened, and the cover or bands drop slack': cf. 740.   τὴν ἱππικήν—Blaydes suspects the reading, as 'ἱππικὴ sine articulo legitur ubique apud nostrum, 27 etc.' Here however the article has an appropriate force='your taste for horses.'

108. οὐκ ἄν—cf. 5, 154: *Ach.* 966, οὐκ ἄν...εἰ δοίη γέ μοι: *Plut.* 928, οὐδ' ἄν εἰ δοίης γέ μοι.

109. φασιανούς—authorities ancient and modern alike are at issue whether horses or birds are meant. Dindorf with others pronounces for horses, his main argument being that φασιανικός is applied to a bird, not φασιανός. But Blaydes' note shows sufficient authority for φασιανὸς ὄρνις, while a Phasian breed of horses appears to be unknown: pheasants are therefore most likely meant.

A rich and luxurious man would keep them like peacocks, for show and for the table. Blaydes cites Aelian *N. A.* xiii. 18, ἐν δὲ τοῖς παραδείσοις τρέφονται μὲν καὶ ταῶς ἥμεροι καὶ χειροήθεις φασιανοί. The son no doubt had other fashionable tastes as well as that for horses. Λεωγόρας—a rich gourmand (*Vesp.* 1268), father of Andocides the orator.

112. εἶναι παρ' αὐτοῖς—i.e. they possess this secret and can impart it (παραδιδόναι) to others: cf. Plat. *Gorg.* 452 C, ἀμφισβητεῖ Γοργίας τὴν παρ' αὐτῷ τέχνην μείζονος ἀγαθοῦ αἰτίαν εἶναι ἢ τὴν σήν. Shortly before this passage παρὰ Γοργίᾳ has the same meaning, not 'in the estimation of Gorgias' as Cope renders it.

'To make the worse appear the better cause was the claim, not of Socrates and his followers, but of other rhetorical teachers and specially of Protagoras, who introduced the custom of teaching his disciples to argue for and against a given thesis with equal plausibility and ingenuity' (Rogers). Socrates however got the credit of such sophistry, as we learn from Plato, *Apol.* 18 B.

113. ὅστις ἐστί—'whatever that may be.' The sense applies to both λόγοι, of which Strepsiades had but little knowledge.

115. νικᾶν λέγοντα—for the construction cf. 99. Here the ἕτερος λόγος is as it were personified and is the subject of νικᾶν.

119. ἰδεῖν—i.e. to face them. As ἰδεῖν is rather 'to see' than 'to

look at' (βλέπειν), Meineke suggests μ' ίδεῖν...διακεκναισμένον, making τοὺς ἱππέας the subject.

120. τοὺς ἱππέας—οἱ γὰρ ἱππεῖς εὔχροοι καὶ ὑποδεδεμένοι καὶ ἐν γυμνασίοις ἐξεταζόμενοι καὶ ἐν παλαίστραις (schol.). τὸ χρῶμα— Meineke considers that τὸν χρῶτα or τὸ σῶμα would accord better with διακεκναισμένος: but it was the faces of the thinkers that particularly disgusted Pheidippides (103), and διακεκναισμένος is 'disfigured' generally.

121. μὰ τὴν Δήμητρα—εἰκότως τὴν Δήμητρα ὄμνυσιν, as it is a question of corn (schol.). ἔδει—future of ἐσθίω: *Pac.* 1357 etc. κατέδομαι, *Ach.* 1112 etc.

122. ὁ σαμφόρας—a horse marked with σάν, the Doric equivalent to σῖγμα: cf. 45. The σαμφόρας may have been a showy expensive horse, as Mr Green suggests, put on the outside (σειραφόρος), as he seems distinguished from the ζύγιος: see 1298.

123. ἐξελῶ σ' ἐς κόρακας—cf. Lys. xiii. 81, ἀπιέναι ἐκέλευσεν ἐς κόρακας ἐκ τῶν πολιτῶν.

125. ἄνιππον ὄντ'—so Blaydes, following Cobet's conjecture; 'nunquam enim post verbum περιορᾶν omittitur participium.' The son now goes away, leaving Strepsiades to make the best of the state of things.

126—221. Strepsiades, undismayed by his son's refusal, applies himself for admission to the school. A disciple, who answers his call, tells him some wondrous stories of the master's wisdom, and at length lets him in. He sees the students, and strange appliances for study, and finally Socrates himself suspended in a basket. The part of the disciple is taken by the actor who has represented Pheidippides.

126. οὐδ' ἐγώ—'I won't give in either,' i.e. any more than you; οὐδέ = 'also not,' as it generally means.

μέντοι—'nevertheless,' 'after all'; or perhaps simply a strong affirmation. πεσών γε κείσομαι—like a thrown wrestler; *Eccl.* 962, καταπεσὼν κείσομαι. The old man is determined not to be floored by his son's refusal.

127. **εὐξάμενος**—prayer was right and natural before a great undertaking. Thus Philocleon is called on to pray before trying to escape, *Vesp.* 388: and the rival tragedians with Dionysus pray before the poetic contest, *Ran.* 871, 885. **διδάξομαι**—'I will get myself taught.' Here διδάξομαι has the strict force of the middle; but it is a true passive, Soph. *Ant.* 726, οἱ τηλικοίδε καὶ διδαξόμεσθα δή;

130. **σχινδαλάμους**—'the nice hair-splittings of subtle logic' (Rogers); so *Ran.* 819, σχινδαλάμων παραξόνια: lit. shavings or splinters.

131. **ἰτητέον**—after a moment's hesitation he nerves himself to the trial. **τί ταῦτ' ἔχων στραγγεύομαι;**—'why do I keep loitering?'; so 509, τί κυπτάζεις ἔχων; *Av.* 541, ληρεῖς ἔχων. ταῦτα is connected with the two words as a cognate accusative, 'thus, in this fashion.'

132. **ἀλλ' οὐχί**—we say '*and* do not knock'; the Greek idiom is with ἀλλά, cf. 227 etc. **παῖ, παιδίον**—knocking, and calling for an attendant; so Dionysus knocks at Heracles' door (*Ran.* 37), and calls παιδίον, παῖ, ἠμί, παῖ. The two passages are much alike: so 1145.

133. **βάλλ' ἐς κόρακας**—not addressed to the knocker, but applying to the circumstance. So we might say, 'Confound it, who is this knocking?': cf. *Vesp.* 835,

βάλλ' ἐς κόρακας, τοιουτονὶ τρέφειν κύνα.

134. **Φειδωνος**—but, according to 65, the grandfather's name was Pheidonides. **Κικυννόθεν**—from Cicynna, a deme of the tribe Acamantis.

136. **ἀπεριμερίμνως—ἀσκόπως, ἀμαθῶς** (schol.); 'without consideration'; cf. note on 101. **λελάκτικας** implies a violent assault on the door, like κενταυρικῶς ἐνήλατο, *Ran.* 38.

137. **ἐξημβλωκας**—'have spoiled, ruined': strictly of an untimely birth 'made abortive.' Socrates was the son of a midwife, and used to say that he followed his mother's trade, by helping others to develop their mental conceptions. **ἐξηυρημένην**—the tenses of εὑρίσκω are perpetually found without the augment, and the old grammarians were at issue as to which forms were right, while some admitted both. It is certainly reasonable to follow the analogy of other verbs in εὑ, and to write ηὗρον, ηὕρηκα.

138. **τηλοῦ τῶν ἀγρῶν**—'far away in the country'; a partitive genitive: cf. ἑκὰς χθονός, ποῦ γῆς; *huc viciniae*, and the like.

140. **ἀλλ' οὐ θέμις κ.τ.λ.**—an unworthy sneer, as if Socrates grudged his teaching to the world at large; so 143.

141. **ἐγὼ γὰρ οὑτοσί—ἑαυτὸν δείκνυσι** (schol.), putting himself

forward as an intending pupil: *Eq.* 1098, καὶ νῦν ἐμαυτὸν ἐπιτρέπω σοι τουτονὶ γεροντανωγεῖν.

143. **μυστήρια**—secrets, not to be divulged to the uninitiated, like the Eleusinian mysteries: cf. τελουμένους, 258.

145. **ψύλλαν ὁπόσους ἅλλοιτο**—the same construction as in 95. Dr Merry points out that this is a gibe at the dictum of Protagoras, πάντων μέτρον ἄνθρωπος. 'This saying represented every one as a law to himself, and denied any fixed principle of truth. Here the flea supplies its own scale for measurement.' **τοὺς αὑτῆς πόδας**—Blaydes says 'vulgata plane soloeca est,' and suggests τῶν αὑτῆς ποδῶν. But the predicative construction of ὁπόσους is quite right: one might say, ἀνήρετ᾿ ὁπόσοι παρεῖεν οἱ ἄνδρες, lit. 'in what number the men were there': cf. Soph. *Ant.* 360, ἄπορος ἐπ᾿ οὐδὲν ἔρχεται τὸ μέλλον, where οὐδὲν specifies the extent to which τὸ μέλλον applies.

146. **τὴν ὀφρύν**—the flea selects the prominent features of the sages, Chaerephon's bushy eyebrows and Socrates' bald head.

148. For the reading see the critical note. Blaydes, who reads πῶς δῆτα διεμέτρησε; 'measured the distance across,' cites Lucian, *Prom.* 6, ψυλλῶν πηδήματα διαμετροῦντας, 'ubi ad hunc locum procul dubio respicitur.'

150. **τὼ πόδε**—its two hind feet, as if the flea were a biped.

151. **ψυχεῖσι**—this is Blaydes' correction, sc. τοῖς ποσί. Most manuscripts have ψυγείσῃ, sc. τῇ ψύλλῃ. Dindorf with one manuscript reads ψυχείσῃ, as the right Attic form. Herwerden has ψυγέντος (τοῦ κηροῦ), Meineke and Kock, ψυχέντος. **περιέφυσαν**—'formed round them.' **περσικαί** are women's shoes; *Eccl.* 319: *Thesm.* 734, περσικὰς ἔχων, of a man dressed like a woman.

152. **ὑπολύσας**—the proper word for taking off shoes: cf. *Vesp.* 1157, where ὑπολύου τὰς καταράτους ἐμβάδας (Cob.) seems the right reading, not ἀποδύου or ὑποδύου. **ἀνεμέτρει**—'he proceeded to measure the distance back.'

153. **ὦ Ζεῦ βασιλεῦ**—his favourite exclamation, see line 2. **τῆς λεπτότητος**—'what a subtle intelligence!' The genitive of exclamation is very common, e.g. *Vesp.* 161, Ἄπολλον ἀποτρόπαιε, τοῦ μαντεύματος. It gives the *cause* of astonishment and is analogous to such phrases as θαυμάζω σε τῆς τόλμης.

φρενῶν—φρήν is a tragic word, generally used by Aristophanes in lyric passages or in parody; see *New Phryn.* p. 9.

154. **τί δῆτ᾿ ἄν**—sc. εἴποις: *Lys.* 399, τί δῆτ᾿ ἄν, εἰ πύθοιο; For other ellipses with ἄν see 5, 108 etc.

157. ὁπότερα—'which was his opinion': ὁπότερα for ὁπότερον, as in Hdt. v. 119.

158. κατά—'at' or 'by.' The scholiast notes that gnats and such insects πάντα διὰ τοῦ στήθους τὴν φωνὴν προΐεται. The sound is of course really produced by the vibration of the wings.

161. διὰ λεπτοῦ δ' ὄντος αὐτοῦ—we should say 'through this narrow passage.' Blaydes illustrates the Greek construction by Thuc. vii. 84, 4, ἐν κοίλῳ ὄντι τῷ ποταμῷ ταρασσομένους.

162. βίᾳ βαδίζειν—'passes violently': cf. Plat. *Phaedr.* 254 A, βίᾳ φέρεται, 'rushes violently.' εὐθύ—with genitive 'straight for'; *Av.* 1421, εὐθὺ Πελλήνης.

163. κοῖλον πρὸς στενῷ—these adjectives are in agreement respectively with the substantives in the next line. The idea is that the ἔντερον of the gnat is a narrow tube ending in a wide mouth, thus forming a trumpet. προσκείμενον is 'fitted on,' like the mouth of a trumpet.

166. ὦ τρισμακάριος κ.τ.λ.—with the nominative ὦ (or ὤ, vid. Stallbaum on Plat. *Phaedr.* 227 D) is an exclamation *about* a person; so *Vesp.* 900. For the following genitive cf. *Vesp.* 1292, ἰὼ χελῶναι μακάριαι τοῦ δέρματος. διεντερεύματος—'insight into the inside' is Blaydes' rendering, in accordance with the scholiast. It is a word coined for the occasion, from ἔντερον, with a supposed allusion to διερευνᾶν, a word of philosophical investigation. τρισμακάριος thus refers to Socrates. But as some inferior manuscripts have τρισμακάριοι, Bentley suggested τρισμακάριαι referring to the ἐμπίδες. διεντέρευμα would then, as Mr Green says, be the 'intestinal passage' through the gnat's body, at whose wondrous internal structure Strepsiades is so surprised. Besides, why should not τρισμακάριος agree with πρωκτός?

167. φεύγων ἂν ἀποφύγοι—*Vesp.* 479, φεύγων, οὐκ ἀποφεύγει: see Blaydes for other instances. Such combinations were not unpleasing to the Greek ear. Strepsiades is thinking still of his own reasons for coming to Socrates.

168. διοῖδε—'sees through' i.e. knows thoroughly.

170. ἀσκαλαβώτου—the same as γαλεώτης, 174, a spotted lizard, *stellio*.

171. τὰς ὁδούς—so 584.

174. ἥσθην—'I like the idea'; so 1240: *Eq.* 696, ἥσθην ἀπειλαῖς. The Greek idiom is more exact than the English. We say 'what do you say?' but the Greek is πῶς εἶπας; τί τοῦτ' ἔλεξας; i.e. at the moment when you spoke: so τί ἐθαύμασας; 185. There was a story of

Thales tumbling into a well while contemplating the heavens. The idea is here transferred to Socrates with a difference.

176. **πρὸς τἄλφιτ'**—to get his supper; cf. 648. **ἐπαλαμήσατο**—'contrived.'

177. **κατὰ τῆς τραπέζης κ.τ.λ.**—the account is not very clear, nor meant to be; it is probably merely intended to astonish Strepsiades. I think the explanation given by Mr S. R. Winans is the most probable (*American Journal of Philology*, xvi. 1). He considers that Socrates is supposed to be skilled in magic arts. He performed in the φροντιστήριον some mystic geomantic process, by which he transferred a piece of meat (θυμάτιον) from the παλαίστρα to the table of his hungry disciples.

τῆς τραπέζης is usually taken to be a table by the altar on which the sacred vessels were placed and the victims cut up. But it is much better to understand it, with Winans, of the table in the φροντιστήριον used for calculations and diagrams. Nothing is said about Socrates leaving his headquarters.

λεπτὴν τέφραν—for drawing figures; sand or dust being the customary and proverbial surface for the geometrician's work: cf. Pers. *Sat.* i. 131, secto in pulvere metas: Cic. *de Nat. Deor.* ii. 18, 48, pulvis eruditus, i.e. the study of geometry: id. *Tusc.* v. 23, 64 (Archimedem) a pulvere et radio excitabo: Sen. *Ep.* 88, itane in geometriae pulvere haerebo?

κατὰ τῆς will thus be 'down over.' Teuffel however takes it as 'down from,' supposing that Socrates takes wood ashes from the table of sacrifice and spreads them on the ground.

178. **κάμψας ὀβελίσκον**—according to the scholiast, Socrates bent the straight spit or skewer, on which there was nothing to cook, into a hook with which to filch away the coat (reading θοἰμάτιον). **διαβήτην λαβών**—one view is that Socrates bent the spit, and then used it as a pair of compasses. But surely, even if ὡς can be implied, the words cannot be equivalent to ὡς διαβήτῃ χρώμενος: and a proper pair of compasses must have been at hand in the φροντιστήριον.

179. **ἐκ τῆς παλαίστρας κ.τ.λ.**—i.e. by his skill in magic, as Winans holds. The other view is that Socrates, standing by the table of sacrifice, distracts the attention of the attendants by drawing his diagrams, and meanwhile appropriates the meat. **θυμάτιον** is Hermann's correction of θοἰμάτιον and is now generally accepted. It makes rather better sense, especially with Winans' view of the passage. θοἰμάτιον has however this to be said for it, that clothes-stealing from the παλαίστρα was a common offence, and as such guarded against by

special penalties. Still this very fact may have led a copyist into error in such an obscure passage. Besides, the article with ἱμάτιον, 'that cloak,' is out of place.

180. τὸν Θαλῆν—' the allusion to Thales now gets a better point. He is apostrophized not as the wise man, but as the geometer who calculated eclipses and in the popular belief taught the Egyptians how to take the height of their pyramids' (Winans).

181. ἀνύσας—'at once'; *Vesp.* 398: with τι, 506 etc.

182. Σωκράτη—the reading of nearly all the manuscripts is Σωκράτην. The grammarians assign Σωκράτη to Plato, Σωκράτην to Xenophon: 'minime tamen sibi constant libri MSS.' (Blaydes). Similar names e.g. Δημοσθένης, Ἑρμοκράτης, Καλλικράτης, generally have the accusative in ην according to manuscript authority.

183. μαθητιῶ—Blaydes gives a long list of verbs in ιᾶν, denoting mental or bodily inclination: we have another instance in line 44.

184. The door is thrown open, and the disciples are discovered at their studies. Their squalid and miserable appearance appals Strepsiades.

ὦ Ἡράκλεις—Heracles is invoked as the averter of ill (ἀλεξίκακος): *Av.* 93, ὦ Ἡράκλεις, τουτὶ τί ποτ' ἐστὶ θηρίον;

186. τοῖς ἐκ Πύλου—see Thuc. iv. 27,—41. The Spartans from Sphacteria had been kept on short rations in the island, and were afterwards imprisoned at Athens. Λακωνικοῖς—adjective used as substantive, so Ἀχαρνικοί, *Ach.* 324.

188. τὰ κατὰ γῆς—the charge of investigating τὰ ὑπὸ γῆς and τὰ ἐπουράνια is repeatedly mentioned in Plato's *Apology*, e.g. 18 B. βολβούς—τὰ λεγόμενα ὕδνα (schol.): ὕδνα according to Liddell and Scott are probably truffles. βολβοί are mentioned as common articles of food, Plat. *Rep.* 372 C: Theocr. xiv. 17 etc.

189. μὴ...φροντίζετε—this is not worthy of your φροντίς. Strepsiades would prefer their considering points which might help him in his difficulties; see 197.

192. ἐρεβοδιφῶσιν—*Pac.* 793, μηχανοδίφης (διφάω). ὑπὸ τὸν Τάρταρον—beneath the lowest deep: Τάρταρος δέ ἐστιν ὁ ὑπὸ γῆν κατώτατος τόπος (schol.).

195. ἀλλ' εἴσιθ'—to the disciples, who are not to waste time out of doors. ἐκεῖνος is 'the master'; so αὐτός, 219.

197. αὐτοῖσι—so in *Vesp.* 172 the line begins with αὐτόν with no emphatic force.

198. πρὸς τὸν ἀέρα—'in the air'; turned to it, πρός implying

direction: cf. 771, πρὸς τὸν ἥλιον : *Vesp.* 772, πρὸς ἥλιον...πρὸς τὸ πῦρ καθήμενος : so σποδίζειν πρὸς τὸ πῦρ, to roast at the fire, Plat. *Rep.* 372 C, πρὸς τὸ φῶς (632), which Blaydes cites in illustration, differs as it has the idea of motion expressed : so πρὸς τὸν ἥλιον, *Thesm.* 69.

199. ἐστίν—the position of this word is very awkward. Blaydes' suggestion of οὕτω would be an improvement.

200. Strepsiades now enters the school and is amazed at the sight of astronomical and geometrical instruments. πρὸς τῶν θεῶν as usual asks a question or makes an appeal. πρός with the genitive is never used of swearing by a god in affirmation.

202. τί ;—'in what?'

203. ἀναμετρεῖσθαι—i.e. to measure; but Strepsiades understands it of portioning out land to the citizens, and asks if he means τὴν κληρουχικήν, the land of conquered countries to which κληροῦχοι were assigned. For such allotments see Dict. Ant. *colonia*, i. 7.

204. ἀστεῖον λέγεις—'a charming idea'; Strepsiades thinks that all the world is to be divided up. Rogers suggests as a Latin translation, 'urbane dicis: urbi enim utile est callidum hoc commentum.' In illustration of the passage he cites Plat. *Phaedr.* 227 D, ὦ γενναῖος, εἴθε γράψειεν κ.τ.λ....ἦ γὰρ ἂν ἀστεῖοι καὶ δημωφελεῖς εἶεν οἱ λόγοι, and Stallbaum's note thereon, 'elegans est ambiguitas in vocabulo ἀστεῖοι, quod et de elegantia atque urbanitate et de communi utilitate capiendum.'

205. σόφισμα—'device, scheme'; Hdt. iii. 152, πάντα σοφίσματα καὶ πάσας μηχανὰς ἐπεποιήκεε: often used in a bad sense of tricks, and so of verbal or logical tricks, quibbles, sophisms. δημοτικόν— 'popular'; the word, like *popularis* and *civilis*, is used both of persons and things.

206. γῆς περίοδος πάσης—'a map of the whole earth'; Hdt. v. 49, χάλκεον πίνακα ἐν ᾧ γῆς ἁπάσης περίοδος ἐνετέτμητο κ.τ.λ.: id. iv. 36, γῆς περιόδους γράψαντας.

208. ἐπεὶ δικαστάς—the special local feature. 'How the oracles are coming to pass,' says Bdelycleon in the *Wasps*, 'for I once heard that every Athenian should have a law-court of his own' (*Vesp.* 799—804).

209. ὡς—usually explained as meaning 'be assured that,' as in *Ach.* 335, ὡς ἀποκτενῶ. There is a nearly similar usage in *Vesp.* 416. Kock however suggests τοῦθ' ὡς ἀληθῶς, 'in very truth,' and Cobet would omit the line. Blaydes approves of Dobree's conjecture of Ἀττική for Ἀττικόν.

210. **Κικυννῆς**—a good illustration of the Greek way of naming a place by its inhabitants, e.g. Λοκροί etc.

211. **ἐνταῦθ' ἔνεισιν**—'here they are down.'

212. **παρατέταται**—'is stretched out': Eur. *Hel.* 1673, παρ' Ἀκτὴν τεταμένην νῆσον.

213. **παρετάθη**—'was stretched on the rack,' distressed and tortured: Liddell and Scott give several instances of metaphorical usage in this sense. The allusion is to the subjugation of the revolted Euboea in 446: see Thuc. i. 114, 2, Περικλέους στρατηγοῦντος κατεστρέψαντο πᾶσαν.

214. **ὅπου 'στίν**;—sc. do you ask? The direct question is repeated indirectly; so 1248: *Ran.* 198, τί ποιεῖς; ὅ τι ποιῶ;

215. **τοῦτο πάνυ φροντίζετε**—i.e. this is a matter well worthy of your φροντίς; cf. 189. Bentley's suggestion of μεταφροντίζετε is very ingenious and tempting, especially as there is a var. lect. μέγα for πάνυ. Strepsiades, he supposes, seeing Sparta close to Athens on the map, imagines that the philosophers have brought it so near and begs them to remove it further. Bentley's conjecture is supported by the scholiast's explaining φροντίζετε by μεταβουλεύεσθε.

217. **νὴ Δί'**—in accordance with Cobet's correction, connected with what follows, instead of with οὐχ οἷόν τε, which would naturally have μὰ Δία.   **οἰμώξεσθ' ἄρα**—i.e. you will suffer from the Spartan invasions, as the scholiast says; or it may be simply a threat on the speaker's part, 'the worse for you.'

218. **φέρε τίς γάρ**—so 342 and 370. Strepsiades now first catches sight of Socrates, who is shown suspended in a basket; in ridicule, it is suggested, of the mechanism by which stage deities appeared. The whole scene reminds one of Dicaeopolis calling on Euripides, *Ach.* 403 sq.

219. **αὐτός**—so pupils and servants styled 'the master.'

220. **ἴθ' οὗτος**—'come, you sir.'   **μέγα**—'loudly'; *Vesp.* 963, λέξον μέγα: *Ach.* 103, λέγε μεῖζον, 'louder.'

221. **μὲν οὖν**—'no, you call him'; μὲν οὖν, 'nay, rather,' modifies what has gone before, strengthening an affirmative or suggesting a negative.

222—274. Strepsiades makes his application to the master, who promises to initiate him in the mysteries of his craft, and invokes the Clouds to aid him.

222. ὦ Σώκρατες κ.τ.λ.—cf. 80.

225. ἀεροβατῶ—this particular gibe is recalled in Plat. *Apol.* 19 C. By **περιφρονῶ** Socrates means 'contemplate,' 'speculate on'; but Strepsiades understands him to mean 'despise.' For this latter sense see Thuc. i. 25, 4. The word takes either the accusative or genitive.

227. εἴπερ—sc. τοῦτο ποιεῖς: if you do look down on the gods, you do it from a basket, not on the level.

229. εἰ μὴ κρεμάσας—'rarius εἰ μή cum participio' is Elmsley's comment. μή alone in the usual construction. Blaydes therefore suggests εἰ μὴ 'κρέμασα καὶ...κατέμιξά γ'. εἰ μὴ (ἐξηῦρον) κρεμάσας is Kock's explanation, which avoids any grammatical difficulty, and is supported by examples.

By 'suspending the intelligence' the philosopher raises it above mere things of earth, and sets it free to range a boundless universe.

230. λεπτήν—note the force of the predicate, 'in subtle admixture'; so 740. **ἐς τὸν ὅμοιον ἀέρα**—'with the kindred air' (Rogers): the air is ὁμοιολεπτομερής, 'subtle like itself,' as the scholiast explains.

232. οὐ γὰρ ἀλλ'—'in very truth'; *Ran.* 58, οὐ γὰρ ἀλλ' ἔχω κακῶς.

233. τὴν ἰκμάδα—the moisture, τουτέστι τὸ νοητικὸν τῆς ψυχῆς. Thus the mind is left dry and barren.

234. πάσχει δὲ ταὐτό—'the same is the case with cress,' it dries up moisture in the ground and in those that eat it; πάσχει almost = ποιεῖ: this is a πάθος, 'condition' or 'property,' of the κάρδαμα.

236. ἡ φροντίς κ.τ.λ.—a hopeless muddle of the lesson. Strepsiades is in fact only half attending, as his head is full of his own needs.

239. ἦλθες δέ—*Pac.* 192, ἥκεις δὲ κατὰ τί;

240. χρήστων—note the accent, to avoid confusion with χρηστῶν from χρηστός. Here and in 434 χρήστης is a lender (χράω); in Demosthenes it is generally a borrower (χράομαι): cf. the epigram Anth. ix. 12. 2, πόδας χρήσας ὄμματα χρησάμενος, on a blind man carrying a lame man on his shoulders.

241. ἄγομαι, φέρομαι—Eur. *Troad.* 1310, ἀγόμεθα φερόμεθα: Dem. *de Cor. trier.* 1232, § 13, πάντας ἀνθρώπους ἄγει καὶ φέρει: so *ago, fero.* **τὰ χρήματ' ἐνεχυράζομαι**—'I have my goods taken in pledge.' The accusative may be simply one of reference and 'limitation,' or rather the special accusative used with words of depriving, defrauding etc.; cf. 24 : *Ach.* 164, τὰ σκόροδα πορθούμενος.

242. ὑπόχρεως—cf. Dem. *Aphob.* i. 821 § 25, where Cobet replaces ὑπόχρεως for ὑπέρχρεως.

243. νόσος μ' κ.τ.λ.—'a galloping consumption seized my money' (Rogers).   δεινὴ φαγεῖν—'lusus est in verbo φαγεῖν, quod de equis pariter ac morbis dicitur' (Blaydes): cf. φαγέδαινα (Aesch. Fr. 231): ἀδηφάγος νόσος (Soph. *Phil.* 313).

246. πράττῃ—Xen. *Mem.* i. 6, 11, οὐδένα τῆς συνουσίας ἀργύριον πράττει, shows the full construction with πράττω and πράττομαι, and vindicates Socrates from the poet's calumny.

247. ποίους θεούς;—a contemptuous question; cf. 367 : *Vesp.* 1202, ποίας χάρακας, 'props indeed!': so πόθεν; 'nonsense,' no real question being intended.

248. νόμισμ'—'current coin,' i.e. gods do not pass current with us. Socrates means an accepted institution, as in Soph. *Ant.* 296; but Strepsiades understands actual coinage, and asks τῷ γὰρ ὄμνυτ'; 'why, what's your current medium for—swearing?' If the text be right, ὄμνυτ' is substituted for ἀγοράζετε or νομίζετε by a comic παρ' ὑπόνοιαν, and τῷ may be regarded as an instrumental dative. ὀμνύναι τινά is the construction for swearing by anyone. Besides this awkwardness of construction, there is a confusion of ideas when the next line comes in: people do not swear by coins. Blaydes therefore reads τῷ νομίζετ'; and suggests as possible τῷ γὰρ χρῆσθε; μῶν—; For dative with νομίζω cf. e.g. Thuc. ii. 38, 1, ἄγωσι καὶ θυσίαις νομίζοντες.

249. σιδαρέοισιν—'the Doric σιδάρεος, for σιδηροῦς, is always retained in speaking of the iron coinage of the Dorian colony, Byzantium, and the scholiast quotes from the Comic writer, Plato,

χαλεπῶς ἂν οἰκήσαιμεν ἐν Βυζαντίοις
ὅπου σιδαρέοις (νομίζουσιν?)'

(*New Phryn.*, p. 49).

The σιδάρεος was a small coin, as we say 'a copper.' If the idea of the gods is not dropped by now, 'a poor, base coinage' is what is suggested.

251. ὀρθῶς—Blaydes gives a conjecture of Meineke, ἅττ' ἐστιν; ΣΤ. ὀργῶ νὴ Δί'. This is suggested by *Av.* 462, καὶ μὴν ὀργῶ νὴ τὸν Δία. No change however is needed.   εἴπερ ἔστι γε—'if it is possible,' as in 322; not 'yes, if there's any truth,' as Rogers translates.

252. ξυγγενέσθαι...ἐς λόγους—*Vesp.* 472, ἐς λόγους ἐλθεῖν ἀλλήλοισι.

254. σκίμποδα—like the Pythia on the sacred tripod: Plat. *Protag.* 310 C, ἐπιψηλαφήσας τοῦ σκίμποδος, 'feeling his way to the bed,' as it was still dark. 'The σκίμπους was a low and mean kind of bed, contemptuously assigned to Socrates in the *Nubes*, called also ἀσκάντης (633), and ὀκλαδίας (folding like a camp-stool, from ὀκλάζω) *Eq.* 1384, 1386 ' (Wayte).

256. ἐπὶ τί;—' what for?' in alarm.

257. ὥσπερ με τὸν 'Αθάμανθ'—there is the same position of the enclitic με *Vesp.* 363, ὥσπερ με γαλῆν κρέα κλέψασαν | τηροῦσιν. Athamas, the faithless husband of *Nephele*, was brought on the stage by Sophocles, crowned with a chaplet, to be sacrificed to Zeus. Strepsiades, as Rogers puts it, fears lest *his* connexion with the Clouds (ξυγγενέσθαι ταῖς Νεφέλαις) is to end in the same way, and with no Heracles to set him free again, as in the case of Athamas. ὅπως μή—'do not': ὅπως or ὅπως μή with the future, as a command or exhortation, is especially common in Aristophanes. It is sometimes found in combination with the imperative; *Ran.* 627, κατάθου τὰ σκεύη χὤπως ἐρεῖς κ.τ.λ. See Goodwin, § 271 sq.

258. οὔκ—' not so,' this is not our purpose; cf. *Vesp.* 9, 77, 250 etc. ἀλλὰ ταῦτα πάντα—Mr Green well points out that there is no need to alter the text into πάντας ταῦτα. The sense is 'all this (chaplet included) is essential at *our* initiations.' ἡμεῖς is emphatic.

260. λέγειν τρίμμα—' a practised hand at speaking'; *Av.* 430: so τρίβων, 869: περίτριμμα δικῶν, 447: Demosthenes calls Aeschines περίτριμμα ἀγορᾶς (*de Cor.* 269 § 127): cf. ἐντριβής. κρόταλον—' a rattle'; so 448: lit. Hdt. ii. 60 etc. It appear to have been like our castanets; see Dict. Ant. παιπάλη—'fine flour,' i.e. a subtle rogue; παιπάλημ' ὅλον, *Av.* 430. So Ajax calls the wily Odysseus ἄλημα, Soph. *Aj.* 381, 390: cf. *Ant.* 320.

According to the scholiast, Socrates accompanies each word with pantomimic action, rubbing some stones together, rattling them over the victim's head, and pouring the dust over him like flour over a sacrifice.

261. ἔχ' ἀτρεμεί—cf. 743: *Av.* 1200, ἔχ' ἀτρέμας. Strepsiades is beginning to kick under his initiation. There are three forms of the adverb, ἀτρέμα, ἀτρέμας and ἀτρεμεί. Here most manuscripts have ἀτρέμας and R ἀτρεμί, while most editors read ἀτρεμεί. οὐ ψεύσει γέ με—i.e. you don't intend to cheat me; your promises, I see, will be kept to the letter.

262. καταπαττόμενος—' I shall be flour indeed with all this peppering' (Rogers).

263. εὐφημεῖν κ.τ.λ.—The metre is changed as Socrates begins a solemn invocation of his divinities. Sacred silence (εὐφημία) is first enjoined on the neophyte: cf. *Ach.* 237, εὐφημεῖτε, εὐφημεῖτε, when Dicaeopolis is beginning to inaugurate his truce: *Eq.* 1316, εὐφημεῖν χρή, when the renovated Demos is about to appear: *Pac.* 96, εὐφημεῖν χρή, when Trygaeus is starting on his beetle to the sky, etc. ἐπακούειν—so most editors, with R and V; cf. 274. In my edition of the *Wasps* I retained ὑπακούει (318) wrongly, as I am now inclined to believe. ὑπακούω is to listen to a request, answer a call, and the like. 'Solennis librorum confusio inter ἐπακούειν et ὑπακούειν' (Blaydes). Dindorf however considers that ἐπακούειν is used rather of the gods hearkening to prayers than of men merely listening.

264. ὦ δέσποτ' ἄναξ—so Bdelycleon addresses Apollo (*Vesp.* 875); and the servant of Trygaeus appeals to Zeus (*Pac.* 90). But Air and Ether are the Zeus of Socrates, and he prays to them, as Euripides, his brother infidel, invokes the Ether as one of his own divinities (*Ran.* 793). The editors cite the lines of Euripides (Fr. 836),

ὁρᾷς τὸν ὑψοῦ τόνδ' ἄπειρον αἰθέρα,
καὶ γῆν πέριξ ἔχονθ' ὑγραῖς ἐν ἀγκάλαις·
τοῦτον νόμιζε Ζῆνα, τόνδ' ἡγοῦ θεόν,

which Cicero translates, *Nat. deor.* ii. 25, 65,

vides sublime fusum, immoderatum aethera,
qui tenero terram circumiectu amplectitur?
hunc summum habeto divom, hunc perhibeto Iovem.

ἔχεις τὴν γῆν μετέωρον—the earth was in the centre of the universe, surrounded by the Air, which in its turn was surrounded by the Ether, 'qui constat ex altissimis ignibus'; see Cic. *Nat. deor.* ii. 36, 91. μετέωρον is predicate with ἔχεις, 'holdest suspended in mid air.'

265. αἰθήρ—cf. 569: *Ran.* 892, where Euripides invokes αἰθήρ, ἐμὸν βόσκημα.

266. τῷ φροντιστῇ—meaning himself; Socrates was eminently the thinker, and the title devolved on his disciples; cf. 414, 456 etc. Strepsiades was scarcely as yet a member of the band.

267. μήπω γε—so 196. τουτὶ πτύξωμαι—τουτί is his ἱμάτιον: part of it passed over (or under) the right arm (*Dict. Ant.* ii. 320, *pallium*); this part he wished to 'wrap round himself' in fear of rain.

268. τὸ δὲ...ἐλθεῖν—the infinitive of exclamation with τό is common in Aristophanes; cf. 819: *Av.* 5 and 7 etc.: also without τό, *Vesp.* 835. τοιουτονὶ τρέφειν κύνα: see Goodwin §§ 787 and 805. μηδὲ κυνῆν is adopted by most editors for the manuscript reading μὴ κυνῆν,

which will not scan. Blaydes however prefers μὴ κυνέην, and shows that the resolved form is admissible in anapaests; e.g. βελέων, *Vesp.* 615. The κυνῆ was mainly for country wear; cf. *Vesp.* 445. Thus Laertes wore a goat-skin κυνῆ when working on the farm, Hom. *Od.* xxiv. 231. In the city the Athenians went with heads uncovered.

269. **πολυτίμητοι**—a regular epithet of gods; cf. 293. Hence the joke in *Ach.* 759, παρ' ἀμὲ πολυτίματος ἅπερ τοὶ θεοί. **τῷδ' εἰς ἐπίδειξιν**—'to show yourselves to this man.' Blaydes gives numerous instances of similar construction with ἄγειν, ἐλθεῖν etc. from Herodotus; and adds Eur. *El.* 1236, ἐς φανερὰν ὄψιν βαίνουσι βροτοῖσιν.

270. **εἴτ' κ.τ.λ.**—Socrates turns to each quarter of the heavens, invoking the clouds, like deities, to appear from wherever they may be. **ἐπ' Ὀλύμπου...χιονοβλήτοισι**—the summit of the Thessalian Olympus, the abode of the epic gods, is covered with perpetual snow. It is roughly speaking north of Athens.

271. **Ὠκεανοῦ...κήποις**—the gardens of the Hesperides may be meant, Ocean 'the father of waters,' and of clouds, being especially the main sea in the far west beyond Atlas; or κῆποι may be used for 'realm.' **ἵστατε**—the regular word with χορούς; Dem. *Meid.* 530 § 15 etc. **νύμφαις**—for their delight, or in their honour. The suggested reading νύμφαι, whether vocative or nominative, is very prosaic.

272. **Νείλου προχοαῖς**—Aesch. *Suppl.* 1025, Νείλου προχοὰς σέβωμεν ὕμνοις. Νείλου follows ὑδάτων, or προχοαῖς ὑδάτων together, the two words forming one idea. The poetic dative of place seems undoubtedly admissible in anapaests; λείπει δ' ἐπί, as the scholiast says. Meineke however inserts 'ν. For προχοαῖς Dindorf reads προχοὰς dependent on ἀρύτεσθε, on the authority of Suidas (on ἀρύτεσθαι). But it seems very clumsy to talk of 'drawing the outflow of a river in golden pitchers.' **χρυσέαις** is here an anapaest, according to Dindorf and Blaydes, but it may be a dissyllable; see Lid. and Scott for the license of ῠ. **ἀρύτεσθε**—the Attic form. The word is, I think, used absolutely here, 'you are drawing (water),' but Lid. and Scott, like Blaydes and Merry, take it with ὑδάτων as a partitive genitive; while Teuffel renders 'aus dem Wasser.' The rhythm of the line is against this view. **πρόχοισιν** —this form seems undoubtedly right, as the best manuscripts have προχόοισιν, and πρόχους is declined like νοῦς. The 3rd declension dative προχοῦσιν, which is read by some here and Eur. *Ion* 435, may be due to the false analogy of χουσίν (from χοῦς, χοός).

273. **Μαιῶτιν λίμνην**—the sea of Azov, due north-east of Athens.

Μίμαντος—ὄρος Θρᾴκης, says the scholiast; but Hom. *Od.* iii. 172, ἣ ὑπένερθε Χίοιο, παρ' ἠνεμόεντα Μίμαντα, shows that it was a promontory in Ionia, east from Athens.

274. ὑπακούσατε—'hearken to my call,' appear, in answer to my prayer. Here ὑπ- has the better manuscript authority. Dindorf, Meineke and others however prefer ἐπακούσατε, which is simply 'hearken.' The question is whether ὑπακούσατε is an appropriate word to address to goddesses; see note on 263. ὑπακούω is certainly used in entreaties to superiors, e.g. *Ach.* 405, where Dicaeopolis is supplicating Euripides; see also line 360. τοῖς ἱεροῖσι χαρεῖσαι—'pleased with our rites.' From the var. lect. Blaydes surmises that the right reading may be τοῖς ἱερεῦσι φανεῖσαι, but, as he points out, χαρεῖς is common in such invocations; e.g. *Thesm.* 978, καὶ Πᾶνα...ἄντομαι...ἐπιγελάσαι ταῖς ἡμετέραισι χαρέντα χορείαις.

Parodos of the Chorus.

275—290. The opening song and the corresponding Antistrophe (299—313) are heard behind the stage. The Clouds are perhaps dimly seen in the background, but the chorus does not fully come on till 328.

275. ἀέναοι—the epithet of waves and streams, and so of clouds which are drawn from them.

276. ἀρθῶμεν—cf. ἄρθητε, 266. φύσιν—'form,' as in 503: so *Vesp.* 1071; and often in tragedy. The accusative 'of respect' follows φανεραί. εὐάγητον—apparently 'bright,' a word not found elsewhere; see Lid. and Scott for εὐᾱγής and εὐᾰγής. Here the α must be long, as the ending of the line corresponds to εὔανδρον γᾶν, 300. Merry considers it the Doric form of εὐήγητον (ἡγεῖσθαι) 'easily drawn.' Blaydes reads εὐάχητον, 'loud-sounding.'

280. ἵνα—for ὅπου, according to the scholiast, 'where resting, we look,' etc.; but 'that,' according to Blaydes, who says we should otherwise have ὅθεν. The following verb ἀφορώμεθα proves nothing, as it may be either indicative or subjunctive.

281. τηλεφανεῖς σκοπιάς—Blaydes, following Green's suggestion, reads τηλεφανοῦς σκοπιᾶς, 'from a conspicuous height'; 'quomodo enim

σκοπιάς prospicere apte dicantur Nubes, quae ipsae has σκοπιάς occupent?' and, as Mr Green says, more often σκοπιά is the height *from* which one looks. Still, from a mountain top the most striking thing is the sight of other peaks; and the singularly beautiful verses as they stand give a glorious suggestion of a mountain view.

282. **καρποὺς ἀρδομέναν**—lit. 'watered as to its fruits (corn).'

283. **κελαδήματα**—Eur. *Phoen.* 212, Ζεφύρου πνοιαῖς...κάλλιστον κελάδημα.

284. **κελάδοντα**—an epic participial form, as if from κελάδω (=-έω): Hom. *Il.* xviii. 576, πὰρ ποταμὸν κελάδοντα etc.

285. **ὄμμα γὰρ**—the sun is shining brightly, and the mists leave the waters and valleys to gather in the form of clouds round the mountain tops. For ὄμμα αἰθέρος, 'the eye of heaven,' cf. Soph. *Ant.* 104: Eur. *Iph. T.* 194, ἱερᾶς ὄμμ' αὐγᾶς ἅλιος. So the noun is νυκτὸς ὄμμα (*ib.* 110), ὀφθαλμός, βλέφαρον. **ἀκάματον**—an epithet of the unvarying, and so unwearying powers of nature: Hom. *Il.* xviii. 484, ἠέλιον τ' ἀκάμαντα: thus Addison,

'The unwearied sun, from day to day,
Does his Creator's power display.'

289. **ἀθανάτας ἰδέας**—the genitive depends on ἀποσεισάμεναι, 'from our immortal form.' If the dative be retained, it must be taken as instrumental with ἐπιδώμεθα, 'in our immortal forms.' But the sense is poor, and the double dative construction thus involved is awkward. For ἰδέας 'form,' cf. *Av.* 1000: the Clouds are now about to appear in human shape.

291. **μέγα σεμναί**—Aesch. *Prom.* 647, μέγ' εὔδαιμον: often in Homer.

292. **βροντῆς**—thunder, the scholiast says, was imitated by pouring pebbles from an ἀμφορεύς into a bronze caldron. The machine was called βροντεῖον or ἠχεῖον.

296. **οὐ μὴ σκώψει κ.τ.λ.**—for this construction, expressing a strong prohibition, cf. Goodwin § 297 sq. and App. II. It is common in Aristophanes, cf. 367, 505: *Vesp.* 397: *Ran.* 202. It is to be noted that the manuscripts mostly have the subjunctive, as in the present passage.

τρυγοδαίμονες—a sort of compound of τρύξ (τρυγῳδοί) and κακοδαίμονες, 'those wretched comedians,' who try to raise a laugh by low and unseemly jokes.

297. **ἀοιδαῖς**—'with' or 'for' songs. Either construction with κινεῖται is strange, 'mira locutio' as Blaydes says. He accordingly reads ἀείδειν, and suggests as possible ἀοιδόν, or ἀοιδὰν, in agreement with θεῶν.

Meincke and others adopt σμῆνος ἀοιδῆς, with θεῶν dependent = 'raised by goddesses.' But 'a swarm of song' is an almost impossible phrase, even if it could mean a singing swarm, while 'a swarm of goddesses' is natural and simple.

300. λιπαράν—λιπαραί, 'bright,' was the cherished epithet of Athens, since Pindar first bestowed the title: *Ach.* 640, ηὕρετο πᾶν ἂν διὰ τὰς λιπαράς, ἀφύων τιμὴν περιάψας, 'a compliment for anchovies,' as being smooth and shiny. The accusatives are governed by ὀψόμεναι.

302. οὗ κ.τ.λ.—the pride and glory of Athens was her devotion to the gods, who were honoured there above all other cities with mysteries and offerings, and temples and feasts. σέβας ἀρρήτων ἱερῶν— 'where is reverence of mystic rites,' not to be divulged to common ears.

303. μυστοδόκος δόμος—the temple at Eleusis in which the initiated were received. ἀναδείκνυται, 'is thrown open.'

305. οὐρανίοις θεοῖς—'the gods of heaven' are contrasted with Demeter and Coré who were worshipped in the mysteries. δωρήματα —sc. ἐστί: for the dative cf. Aesch. *Pers.* 523, γῇ τε καὶ φθιτοῖς δωρήματα: Soph. *Trach.* 668, τῶν σῶν Ἡρακλεῖ δωρημάτων.

307. πρόσοδοι—'processions,' as at the Panathenaea; *Pac.* 396, καί σε θυσίαισιν ἱεραῖσι προσόδοις τε μεγάλαισι διαπαντός, ὦ δέσποτ', ἀγαλοῦμεν ἀεί.

309. εὐστέφανοι—the priests, the altar, and the victim were crowned with garlands.

310. παντοδαπαῖς ἐν ὥραις—other cities had special seasons of sacred ceremony, but at Athens there was a perpetual round of feast and sacrifice: διὰ τὸ πάντας θρησκεύειν τοὺς θεοὺς θύουσι καὶ πανηγυρίζουσιν ἀεί (schol.). Blaydes reads παντοδαπαῖσιν for παντοδαπαῖς ἐν, and makes a similar alteration in line 285. He observes 'librarii saepe praepositionem ἐν inferserunt.'

311. ἦρί τ'...Βρομία χάρις—τὴν παροῦσαν ἑορτὴν λέγει (schol.). The great Dionysia, 'the delight of Bromius' or Bacchus, were held in the month Elaphebolion in the early spring. The *Clouds* came out at this festival. ἐπερχομένῳ—'recurring': the form is rare: Aesch. *Prom.* 98, ἐπερχόμενον: see Horton-Smith, *Conditional Sentences* p. 464, on the use of ἔρχομαι in Attic Greek.

312. ἐρεθίσματα—contests, lit. 'provocations,' the competition of rival choirs.

314—509. The Clouds having come at the Master's call amaze and terrify Strepsiades. He is taught the meaning of their changing forms, and learns that they alone are deities. In the end he surrenders himself to their teaching.

316. ἀνδράσιν ἀργοῖς—poets and philosophers, says the scholiast, who deal with nothing but words; οἱ γὰρ ἀργοὶ κεχήνασιν εἰς τὰς νεφέλας.

317. γνώμην—'intelligence'; σύνεσιν καὶ φρόνησιν, ὡς τὰ δέοντα νοεῖν (schol.): Green and Merry render it 'sententiousness.' διάλεξιν—λόγων ἐμπειρίαν, ὥστε τὰ νοηθέντα φράζειν 'argument,' power of discussion.

318. τερατείαν—παραδοξολογίαν, making marvellous statements. κροῦσιν—ἀπάτην: ποικιλίαν καὶ στροφὰς λόγων, δι' ὧν τοὺς διαλεγομένους σοφιζόμεθα καὶ ἀπατῶμεν. κατάληψιν—εὕρεσιν (schol.), 'comprehension' or 'conception.' Merry renders it 'over-mastering,' comparing *Eq.* 1379,
γνωμοτυπικὸς καὶ σαφὴς καὶ κρουστικὸς
καταληπτικός τ' ἄριστα τοῦ θορυβητικοῦ,
'masterful over the noisy mob.'

319. ταῦτ' ἄρα—'this then is why my soul is winged.' The voice of the Clouds has raised Strepsiades into an airy realm, μετέωρα φρονεῖ ἤδη, as the scholiast says. For ταῦτα 'therefore,' cf. 335, 353 etc.

320. λεπτολογεῖν—'refine.' Blaydes points out that we should expect the middle form, on the analogy of σεμνολογεῖσθαι, μικρολογεῖσθαι etc., cf. 1496. The active form λεπτολογεῖν is however found in Lucian, and Aristophanes has καταλεπτολογήσει, *Ran.* 828. καπνοῦ—of fleeting nothings: Soph. *Ant.* 1171, καπνοῦ σκιᾶς οὐκ ἂν πριαίμην. So light-headed, empty spendthrifts are called καπνοί.

στενολεσχεῖν—'discourse subtly': 'comice formatum ut ἀδολεσχεῖν' (Blaydes).

321. γνωμιδίῳ γνώμην νύξασ'—'having pricked wit with a witticism' (Merry). This represents the verbal play, but γνωμίδιον is rather a little idea or maxim, sententiola. νύξασ' suggests either testing (pricking a bubble) or provoking. The editors cite Cic. *de or.* ii. 38, 158, ipsi (dialectici) se compungunt suis acuminibus. ἑτέρῳ λόγῳ ἀντιλογῆσαι—'to contradict another argument,' or '*with* another argument': συνάψας ἕτερον λόγον τῷ ῥηθέντι ἀντιθεῖναι (schol.).

323. πρὸς τὴν Πάρνηθ'—'the theatre being open to the sky, Socrates was able to direct the gaze of Strepsiades towards Mount Parnes, on the Boeotian frontier, and to pretend that the Clouds were to be seen 'coming softly down' the hill side, 'trailing aslant through the hollows or the thickets,' on their way to the theatre. It may be doubted whether Parnes was actually visible to the spectators. Probably the Acropolis hid the view' (Merry). ἤδη γὰρ ὁρῶ—'fingit haec Aristophanes,' is Hermann's comment, i.e. the Clouds are not really seen till they come on by the usual entrance for the chorus.

324. αὗται—predicative, 'there they come in troops, through the valleys and the woodlands, sideways there.' Photius has preserved a fragment from an edition of this play in which the Clouds are represented as irritated by their discourteous reception:

ἐς τὴν Πάρνηθ' ὀργισθεῖσαι φροῦδαι κατὰ τὴν Λυκαβηττόν,

i.e. they sail over Lycabettus, which was close on the north-east of Athens, on their way back to Parnes.

326. ὡς οὐ καθορῶ—either '(I ask), since I can't see them'; or 'know that I can't see them' (cf. 209). παρὰ τὴν εἴσοδον—by which the chorus entered. The Clouds now come crowding in like the chorus in the *Birds* (296),

ὦναξ Ἄπολλον τοῦ νέφους. ἰοὺ ἰού.
οὐδ' ἰδεῖν ἔτ' ἔσθ' ὑπ' αὐτῶν πετομένων τὴν εἴσοδον.

μόλις οὕτως—sc. ὁρῶ αὐτάς. Hermann's emendation is generally adopted, but the reading is not quite satisfactory. Blaydes has νῦν ὁρῶ ἤδη μόλις αὐτάς. οὕτως is 'even as it is,' even now; or possibly it modifies μόλις, like μάψ οὕτως, ἁπλῶς οὕτως etc. 'just, merely.'

327. εἰ μὴ λημᾷς κολοκύνταις—'unless your eyes are bleared with pumpkins': *Plut.* 581, Κρονικαῖς λήμαις λημῶντες. Hence Lucian has χύτραις λημῶντες, and such expressions became proverbial; see quotations in Blaydes.

328. κατέχουσι—'fill,' 'cover'; cf. 572.

331. βόσκουσι—'keep'; often, but not necessarily, used in a contemptuous sense. σοφιστάς—what they were we are told, seers, doctors, dithyrambic poets. We may render the word 'professors' for the nonce.

332. θουριομάντεις—one Lampo is especially meant. He was a seer, and was sent by Pericles in 444 in charge of a colony to the site of the ancient Sybaris, which received the name of Thurii. The scholiast on *Av.* 521 adds, ἔτυχε δὲ καὶ τῆς ἐν πρυτανείῳ σιτήσεως. ἰατροτέχνας—such as Hippocrates, whose posterity were fed in the prytaneum.

He wrote, says the scholiast, περὶ ἀέρων, τόπων καὶ ὑδάτων. **σφραγιδονυχαργοκομῆτας**—from σφραγίς, ὄνυξ, ἀργός, κομήτης, 'lazy longhaired fellows with onyx rings,' or 'with rings to their very nails,' or 'with rings and well-trimmed nails.' It would seem that the prophets and physicians posed as exquisites in dress and appointments.

333. **κυκλίων τε κ.τ.λ.**—the 'tune-twisters of cyclic choruses' are dithyrambic poets. They too competed at the festivals, and their choruses were furnished by the *choregi*. κάμπτειν and καμπή are often used of 'turns and twists' in speech or verse; cf. 970. The dithyrambic bards were 'fed by the Clouds,' for their themes were air and sky and storms, as Strepsiades goes on to show: cf. too *Av.* 1387: *Pac.* 830, where the souls of dithyrambic poets are said to 'flutter in the air.'

ἄνδρας μετεωροφένακας—in apposition with the accusative before. The 'air-humbugs' are here the poets, as the following context plainly shows. For μετεωροφέναξ cf. μετεωροσοφιστάς (360): Plat. *Rep.* 488 E, μετεωροσκόπον τε καὶ ἀδολέσχην: *ib.* 489 C, τοὺς ἀχρήστους λεγομένους καὶ μετεωρολέσχας: and a number of like disparaging terms in Blaydes.

335. **ταῦτ' ἄρ'**—cf. 319. Now follow specimens or parodies of dithyrambic diction. **στρεπταίγλαν**—'ray-turning hostile onset,' τὴν στρέφουσαν τὴν αἴγλαν καὶ ἀφανίζουσαν (schol.), i.e. diverting and obscuring the sun's beams.

336. **πλοκάμους θ'**— 'locks of hundred-headed Typho'; clouds torn by whirlwinds. **πρημαινούσας**—connected with πρήθω, πρηστήρ, and formed like τετρεμαίνω (294).

337. **ἀερίας διεράς**—these adjectives agree with νεφέλας implied: 'then they called them (ἐποίουν) airy, liquid.' Reisig reads ἀερίας διερᾶς 'of the moist atmosphere,' making ἀερία a substantive: Meineke and others have ἀερίους διερούς, in agreement with οἰωνούς. **γαμψούς**— 'hooked fowls which swim in air,' i.e. they write of such, or actually called the clouds such names.

338. **ἀντ' αὐτῶν**—'in return for these' the Clouds rewarded them with sumptuous fare. **κατέπινον**—'swallowed' generally. The poets were entertained by men of wealth, and in particular by the *choregus* while the chorus was training.

339. **κεστρᾶν**—the κέστρα was a costly fish, and the banquet is a refined and dainty one. The Athenians generally were not great meat-eaters but preferred fish and game. **τέμαχος** is properly used of fish, not meat: *Eq.* 283, ἄρτον καὶ κρέας καὶ τέμαχος. **κιχηλᾶν**—

Doric for κιχλῶν, the whole line being Doric in imitation of these dithyrambics.

340. διὰ μέντοι τάσδ'—'yes, but it's thanks to these goddesses.' τί παθοῦσαι—τί παθὼν τοῦτο ποιεῖς; 'what possesses you, induces you to do this?' τί μαθὼν τοῦτο ποιεῖς; 'with what idea, on what principle, do you do it?'

341. εἴξασι—*Av.* 96 and 383: Eur. *Hel.* 497: Plat. etc. cf. εἴξεις (1001).

342. ἐκεῖναι—sc. νεφέλαι, 'for *they* (γ') are not like this.' ἐκεῖναι are the clouds he is used to, αὗται (infr.) those which appear on the stage.

343. δ' οὖν—*ceterum*, 'however,' 'any way.' This is the best supported reading and makes good sense. ἐρίοισιν πεπταμένοισι: Hom. *Od.* vi. 45, αἴθρη πέπταται ἀνέφελος: Verg. *G.* i. 397, tenuia nec lanae per caelum vellera ferri.

344. αὗται δὲ—the vowel is lengthened before ρ, as in *Thesm.* 781, τουτὶ τὸ ῥῶ μοχθηρόν, a license derived from epic poetry. ῥῖνας ἔχουσι—they had grotesque masks with enormous noses, according to the scholiast.

346. ἤδη...εἶδες—766, ἤδη...ἑόρακας; *Kan.* 62, ἤδη ποτ' ἐπεθύμησας; Κενταύρῳ ὁμοίαν—'saepissime in hoc genere metri corripitur et longa vocalis et diphthongus ante vocalem, ut in 352, λύκοι ἐξαίφνης: 355, Κλεισθένη εἶδον: 365, μόναι εἰσί etc.' (Blaydes). The clouds assume the shapes of all sorts of animals in the sky, why then may they not appear like women? The editors illustrate this passage by Cic. *de div.* ii. 21, 49, and Shakespeare, *Antony and Cleopatra*, iv. 12, 3,

'Sometime we see a cloud that's dragonish,
A vapour sometime like a bear or lion,' etc.

also the well-known scene in *Hamlet* iii. 2, 360.

348. πάνθ' ὅ τι—'all kinds of things, whatever they please': Eur. *Ion* 233, πάντα θεᾶσθ' ὅ τι καὶ θέμις. There is no need to alter πάνθ' to πᾶν 'anything,' which Cobet thinks necessary.

349. τῶν λασίων τούτων—'those shaggy fellows'; cf. 296. τὸν Ξενοφάντου—according to the scholiast this was Hieronymus, a dithyrambic poet: cf. *Ach.* 389.

351. Σίμωνα—satirized by Eupolis also for peculation: in line 399 he appears as a perjurer.

352. τὴν φύσιν—'speciem, figuram,' according to Blaydes, as in 505, and often. But here it is rather his nature (character), which

is represented by the shape taken by the Clouds. ἐγένοντο—i.e.
they at once assume the shape of wolves: *Vesp.* 97,

ἦν ἴδῃ γέ που γεγραμμένον
υἱὸν Πυριλάμπους ἐν θύρᾳ Δῆμον καλόν,
ἰὼν παρέγραψε πλησίον κημὸς καλός.

These are not strictly gnomic aorists, implying repetition, but denote that the consequence follows the cause or occasion at once.

353. ταῦτ' ἄρα—cf. 319 etc.: ταῦτα is repeated, as in 1052. Κλεώνυμον—a big coward, a perpetual butt of Aristophanes, *Ach.* 88: *Eq.* 1290: *Vesp.* 19 etc.

355. Κλεισθένη—satirized for his effeminate ways and appearance, *Ach.* 18: *Eq.* 1374: *Vesp.* 1187 etc.

356. τινὶ κάλλῳ—Thuc. i. 70, 1, καὶ ἅμα, εἴ τινες καὶ ἄλλοι, ἄξιοι νομίζομεν εἶναι.

357. οὐρανομήκη—'heaven-high'; cf. 459: Hom. *Od.* v. 239, and Hdt. ii. 138, of tall trees. Ar., *Rhet.* iii. 7, 11, instances it as a compound word, suitable to the language of emotion; συγγνώμη γὰρ ὀργιζομένῳ κακὸν φάναι οὐρανομῆκες (see Cope's note). ῥήξατε—so 960: Hdt. i. 85 etc.: so *rumpere* vocem, questus etc. Verg.: Tac. *Ann.* vi. 20, rupta voce.

358. παλαιογενές—no compliment, as the scholiast points out, but implying that Strepsiades is old and silly. The chorus in fact utter the poet's feeling towards his characters. θηρατά—ἀντὶ τοῦ ἰχνευτὰ λόγων, ἢ ζηλωτὰ, ἢ μετιὼν λόγους (schol.).

359. λήρων ἱερεῦ—'high priest of subtlest nonsense.'

360. μετεωροσοφιστῶν—see note on 333.

361. πλὴν ἤ—praeterquam: *Thesm.* 532: Hdt. ii. 112. The phrase is not common, though it is logically right, as πλήν implies comparison. πλὴν εἰ is a common variant in the manuscripts, and is read here by Meineke and Kock. Προδίκῳ κ.τ.λ.—this may be genuine praise, as Rogers following Bergler thinks, but probably not. The passage in the *Birds* (692) where Prodicus is mentioned has a depreciatory ring, and he is classed with 'idle talkers' in the lines from the *Tagenistae* (Frag. 418, Poet. Sc.)

τὸν ἄνδρα τόνδ' ἢ βιβλίον διέφθορεν,
ἢ Πρόδικος ἢ τῶν ἀδολεσχῶν εἷς γέ τις.

Prodicus was a native of Ceos and one of the most respected of the Sophists. To him is due the well-known allegory of the Choice of Hercules (Xen. *Mem.* ii. 1, 21). He wrote περὶ ὀρθότητος ὀνομάτων, distinguishing between apparent synonyms. This subtlety lent itself naturally to Plato's banter, as we find in the *Protagoras*; but the work was probably good and useful. Prodicus' 'fifty drachma lecture' is mentioned in the *Cratylus* 384 B, and Ar. *Rhet.* iii. 14, 9.

τῷ μὲν...σοὶ δέ—commentators follow the scholiast in calling the construction 'anacoluthous,' as if πλὴν ἢ Προδίκῳ καὶ σοί should have preceded. It is however rather 'chiastic,' ἤ σοι being understood with ἄλλῳ in line 360, and then the order of the persons reversed. Rogers expresses the construction well:—

'Since there is not a sage for whom we'd engage our wonders more
  freely to do,
Except, it may be, for Prodicus: he for his knowledge may claim
  them, but you,
Because as you go, you glance to and fro, and in dignified arrogance
  float.'

362. βρενθύει—'stalk with an air'; *Pac.* 26: 'give oneself airs,' *Lys.* 887. Alcibiades adapts this passage when he is describing the demeanour of Socrates in the retreat from Delium, Plat. *Symp.* 221 B, ἔπειτα ἔμοιγε ἐδόκει, ὦ Ἀριστόφανες, τὸ σὸν δὴ τοῦτο, καὶ ἐκεῖ διαπορεύεσθαι ὥσπερ καὶ ἐνθάδε, βρενθυόμενος καὶ τὠφθαλμὼ παραβάλλων, ἠρέμα περισκοπῶν καὶ τοὺς φιλίους καὶ τοὺς πολεμίους. In peace and war alike Socrates glanced keenly and quietly from side to side; ταυρηδὸν ὑποβλέψας ὥσπερ εἰώθει is said of him, Plat. *Phaed.* 117 B.

363. κἀνυπόδητος—cf. 103.   κἀφ' ἡμῖν—'in reliance on us,' or, 'on the strength of (your friendship with) us,' like κομᾶν ἐπί τινι etc. (Blaydes).

364. ὦ γῆ, τοῦ φθέγματος—cf. 153: *Ach.* 64, ὠκβάτανα, τοῦ σχήματος.

365. φλύαρος—'rubbish': *Lys.* 860, ληρός ἐστι τἄλλα πρὸς Κινησίαν, 'to Cinesias,' i.e. compared with him.

367. ποῖος Ζεύς;—a contemptuous question, as in 247.   οὐ μὴ ληρήσεις;—see note on 296.

368. ἀπόφηναι—elsewhere Aristophanes uses the active. Blaydes therefore suspects the reading, the more so as ἔμοιγ' has no appropriate force.

370. ὕοντ'—sc. τὸν θεὸν or τὸν Δία. Both expressions are found, though ὕει is generally used alone as if impersonal: Hdt. ii. 13, εἰ μὴ ἐθελήσει ὕειν ὁ θεός: Theogn. 25, οὐδὲ γὰρ ὁ Ζεὺς οὔθ' ὕων πάντεσσ' ἀνδάνει οὔτ' ἀνέχων.   ἤδη τεθέασαι;—='have you ever seen?' cf. 766, 1061.

371. χρῆν—so ἐξῆν, ἔδει etc. (without ἄν), of what ought or might

be done (but is not): see Goodwin, § 415 sq., 419. αἰθρίας—cf. νυκτός, χειμῶνος, etc. and perhaps φρουρᾶς line 721. The ι is here long, as in κονίας, *Ach.* 18. The editors cite Lucr. vi. 400,

denique cur nunquam caelo iacit undique puro
Iupiter in terras fulmen sonitusque profundit?

372. **προσέφυσας**—ἥρμοσας, προσήρμοσας, is the scholiast's explanation; 'you have fitted (adapted) this illustration admirably to your present argument': cf. Aesch. *Suppl.* 276, καὶ ταῦτ' ἀληθῆ πάντα προσφύσω λόγῳ, where Professor Tucker notes that the sense is derived from that of making one thing 'grow on to' another: i.e. so that the tale is all of a piece, welded together.

375. **ὦ πάντα σὺ τολμῶν**—for Socrates would rob Zeus of his thunder; cf. Soph. *O. C.* 761, ὦ πάντα τολμῶν: Aesch. *Sept.* 671, φωτὶ παντόλμῳ φρένας.

376. **φέρεσθαι**—like *ferri*, 'to move, rush,' used of the motion of heavenly bodies, the sweep of winds, and the like.

377. **κατακρημνάμεναι**—'hanging down'; κρήμναμαι (=κρέμαμαι) occurs Eur. *El.* 1217: Aesch. *Sept.* 229, κρημναμενᾶν νεφελᾶν: Eur. *Here. Fur.* 520, ἐκκρήμνασθε etc.

δι' ἀνάγκην—best taken with what follows (Green); most editors however put the comma after ἀνάγκην. Either way 'ἀνάγκη was used by the physical philosophers of the day to express what we now call natural laws, such as gravitation; Democritus affirming that πάντα κατ' ἀνάγκην γίγνεσθαι' (Merry), Diog. Laert. ix. 7, 45. **βαρεῖαι**—'being laden,' by reason of their weight.

378. **εἰς ἀλλήλας κ.τ.λ.**—so Anaxagoras (Diog. Laert. ii. 9) called thunder σύγκρουσις νεφῶν and lightning ἔκτριψις νεφῶν: the Epicureans held similar views later; cf. Lucr. vi. 96,

principio tonitru quatiuntur caerula caeli
propterea quia concurrunt sublime volantes
aetheriae nubes contra pugnantibu' ventis.

379. Strepsiades is not satisfied with the 'how'; he wants the 'why,' and he still believes there must be a personal will at the head of things.

380. **αἰθέριος δῖνος**—the 'etherial whirl,' meaning the motion and revolution of the heavens, was the physical dogma of the day; ἐθρυλεῖτο παρὰ τοῖς φυσικοῖς (schol.). It was known through Euripides, e.g. *Alc.* 244, οὐράνιαι δῖναι νεφέλας δρομαίου: cf. Lucr. v. 622, cum caeli turbine ferri. δίνη was the more common word; but δῖνος is adopted here, as sounding like a proper name and resembling δῖος and Διός. The

scholiast says that Strepsiades takes δῖνος to mean a round earthen pot; see also 1473.

ἐλελήθειν—so Cobet, followed by Meineke and Kock: most manuscripts have ἐλελήθει, so Merry and Blaydes: Teuffel reads ἐλελήθη. See note on 1347.

381. ὁ Ζεὺς οὐκ ὤν κ.τ.λ.—i.e. his non-existence etc.; cf. 1241, Ζεὺς ὀμνύμενος, 'swearing by Zeus': *Vesp.* 27,
δεινόν γέ τουστ' ἄνθρωπος ἀποβαλὼν ὅπλα.

382. ἀτάρ—a particle of transition rather than of opposition, 'but still,' 'but, by the way.'

384. πυκνότητα—'compression' (Merry); see 406: also the explanation of the sound in 164.

385. τῷ—i.e. τίνι, 'by what (proof)?': *Plut.* 48, τῷ τοῦτο κρίνεις; Eur. *Ion* 1344, τῷ τόδε γνῶναι με χρή; ἀπὸ σαυτοῦ—another of the master's 'homely illustrations'; cf. 234.

386. Παναθηναίοις—at this festival each city which was a colony of Athens sent an ox for sacrifice, so that there was feasting in plenty throughout the town.

387. διεκορκορύγησεν—so κορκορυγή, 'rumbling,' *Pac.* 991: *Lys.* 491.

388. δεινὰ ποιεῖ—sc. ἡ γαστήρ. δεινὸν or δεινὰ ποιεῖν is to make an outcry or uproar; δεινὰ ποιεῖσθαι to take a thing ill, be indignant; cf. 583: *Ran.* 1093, δεινὰ ποιῶν: see note on Thuc. v. 42, 3, οἱ Ἀθηναῖοι δεινὰ ἐποίουν νομίζοντες ἀδικεῖσθαι. The active refers to external manifestations, noises etc., while the middle expresses the subjective feeling.

390. ἐπάγει—'brings in,' 'brings up.'

392. τυννουτουΐ—'(only) so big'; συναγαγὼν δὲ τοὺς δακτύλους φησὶ τοῦτο (schol.): *Ach.* 367: *Ran.* 139. For the illustration cf. Lucr. vi. 128 sq.

393. μέγα—'loud'; cf. *Vesp.* 963, λέξον μέγα, 'speak up.'

396. τοὺς δὲ ζῶντας περιφλύει—'alios autem vivos amburit (i.e. salva vita): quasi praecessisset τοὺς μέν' (Blaydes). περιφλύει δὲ ἐπιπολῆς καίει (schol.), 'scorches.'

398. Κρονίων ὄζων—'smelling of old-world notions.' The Cronia was a feast held in Hecatombaeon; while Κρόνος and such words denote anything out of date; cf. 929 and 1070: *Plut.* 581, Κρονικαῖς λήμαις λημῶντες.

βεκκεσέληνε—'pre-Adamite booby,' if we may so say. The first half of this comic word is generally taken as an allusion to βεκός, which the Egyptian king learned, by experimenting with two infants, to be the *oldest* word for bread (Hdt. ii. 2); it may however be simply chosen for its contemptuous sound. The second half suggests προσέληνοι, which the Arcadians claimed to be.

399. εἴπερ κ.τ.λ.—such reasoning was naturally adopted by the Epicureans : see especially two well-known passages in Lucr., vi. 386 sq. and 416 sq. For the position of δῆτ' cf. *Eq.* 18 and 810. Σίμων'— see 351.

400. Κλεώνυμον—cf. 353. Θέωρον—*Ach.* 134 : *Vesp.* 42 etc. : ' ut periurus, rapax, moechus, adulator saepius carpitur ' (Richter).

401. Σούνιον κ.τ.λ.—from Hom. *Od.* iii. 278,

ἀλλ' ὅτε Σούνιον ἱρὸν ἀφικόμεθ' ἄκρον Ἀθηνέων·

Hence the long a in ἄκρον and the Ionic form Ἀθηνέων.

402. τί μαθών ;—see note on 340. Here the manuscript authority is much stronger for μαθών than for παθών. δρῦς γ'—γ' is only in a few manuscripts, but is required for emphasis, cf. 342.

403. ἀτάρ κ.τ.λ.—the line stands in the text as it is generally edited. Possibly however ἀτάρ (382) is the transition to the question ' what *is* the lightning ?' and εὖ σὺ λέγειν φαίνει should be printed as a parenthesis. If it were εὖ γάρ (which would not scan) there would be no doubt. For εὖ σύ Teuffel and Blaydes read εὖ γε.

404—407. Cf. Lucr. vi. 124 sq. and 276 sq. Teuffel also cites Arrian from Stob. *Eth. Phys.* i. 29, 2, ξηροὶ ἀτμοὶ ἐν νέφει ἀποληφθέντες, ἔπειτα ῥηγνύντες βίᾳ τὸ νέφος βροντάς τε καὶ ἀστραπὰς ἐξέφηναν. Kock adds the dictum of Metrodorus from Plut. *Mor.* 893 E, ὅταν εἰς νέφος πεπηγὸς ὑπὸ πυκνότητος ἐμπέσῃ πνεῦμα, τῇ μὲν θραύσει τὸν κτύπον ἀποτελεῖ τῇ δὲ πληγῇ καὶ τῷ σχισμῷ διαυγάζει.

405. ὑπ' ἀνάγκης—cf. δι' ἀνάγκην, 377.

406. ἔξω φέρεται σοβαρός—' bursts out violently ' : *Plut.* 872, ὡς σοβαρὸς εἰσελήλυθεν. πυκνότητα—see 384.

407. τοῦ ῥοίβδου καὶ τῆς ῥύμης—*Av.* 1182, ῥύμῃ τε καὶ πτεροῖσι καὶ ῥοιζήμασι. The sound of such words represents the sense, as our rush, roar and the like.

408. Διασίοισιν—cf. 864 : Thuc. i. 126, 6, Διάσια ἃ καλεῖται, Διὸς ἑορτὴ Μειλιχίου μεγίστη : it was held on the 23rd of Anthesterion.

409. ὤπτων—R has the participle ὀπτῶν, which is read by Teuffel and Meineke, the latter putting no stop after the line before: cf. *Ach.* 24, ἀωρίαν ἥκοντες, εἶτα δ' ὡστιοῦνται. γαστέρα—a paunch or haggis : it had to be pricked or slit to let out the steam : Hom. *Od.*

xviii. 44, γαστέρες αἶδ' αἰγῶν κέατ' ἐν πυρί: cf. ib. xx. 25 sq. ἔσχων—παρὰ τοῖς ἀρχαίοις ἔσχων ἀντὶ τοῦ ἐσχαῖον καὶ ἐκέντουν (Phryn.): σχᾶται is found in Hippocrates.

410. ἡ δ' ἄρ'—'and so it got inflated'; ἄρα, 'accordingly.' διαλακήσασα—*Pac.* 381, λακήσομαι: Theocr. ii. 24, λακεῖ μέγα.

414. εἰ μνήμων εἶ—'this list of virtues that the chorus commends to Strepsiades represents just those that his contemporaries assigned to Socrates; Xen. *Mem.* i. 2, 1: so Plat. *Symp.* 220 A, B' (Merry). So Diogenes Laertius (ii. 5, 27) says of Socrates, οἱ κωμῳδοποιοὶ λανθάνουσιν ἑαυτοὺς δι' ὧν σκώπτουσιν ἐπαινοῦντες αὐτόν. He cites the present passage, with sundry variations, which may be due to quoting from memory or, as Teuffel suggests, to his having the former edition of the *Clouds* before him.

τὸ ταλαίπωρον—indifference to bodily needs was especially practised and enjoined on his disciples by Socrates, whose own hardiness was proverbial.

417. καὶ γυμνασίων—this must mean the abuse of γυμνάσια, if the reading be right. Diogenes however has κἀδηφαγίας 'gluttony.' Naber suggests καὶ βαλανείων, which agrees with 991 and 1054. Other suggestions are κἀγυμνασίας and καὶ συμποσίων, which last is adopted by Blaydes.

ἀνοήτων—'follies' i.e. sensual excess.

419. πράττων—in public matters and political life.

420. οὔνεκά γε—'for' i.e. so far as concerns: *Ach.* 958, εὐδαιμονήσεις συκοφαντῶν γ' οὔνεκα. Bergler and other editors quote a list of qualities like these as claimed by a would-be pupil in Aristophon's *Pythagorist*, Athen. vi. 238 C (34).

421. τρυσιβίου—'wearing out life,' i.e. hardy. θυμβρεπιδείπνου—'sage-dining'; λάχανα μόνα τρωγούσης εὐτελῆ (schol.): *Ach.* 254, βλέπουσα θυμβροφάγον (=θύμβραν): *Eccl.* 1178, λαβὼν λέκιθον ἵν' ἐπιδειπνῇς.

422. ἀμέλει—practically an adverb going with what follows, 'with absolute confidence I would' etc.; cf. 488. Most editors however put a comma after ἀμέλει (or θαρρῶν), making ἀμέλει a real imperative, 'have no concern, I would' etc.

ἐπιχαλκεύειν παρέχοιμ' ἄν—'I would let myself be hammered on,' like iron on an anvil, i.e. I could stand any amount of moulding and fashioning. The construction with παρέχω without ἐμαυτόν is not uncommon; e.g. Soph. *Aj.* 1146, πατεῖν παρεῖχε τῷ θέλοντι: Plat. *Charm.* 176 B, ἣν ἐπᾴδειν παρέχῃς Σωκράτει.

423. ἄλλο τι—you will then acknowledge no gods but what we do? The construction is understood in two ways: (1) ἄλλο τι is taken as = *nonne*? sc. ἄλλο τι δῆτα (ποιήσεις ἤ) οὐ νομιεῖς etc.: so Teuffel, and most editors: (2) the order is οὐ νομιεῖς ἄλλο τι οὐδὲν θεόν (or οὐδὲν οὖν νομιεῖς). This is the view taken by Dindorf, who urges that the Platonic interrogative ἄλλο τι (ἤ) is 'alienissimum quum omnino ab Aristophane tum praesertim ab hoc loco.' Blaydes indeed suggests that the phrase is a mannerism intentionally abscribed to Socrates here, but this seems fanciful; it is rather a mannerism of Plato's. But for the balance of authority in favour of (1) I should accept Dindorf's view. It involves however a harsh order of words, unlike the beautiful clearness of Aristophanes.

οὐδέν is better in any case than οὐδένα because of the following ἅπερ, and is necessary with (2).

νομιεῖς—'acknowledge'; *Eq.* 1338, ἐμὲ νομίζοις ἂν θεόν: Plat. *Ap. Socr.* 24 B, Σωκράτη φησὶν ἀδικεῖν θεοὺς οὓς ἡ πόλις νομίζει οὐ νομίζοντα.

424. τὸ χάος τουτί—hitherto Strepsiades has been taught only the divinity of the Clouds. Now three powers are cited, as three are appealed to in 264, 5 and 627: 'mos erat per tres deos, ut idoneum testium numerum, iurare' (Blaydes). γλῶτταν—so Euripides invokes αἰθὴρ ἐμὸν βόσκημα καὶ γλώττης στρόφιγξ (*Ran.* 892).

426. οὐδὲ σπείσαιμ'—so Cobet, for οὐδ' ἂν of most editions. The second ἂν is omitted *Eq.* 1057.

ἐπιθείην—*Vesp.* 96, λιβανωτὸν ἐπιτιθεὶς νουμηνίᾳ.

427. δρῶμεν—conjunctive, 'what we are to do.'

430. ἑκατὸν σταδίοισιν—*Ran.* 91, Εὐριπίδου πλεῖν ἢ σταδίῳ λαλίστερα.

432. ἐν τῷ δήμῳ—in the ἐκκλησία: *Vesp.* 594, ἐν τῷ δήμῳ γνώμην ἐνίκησεν: cf. 99.

433. μή μοί γε—'no moving great resolutions for me': cf. 84: *Vesp.* 1179, μή μοί γε μύθους.

434. ἀλλ' ὅσα—'just enough to,' sc. τοσαῦτα μόνα (ἐπιθυμῶ λέγειν) ὅσα: *Vesp.* 1288, οὐδὲν ἐμοῦ μέλον, ὅσον δὲ μόνον εἰδέναι. στρεψοδικῆσαι—'to wrest the right for myself' (Green): *Av.* 1468, στρεψοδικοπανουργίαν. Hence the name Strepsiades (schol.).

435. ἱμείρεις—a lofty, tragic word; 'nusquam alibi in comoedia Graeca superstite occurrit' (Blaydes).

436. προπόλοισιν—'ministers'; *Plut.* 670, τοῦ θεοῦ ὁ πρόπολος.

437. δράσω—cf. *Vesp.* 385, δράσω τοίνυν ὑμῖν πίσυνος.

438. κοππατίας—cf. 23. ἐπέτριψεν—'ruined.'

439. χρήσθων—'let them use (me),' with cognate accusative ὅ τι βούλονται: *Thesm.* 212, ἐμοὶ δ' ὅ τι βούλει χρῶ λαβών. According to the reading adopted by Meineke this cognate goes with the following infinitives and there is no stop after βούλονται; see critical note. Blaydes marks a lacuna after νῦν οὖν, or suggests νῦν μοι χρήσθων, 'vix enim omitti potest pronomen.'

440. τοὐμόν—so Cobet and others: the manuscripts have τό γ' ἐμόν, 'yea, this my own.'

441. παρέχω τύπτειν—cf. 422: the active infinitive is the regular construction: Plat. *Euthyd.* 285 C, παρέχειν ἐμαυτὸν τοῖς ξένοις δέρειν. Here the subject of πεινῆν etc. is ἐμέ, while αὐτούς comes in again as the subject of δέρειν. Dr Merry thus represents the clause, 'I hand over this body of mine to them for beating, for hunger, thirst' etc. Note the irregular contraction of πεινῆν, διψῆν.

442. ῥιγῶν—see *Vesp.* 446: ῥιγόω has generally an irregular contraction with ω, ῳ, instead of ου, οι. ἀσκὸν δείρειν—'to beat (or flog) into a wine skin'; ἤθελον ἀσκὸς δεδάρθαι, from a fragment of Solon: *Eq.* 370, δερῶ σε θύλακον.

443. εἴπερ διαφευξοῦμαι—cf. 1035: Soph. *Oed. Col.* 54, εἴπερ ἄρξεις τῆσδε γῆς, 'if you mean to be king.'

445. ἴτης—'go-ahead'; δι' αὐτῶν χωρῶν πραγμάτων (schol.): Plat. *Protag.* 349 E, καὶ ἴτας γε ἐφ' ἃ οἱ πολλοὶ φοβοῦνται ἰέναι. ἰταμός is more common.

447. περίτριμμα—cf. 260. Dem. (*de Cor.* 269 § 127) calls Aeschines περίτριμμα ἀγορᾶς.

448. κύρβις—'a walking statute-book: the κύρβεις were triangular pyramids of wood revolving on a pivot, whereon were written the laws of Solon' (Merry): cf. *Av.* 1354. κίναδος—*Av.* 430: Soph. *Aj.* 103: Dem. etc. τρύμη—lit. 'a hole'; ὁ τετρημένος σφόδρα καὶ πεπερονημένος ἐν τοῖς πράγμασιν, ὃν ἡμεῖς τρύπανόν φαμεν (schol.). τρύπανον is an auger, and the meaning may be a fellow who will pierce and force his way, 'sharp as a needle' as Mr Green says.

449. μάσθλης—*Eq.* 269, ὡς δ' ἀλαζών, ὡς δὲ μάσθλης: lit. a soft and supple strap. γλοιός—lit. coagulated oil; hence a slippery fellow, or perhaps a dirty rogue.

450. κέντρων—either a 'goader,' or one who is whipped or goaded, as in Soph. Frag. 309, μαστιγίαι, κέντρωνες. ἀργαλέος—'an awkward customer' (Merry).

451. ματτυολοιχός—'a licker up of dainty dishes.' This is Bentley's conjecture, and is adopted by Kock, Meineke, Green, and

G. C. 8

other editors. It is not free from objections, as ματτύη, 'cibi genus,' (Mart. xiii. 92, 2, inter quadrupedes mattya prima lepus), was a Macedonian word, not yet introduced in Athens. Besides, daintiness is not a quality which Strepsiades would claim, but rather indifference to dainties. The word may however merely mean 'a trencher-scraper,' one who can look out for himself.

The manuscript reading is ματιολοιχός, which is explained by the scholiast as μικρολόγος or μάταια βουλευόμενος καὶ λοχῶν, and by the old grammarians as ὁ περὶ τὰ μικρὰ πανοῦργος καὶ λίχνος· μάτιον γὰρ τὸ μικρόν.

455. ἔκ μου χορδήν—*Eq.* 372, περικόμματ' ἔκ σου σκευάσω: Plaut. *Mil.* i. 1, 8, sarctum facere ex hostibus.

456. παραθέντων—'let them serve up.'

459. οὐρανόμηκες—cf. 357.

465. ἆρα...ἆρα—'shall I then?'

468. ὥστε γε—'yea, so that' etc. ἐπὶ ταῖσι θύραις καθῆσθαι— coming to the doors, or sitting at the doors of any one, means applying for his counsel or help. The old gibe was that riches were better than wisdom, for philosophers haunted the doors of the rich, but the rich did not frequent the doors of the wise.

470. ἀνακοινοῦσθαι—'to communicate,' with or without accusative expressed, and with dative of the person: so the active, 197. ἐς λόγον ἐλθεῖν—'to confer'; cf. 252.

472. πράγματα—'causes': the accusative follows ἀνακοινοῦσθαι, ἐς λόγον ἐλθεῖν being thrown in parenthetically (Green). Dr Merry however takes πράγματα etc. as dependent on συμβουλευσομένους. ἀντιγραφάς—strictly the defendant's 'plea' or rejoinder, but often used more generally: see Dict. Ant. πολλῶν ταλάντων—'worth many talents,' i.e. involving great sums.

475. ἄξια σῇ φρενί—'wishing to take counsel with you on matters meet for your great wisdom' (Green); cf. *Ach.* 8, ἄξιον γὰρ Ἑλλάδι: *Eq.* 616, ἀξιόν γε πᾶσίν ἐστιν ἐπολολύξαι. Teuffel and Blaydes put a comma after ἄξια σῇ φρενί, making it appositional with the words before.

476. ἀλλ' ἐγχείρει—turning to Socrates, 'take in hand, begin.' προδιδάσκειν—here the preliminary lessons may be implied; but the word is often equivalent to διδάσκειν, the προ suggesting the teacher's leading and the scholar's progress.

479. μηχανάς...προσφέρω—of plans and means, Eur. *Iph. T.* 112, πάσας προσφέροντε μηχανάς. Hearing of the 'engines' which are to be

'brought to bear' on him Strepsiades cries out as if in fear of an armed assault: Thuc. ii. 58, 1, μηχανὰς τῇ Ποτιδαίᾳ προσέφερον: ii. 76, 4, μηχανὰς προσῆγον τῇ πόλει. According to Poppo scaling-ladders are especially meant.

481. τειχομαχεῖν μοι—like μάχεσθαί μοι. τειχομαχεῖν occurs three times in Thucydides, without a case following.

485. σχέτλιος—'poor wretch.'

487. ἀποστερεῖν—Teuffel suggests that there may be a joke in ἀποστ-ερεῖν (=λέγειν). Meineke and Kock suspect the genuineness of 486, 7: Green puts them after 488.

488. ἀμέλει—cf. 422.

489. ἄγε νῦν ὅπως κ.τ.λ.—*Ach.* 253, ἄγ' ὅπως...οἴσεις: Goodwin § 273.   προβάλω—Socrates means 'propound'; in which sense προβαλεῖ is perhaps the true reading *Vesp.* 21, as suggested by Green. The word is also used of throwing things to a dog, 'when I drop you a scrap of wisdom'; cf. *Vesp.* 916. With the following ὑφαρπάσει, 'snap up,' this naturally suggests κυνηδόν.

493. δέδοικά σ'—the subject of the subordinate sentence is made the object of the main verb: Thuc. iv. 1, 1, φοβούμενοι τοὺς Ἀθηναίους, μὴ ἐπέλθωσιν. Teuffel cites Ter. *Eun.* 610, metuo fratrem ne intus sit.

The manuscripts vary between δέῃ and δέει: most editors read δέει, 'I fear you (actually) need whipping'; see Goodwin § 365 and 369.

494. τί δρᾷς—Dr Blaydes takes this as conjunctive, 'what are you to do?' while 'pro indicativo perverse accipit senex rusticus.' But more probably Socrates is simply asking if whipping does his pupil good, or perhaps if it is likely to get the teacher into trouble.

495. ἐπισχὼν ὀλίγον—he does everything in an orderly and deliberate way: [Dem.] *Energ.* 1150 § 38, ἐπιμαρτυράμενος τοὺς παρόντας ἠμυνάμην. The simple μαρτύρομαι occurs 1222, 1297.

496. ἀκαρῆ—sc. χρόνον: *Plut.* 244, ἐν ἀκαρεῖ χρόνῳ.   διαλιπών—Isocr. *de pac.* 10, ὀλίγον χρόνον διαλιπόντες, πάλιν κ.τ.λ. δικάζομαι—'I bring my action.'

497. ἴθι νῦν—Socrates is satisfied of his pupil's fitness, or else thinks further questions useless. He bids him take off his cloak, to prepare for philosophic training, or as one about to be initiated (schol.). Strepsiades however fears a beating. This cloak is somehow missing afterwards, see 856 and 1498, and Strepsiades loses his shoes as well, 719.

This passage in some degree supports the rendering θοἰμάτιον, 179.

8—2

498. γυμνούς—in the χιτών only, so 965. ἔθος ἦν τοῖς τότε φιλοσόφοις ἐν χιτώνιον μόνον ἐνδεδυμένους καὶ ἡμιγύμνους καθημένους φιλοσοφεῖν (schol.). νομίζεται—1416, 1420.

499. φωράσων—searchers for stolen goods had to leave their clothes behind, that they might not carry property in with them and then pretend to have found it: Plat. *legg.* 954 A, φωρᾶν ἂν ἐθέλῃ τίς τι παρ' ὁτῳοῦν, γυμνὸς ἢ χιτωνίσκον ἔχων, ἄζωστος κ.τ.λ.

503. τὴν φύσιν—Socrates means 'in character,' but Strepsiades understands 'appearance'; see 276.

504. ἡμιθνής—ἐπεὶ ἰσχνὸς καὶ ὠχρὸς τὴν ἰδέαν ὁ Χαιρεφῶν· ὅθεν νυκτερὶς ἐκαλεῖτο καὶ πύξινος (schol.): cf. 103.

505. οὐ μή...ἀλλ'...;—cf. *Ran.* 462, οὐ μὴ διατρίψεις ἀλλὰ γεύσει τῆς θύρας; see also 296 and 367.

506. ἀνύσας τι—cf. 181. δευρί—Socrates turns to the door of the Contemplatory, which seems to have been more or less underground, see 632. θᾶττον—'at once,' *ocius*. τὼ χεῖρε—τώ, τοῖν are the dual forms for all genders.

507. μελιτοῦτταν—μᾶζαν μέλιτι μεμαγμένην: *Av.* 567: *Lys.* 601.

508. ἐς Τροφωνίου—the oracle of Trophonius was in an underground cave at Lebadaea in Boeotia. Those who consulted it took with them cakes to soothe the serpents which beset the place. The horrors of the cave and the mysterious terrors of the oracle are described by Pausanias, ix. 39, 2—14, and further traditions are recorded by the scholiasts: see Dr Blaydes' edition, and also Dr Merry's note.

509. κυπτάζεις—*Pac.* 731, περὶ τὰς σκηνὰς κυπτάζειν. ἔχων— cf. 131.

Socrates and his pupil now enter the house, and the chorus come forward. As the actors retire they wish good luck to the neophyte in his bold venture, and then the leader delivers the Parabasis.

Parabasis, lines 510—626.

In the *Wasps* and the *Birds* we have a parabasis complete in all its parts: see Dict. Ant. *chorus* p. 422. Here the πνῖγος or μακρόν alone

l. 523] NOTES 117

is wanting. See note on 562. The arrangement is as follows:—κομμάτιον, 510—516: παράβασις proper, 517—562: στροφή or ὡδή, 563—574: ἐπίρρημα, 575—594: ἀντιστροφή or ἀντωδή, 595—606: ἀντεπίρρημα, 607—626.

510—517.—*τοῦτο διὰ τὸ εἰσάγεσθαι τὸν χορὸν ἐξιόντων τῶν ὑποκριτῶν ὀνομάζεται κορωνίς* (schol.). κομμάτιον is the usual term. It was sung as the chorus were turning to face the audience.

510. ἀλλ' ἴθι χαίρων—the usual formula; *Eq.* 498, ἀλλ' ἴθι χαίρων: so *Pac.* 729, *Vesp.* 1009, ἀλλ' ἴτε χαίροντες.

513. προήκων κ.τ.λ.—Plut. *Alc.* 18, ἡλικίᾳ προήκων: *Anth. Pal.* vii. 163, 7, ἐς βαθὺ γῆρας ἵκοιτο.

515. νεωτέροις κ.τ.λ.—'is getting his mind imbued with new pursuits' (Blaydes); cf. 1399, καινοῖς πράγμασιν ὁμιλεῖν: *Vesp.* 1471, τὸν φύσαντα σεμνοτέροις κατακοσμῆσαι πράγμασι, 'conditions.' τὴν φύσιν αὐτοῦ—so 905, τὸν πατέρ' αὐτοῦ: *Pac.* 880. τὴν αὐτοῦ φύσιν is the usual order, but ἡ φύσις αὐτοῦ, ἐμοῦ etc.: see 905, and my note on Thuc. v. 71, 1. χρωτίζεται—middle, as in 127. The active χρωτίζω is quoted from Plutarch by Liddell and Scott.

520—562. The chorus facing the spectators, the leader addresses the audience in the poet's name. This part of the Parabasis belongs to the second edition of the *Clouds*. The play had not deserved to fail, says the poet, for it was the best and most careful of his works. He hopes now for a better verdict, even as his earlier plays have met with welcome and encouragement.

This is free from vulgarity and coarseness; it is full of fresh ideas. Old adversaries are not attacked again; while it is the poet's rivals who imitate his former comedies, and now assail Hyperbolus as he encountered Cleon.

The Parabasis of the *Wasps*, exhibited in 422, has a still further vindication of the merits of the *Clouds*, with complaints of unappreciative critics, and many of the verses in the *Wasps* are repeated in the *Peace*, which appeared in 421.

519. Διόνυσον—ἐπεὶ ἐν Διονυσίοις παρῆλθε τὸ δρᾶμα (schol.). ἐκθρέψαντα—cf. 532: *Ran.* 886, Δήμητερ ἡ θρέψασα τὴν ἐμὴν φρένα.

520. οὕτω...ὡς—the usual formula in prayers and invocations, so ita, sic...ut. οὕτω states the wish, ὡς the condition. We generally invert the order and say 'if...then.'

σοφός—used, like δεξιός, of good taste and judgment and refinement in the poet and the critic.

523. πρώτους—instead of producing the play elsewhere, in the

Piraeus for instance or in Aegina, or perhaps at the rural Dionysia; ὑμᾶς being the audience at the great Dionysia. ἀναγεῦσ' ὑμᾶς— 'to give you a taste of it'; 'a second taste' might seem implied from the composition of the word, which is not found elsewhere; but this does not agree with εἶτ' ἀνεχώρουν. The cognate αὐτήν is implied: cf. Eur. *Cycl.* 149, βούλει σε γεύσω πρῶτον ἄκρατον μέθυ; ποτίζω is constructed in the same way.

524. εἶτ'—'and after all'; 'cum indignatione dictum, ut in 1214' (Blaydes). ὑπ' ἀνδρῶν φορτικῶν—the converse of σοφός and δεξιός, boorish, vulgar, illiterate. Some authorities understand the judges, others the rival poets. I rather incline to the latter view, as Aristophanes often complains of φόρτος and φορτικά in other people's plays, while it would not be judicious to call the judges or the audience φορτικοί.

526. ταῦτ' ἐπραγματευόμην—'I took all this trouble.'

527. οὐδ' ὥς—not even after this defeat.

528. ἐνθάδ'—in this same theatre. οἷς ἡδὺ καὶ λέγειν—'to (before) whom it is a pleasure even to speak,' i.e. to perform, even without a victory. This is the scholiast's explanation, and there is no variation of reading. The sense however is not very clear, and οἷς λέγειν is not common Greek for πρὸς οὕς or παρ' οἷς. Blaydes suggests οὕς, Herwerden οἷσιν δίκης μέλει, while Kock proposes ψέγειν for λέγειν.

529. ὁ σώφρων κ.τ.λ.—'my Modest Man and my Rake'; characters in the Δαιταλῆς, the poet's first play, B.C. 427. πρῶτον δρᾶμα γράψας, σῶφρον μειράκιον εἰσάγει καὶ ἕτερον ἄχρηστον (schol.). ἄριστ' ἠκουσάτην—εὐδοκίμησαν, 'won high praise'; the play however only took the second place.

530. κοὐκ ἐξῆν—either he had not attained full citizenship, and so could not apply for a chorus in his own name (Teuffel), or it was his own prudence and modesty that kept him back: *Eq.* 545, σωφρονικῶς κοὐκ ἀνοήτως ἐσπηδήσας ἐφλυάρει: so the scholiast, οὔπω ἐπέτρεπον ἐμαυτῷ λέγειν διὰ τὴν αἰδῶ (Green). Aristophanes was nineteen in 427.

531. ἐξέθηκα—Eur. *Phoen.* 36, τὸν ἐκτεθέντα παῖδα. The παῖς ἑτέρα was either Philonides or Callistratus; the scholia are confused. ἀνείλετο—*Act. Apost.* vii. 21, ἐκτεθέντος δὲ αὐτοῦ ἀνείλετο αὐτὸν ἡ θυγάτηρ Φαραώ (Blaydes).

533. ἐκ τούτου—'since then,' ἐξ ὅτου, 528. παρ' ὑμῖν—'with you,' in your minds. We should rather expect παρ' ὑμῶν, which many

editors adopt. **γνώμης ὅρκια**—'pledges of good judgment,' or of appreciative feeling : ὅρκια πιστά is a regular Homeric expression.

534. **Ἠλέκτραν κατ' ἐκείνην**—'like Electra in the play': *Ran.* 463, καθ' Ἡρακλέα. ἐκείνην, *illam*, the well-known character. Note the omission of the article with a proper name.

536. **γνώσεται...βόστρυχον**—As Electra in the *Choephori* (164 sq.) recognised her brother's lock of hair, so my play, if kindly welcomed, will recognise the wonted appreciation of the audience.

540. **τοὺς φαλακρούς**—Aristophanes was bald, and his rivals apparently made a jest of it. Eupolis at any rate, according to the scholiast on 554, claimed to have 'helped the bald man to write his *Knights*'; and we find in the *Peace* a good-humoured vindication of the credit which Aristophanes had won for the bald-headed tribe (*Pac.* 765 sq.). **εἵλκυσεν**—either 'danced,' ἀσέμνως ὠρχήσατο, as in *Pac.* 328, ἐν τουτὶ μ' ἔασον ἑλκύσαι : or ' brought in,' εἰσήγαγεν, cf. 553. Aristophanes vindicates the dignity and refinement of his own plays in contrast to the buffoonery of others in a somewhat similar passage in the *Wasps*, 55—66.

Mr Green notes that ' in his later plays, Aristophanes certainly did much of what he here blames in the other comic writers. He seems to have started with an idea of reforming the public taste, which he found a task impossible, and so had to give in.'

541. **ὁ λέγων τἄπη**—i.e. in the dialogue, as opposed to the choral songs. Some particular incident is doubtless meant; in a play of Eupolis, says the scholiast, or of Hermippus.

542. **ἀφανίζων**—'concealing,' or 'carrying off' as we say ; περικαλύπτων τῷ γέλωτι καὶ τῇ παιδιᾷ (schol.).

543. **οὐδ' εἰσῇξε**—ἥτις is the subject, the two lines before being parenthetical. **δᾷδας**—we have however a torch in line 1492, and cries of ἰού there and at the beginning of the play. The scholiast says that these were not introduced in the first edition of the *Clouds* ; and adds that Aristophanes brings in such things in their proper places, μετὰ λόγου· οὗτοι δὲ ἀκαίρως.

545. **οὐ κομῶ**—οὐ μέγα φρονῶ, with a joking allusion to his own baldness: χαριέντως δὲ λέγει ἐπεὶ φαλακρὸς ἦν (schol.). Compare the passage in the *Wasps*, 1022, ἀρθεὶς δὲ μέγας κ.τ.λ.: and note on 14.

549. **μέγιστον ὄντα**—Cleon was 'at the height of his power' and popularity after his success at Pylos in 425, when Aristophanes assailed him fiercely in the *Knights*. **ἔπαισ' ἐς τὴν γαστέρα**—*Eq.* 273, γαστρίζομαι : 454, παῖ' αὐτὸν καὶ γάστριζε.

550. **κοὐκ ἐτόλμησ'**—'I wasn't hard enough' (Merry). **ἐπεμπηδῆσαι**—Soph. *Aj*. 1348, οὐ γὰρ θανόντι καὶ προσεμβῆναί σε χρή; **κειμένῳ**—meaning, I think, 'when I had got him down.' Most editors however take it to refer to Cleon's death. He never met with a political downfall.

We find the poet again in the *Wasps* (62) disclaiming a further attack on Cleon; but he scarcely kept his word, though he did not repeat the sustained and organised assault of the *Knights*.

551. **παρέδωκεν λαβήν**—*Eq.* 841, λαβὴν δέδωκε: with ἐνδιδόναι, *ib.* 847: *Lys.* 671: so *ansa, ansas dare* (Cic.). **Ὑπέρβολος**—a lamp-seller (*Eq.* 739), who was now the demagogue of the day, and a sort of second-rate Cleon: see note on *Vesp.* 1007.

552. **δείλαιον**—predicative, as in line 12. **κολετρῶσ'**—κατὰ κόλου τύπτουσι, καταπατοῦσι (schol.). **τὴν μητέρα**—contemptuously mentioned, *Thesm.* 840.

553. **Εὔπολις κ.τ.λ.**—Eupolis, the contemporary and rival of Aristophanes, put on the stage the *Maricas*, in which he attacked Hyperbolus and his mother. Aristophanes complains that it was an adaptation, and a bad one, of his *Knights*. The *Maricas* appeared in 421, two years after the *Clouds*, which shows that we have here a passage belonging to the second *Clouds*. **παρείλκυσεν**—εἰς τὸ θέατρον εἰσήγαγεν (schol.): παρά perhaps suggests awkwardness and force, 'lugging in' (Green). Liddell and Scott say 'spun out.'

554. **ἐκστρέψας**—μεταβαλών (schol.); cf. 88. The idea is that Eupolis altered and spoilt the play. **κακὸς κακῶς**—so *Ach.* 253 etc.

555. **αὐτῷ**—i.e. the play, the sense of αὐτό or αὐτά, like that of our 'it' or 'this,' being often implied in the context; or it may be τῷ Μαρικᾷ. **γραῦν μεθύσην**—the mother of Hyperbolus, according to the scholiast; in any case a character brought in **τοῦ κόρδακος οὕνεχ'**, to perform a vulgar dance (540).

556. **Φρύνιχος**—Phrynichus the comic poet is meant, according to the scholiast; he seems to have travestied the tragic Andromeda, who was exposed to a sea monster. Possibly however an *Andromeda* of the tragic Phrynichus is alluded to.

557. **Ἕρμιππος**—a comic writer of the time of Pericles. In his play of the *Baking-women* he falls foul of Hyperbolus and his mother. **ἐποίησεν εἰς**—'wrote upon,' lit. 'in reference to'; Hdt. i. 86, ἐς ἑωυτὸν λέγων. ἐπήδησεν is an amendment suggested.

558. **ἄλλοι πάντες**—'others, every one'; Blaydes and Teuffel read

ἄλλοι with Meineke.   ἐρείδουσιν εἰς—ἐρείδω is here intransitive, 'press upon,' 'pitch into.'

559. τὰς εἰκούς κ.τ.λ.—*Eq.* 864 sq., where Cleon is compared to an eel-catcher, who stirs up the mud in order to fish in troubled waters.

562. ἐς τὰς ὥρας—for the time to come; εἰς τοὺς μετὰ ταῦτα ἐνιαυτούς (schol.): *Ran.* 381, σώζειν φῂσ' ἐς τὰς ὥρας: *Thesm.* 950, ἐκ τῶν ὡρῶν ἐς τὰς ὥρας. Another view is 'till next season,' i.e. till the next comic contest.   δοκήσετε—so *Ran.* 737: δοκήσας, *ib.* 1485. The μακρόν or πνῖγος (*Vesp.* 1051) is wanting, and the *strophe* follows at once. It is an invocation of the mighty gods who have some affinity with the Clouds.

563. μέν—with the force of 'first'; there is no corresponding δέ, the other powers invoked are introduced with τε etc. The Clouds, whom the philosophers called the only deities, themselves appeal to Zeus and the other gods.

566. ταμίαν—Hom. *Il.* iv. 84, ταμίης πολέμοιο: *Od.* x. 21, ταμίην ἀνέμων.

567. μοχλευτήν—'upheaver'; cf. 1397.   Poseidon was ἐνοσίχθων, ἐννοσίγαιος, the lord of earthquakes as well as of storms: *Ach.* 510, σείσας Ποσειδῶν.

570. αἰθέρα—see 264. The scholiast says that the ἀήρ is here meant, ὁ γὰρ αἰθὴρ ἀνέφελος, καὶ βιοθρέμμων ὁ ἀήρ, οὐχ ὁ αἰθήρ.

571. ἱππονώμαν—τὸν νωμῶντα τὸ ἅρμα (schol.); the sun-god: the form occurs Soph. *Aj.* 232: Eur. *Hip.* 135.

572. κατέχει—'fills,' 'pervades.'

575—594. *epirrhema,* recited by the leader of the chorus. The Clouds complain that they are not duly honoured for their good will and good service to the Athenians.

575. ὦ σοφώτατοι—cf. *Pac.* 603, ὦ σοφώτατοι γεωργοί κ.τ.λ. *Ran.* 700, ὦ σοφώτατοι φύσει.   πρόσσχετε—2nd aorist: many editors read πρόσχετε = προσέχετε, which last is found in most manuscripts. There is the same question of reading *Vesp.* 1015, in a passage of somewhat similar tone.

576. ἐναντίον—'to your face.'

577. ὠφελούσαις—Blaydes adopts the reading of R, ὠφελοῦσαι as a pendent nominative.

579. ἔξοδος—'expedition'; *Pac.* 1181, αὔριον δ' ἔσθ' ἡ 'ξοδος.

580. βροντῶμεν—thunder and rain were ominous, and stopped proceedings in the assembly, cf. *Ach.* 169,

ἀπαγορεύω μὴ ποιεῖν ἐκκλησίαν
τοῖς Θραξὶ περὶ μισθοῦ, λέγω δ' ὑμῖν ὅτι
διοσημία 'στὶ καὶ ῥανὶς βέβληκέ με·
so in case of an earthquake, Thuc. v. 45, 4: 50, 4.

582. ἡνίχ' ᾑρεῖσθε στρατηγόν—this apparently refers to Cleon's command at Pylos in 425 (Thuc. iv. 28). The passage belongs to the first *Clouds*, as Cleon is spoken of as alive in line 591; he fell at Amphipolis in 422. We have no record of portents happening at the time of Cleon's appointment; some storm may be meant, which hid the light of the sun and moon. **ὀφρῦs**—*Plut.* 756, ὀφρῦς ξυνῆγον ἐσκυθρωπαζόν θ' ἅμα.

583. **κἀποιοῦμεν δεινά**—cf. note on 388. **βροντὴ δ'**—from the *Teucer* of Sophocles (Frag. 507). The thunder bursts through where the lightning has cloven a path.

584. **ἡ σελήνη**—according to Teuffel there was an eclipse of the moon in Oct. 425; which was not the time of Cleon's appointment. An eclipse certainly seems meant by **ἐξέλειπε**, which is the regular word; as in Thuc. ii. 28, ὁ ἥλιος ἐξέλιπε. **ὁ δ' ἥλιος κ.τ.λ.** may however only mean that the sun was obscured by storms. Of course the two eclipses could not occur close together.

586. **στρατηγήσει**—Blaydes reads στρατηγήσοι, the future optative representing the simple future in reported speech after a past tense, as *shall* becomes *should*. The indicative however is often retained in such cases; see Goodwin, § 689.

588. **προσεῖναι**—'belongs to,' is a constant quality. The legend was that Poseidon when defeated by Athene in the contest for the patronage of the new city laid on the Athenians the curse of perpetual ill-counsel; but Athene turned the curse into a blessing, by decreeing that their ill counsels should always turn out well: cf. *Eccl.* 473. This became proverbial, λεγόμενον ἐπιχώριον (schol.).

590. **τοῦτο**—Cleon's election. Being in office he can be arraigned for peculation. **ξυνοίσει**—may turn out well, profit.

591. **λάρον**—*Eq.* 956, λάρος κεχηνὼς ἐπὶ πέτρας δημηγορῶν is the device on Cleonymus' ring. A greedy parasite is described as πεινῶντι λάρῳ ὄρνιθι ἐοικώς, Athen. 134 § 13. **δώρων ἑλόντες**—*Vesp.* 1207, εἷλον λοιδορίας.

592. **τῷ ξύλῳ**—*Eq.* 1049, δῆσαι πεντεσυρίγγῳ ξύλῳ: *Lys.* 680, τετρημένον ξύλον: a wooden frame with five openings to confine the neck and hands and feet; Dict. Ant. *nervus*. The κύφων, *Plut.* 476, held the neck.

593. ἐς τἀρχαῖον—'in statum pristinum'; *Eq.* 1387, ἐς τἀρχαῖα δὴ καθίσταμαι. In construction the words are loosely connected with the following line, and particularly with ξυνοίσεται.   εἴ τι κάξη-μάρτετε—if you *did* err at all.

594. ἐπὶ τὸ βέλτιον...ξυνοίσεται—Hdt. vii. 8, ἡμῖν συμφέρεται ἐπὶ τὸ ἄμεινον.

595—606. In the *antistrophe* the chorus invoke Phoebus, Artemis and Athene, and finally Dionysus, the patron of the stage.

595. ἀμφί μοι—sc. ἕσο (=ἴσθι) or χόρευσον (schol.), 'be about me,' i.e. vouchsafe thy presence (Merry). Another view is that σε is implied after ἀμφί, and 'my song shall be' or the like is the sense. This agrees with other odes beginning in this way. Thus the scholiast quotes from Terpander ἀμφί μοι ἄνακτα ἑκατήβολον as the beginning of an ode; and we have the beginnings of the Homeric hymns, ἀμφί μοι Ἑρμείαο φίλον γόνον ἔννεπε, Μοῦσα etc. So usual was this dithyrambic exordium that the terms ἀμφιάνακτες and ἀμφιανακτίζειν were applied to the poets and their preludes.

596. Κυνθίαν—Strab. x. 5, 2, ἡ Δῆλος ἐν πεδίῳ κειμένην ἔχει τὴν πόλιν καὶ τὸ ἱερὸν τοῦ Ἀπόλλωνος. ὑπέρκειται δὲ τῆς πόλεως ὄρος ὑψηλὸν ὁ Κύνθος καὶ τραχύ. It is really of no great height.

597. ὑψικέρατα—as if from ὑψικέρας -ᾱτος: the form is found in Pind. *Frag.* 285, whence Aristophanes may have borrowed it. χρυσόκερατα is read by Paley after Elmsley, Eur. *Hel.* 382. With 'high-horned,' i.e. high-peaked, Mr Green compares the German names Matterhorn, Weisshorn etc.

599. πάγχρυσον...οἶκον—the great temple of Artemis built or rebuilt in the 6th century B.C. It was burnt the night that Alexander the Great was born in 356, and rebuilt during his time.   Λυδῶν—for Ephesus, though the chief city of Ionia, was anciently spoken of as in Lydia; Hdt. i. 142, αἱ δὲ ἐν τῇ Λυδίῃ Ἔφεσος, Κολοφών κ.τ.λ.

602. αἰγίδος ἡνίοχος—generally taken as ='wielder of the aegis,' ἡνίοχος being used of one who sways, directs etc.; see Liddell and Scott. Mr Green, citing Aesch. *Eum.* 403—5, where Athene is borne on the aegis, says 'charioted on thy aegis' would be better. But I think Dr Merry is right in saying that 'the meaning there is rather that the movement of the goddess swelled out the folds of the aegis.' πολιοῦχος—*Eq.* 581, ὦ πολιοῦχε Παλλάς.   Ἀθάνα--elsewhere Aristophanes uses the older form Ἀθηναία, *Pac.* 271 etc. The form Ἀθηνᾶ, which occurs in Thucydides, is a contraction of this.

604. σὺν πεύκαις —'there was a streaming light, a meteor of some

kind, occasionally visible on the bipeaked hill, which was referred in the neighbouring legends to Dionysus with torches in either hand, leading his revellers to the nightly dance. This was a constant theme with the Attic poets' (Rogers).   σελαγεῖ is the 2nd person, cf. 285.

607—626. *antepirrhema*—The chorus deliver a commission from the moon to the Athenians. She does them good service both in private and in public, but they disregard her, and bring on her complaints from the other gods from the confusion of the calendar.

608. φράσαι—with the following χαίρειν, 'to bid you hail'; *Plut.* 322, χαίρειν ὑμᾶς προσαγορεύειν.

609. πρῶτα μέν—followed by εἶτα without δέ, a common form, with a slight anacoluthon in the construction. In 612 it is followed by ἄλλα τ', with a similar anacoluthon.   τοῖς ξυμμάχοις—who would be present at the great Dionysia (*Ach.* 502).

611. οὐ λόγοις—not like the orators and demagogues.

612. τοῦ μηνός—*Ach.* 859, τοῦ μηνὸς ἑκάστου.   οὐκ ἔλαττον ἤ δραχμήν—cognate accusative, sc. ὠφελοῦσα.

614. σεληναίας—σεληναίης is read in most manuscripts, but σεληναία, like Ἀθηναία, is the old Attic form. Some manuscripts have σεληναῖον, but the substantive is much more in place.

615. ὑμᾶς δ' οὐκ ἄγειν—nine or ten years before Meton the astronomer had endeavoured to improve the system by which the solar and lunar year were harmonised, all religious festivals being regulated by the lunar year. The details are clearly summarised in Dr Merry's edition of the *Clouds*; and further particulars may be found in Dict. Ant. *calendarium*. It does not appear that Meton's changes were formally adopted by the state, but some modifications of the calendar were plainly introduced about this time. There is a somewhat similar complaint implied, *Pac.* 414.

616. κυδοιδοπᾶν—συνταράττειν, ἀπὸ τοῦ κυδοιμοῦ (schol.): *Pac.* 1152, κἀκυδοιδόπα, of a γαλῆ stealing things.

618. ψευσθῶσι δείπνου—Soph. *Aj.* 178, ἐνάρων ψευσθεῖσα.

619. κατὰ λόγον—'there was an error in excess at the end of the cycle of 1½ days—a very appreciable quantity. The gods might well grumble, as this would be sufficient to disarrange the whole calendar. We might illustrate it by supposing Shrove Tuesday pushed forward to Ash Wednesday or vice versa' (Merry).

620. στρεβλοῦτε—i.e. examining slaves by torture, and conducting judicial business when the courts ought to be closed.

621. ἀγόντων—'keeping, observing': Aesch. *Ag.* 1592, κρεουργὸν ἧμαρ ἄγειν.

622. ἢ τὸν...ἢ—most manuscripts have a second τὸν before Σαρπηδόνα. The metre requires its omission; and the irregularity thus caused is justified by such lines as 104, 1418, 1465. Meineke reads ἤτοι Μέμνον', but ἤτοι...ἢ, according to Blaydes, is not found in comedy. Memnon son of Tithonus, and Sarpedon son of Zeus, both fell before Troy. So highly were they honoured by the gods that on the day of their death ἐν πένθει καὶ νηστείᾳ διάγειν τοὺς θεοὺς κατ' ἔτος (schol.).

624. τῆτες—*Ach.* 15: *Vesp.* 400. ἱερομνημονεῖν—the ἱερομνήμων was a commissioner appointed by lot to the Amphictyonic council. It was an office of high distinction; see Dict. Ant. *Amphictyones*. κἄπειθ'—note καί following a participle; *Eq.* 392, τοιοῦτος ὤν...κᾆτ' ἀνὴρ ἔδοξεν εἶναι.

625. τὸν στέφανον ἀφῃρέθη—he might wear a laurel chaplet as one returning from a sacred mission (*Plut.* 20); or as a mark of office, see Dem. *Meid.* 524 § 32. How he lost it we do not know. It has been suggested that he had his chaplet blown off by a gust of wind, which the Clouds here claim to have caused. Or the meaning may be that he was not rewarded with a crown of honour on his return from Delphi.

627. The chorus files off, and Socrates comes out of the Contemplatory, complaining of the hopeless dulness of his pupil: Strepsiades is still inside. Socrates swears μὰ τὴν ἀναπνοήν κ.τ.λ., appealing to his gods, the powers of nature; see 264 and 424. For the run of the verse cf. *Av.* 194, μὰ γῆν, μὰ παγίδας, μὰ νεφέλας, μὰ δίκτυα.

629. ἄπορον—helpless, shiftless, without a πόρος. Like most Greek adjectives it is usually active in force when used of a person; passive however Eur. *Bacch.* 800, ἀπόρῳ γε τῷδε συμπεπλέγμεθα ξένῳ etc. 'Awkward' does for both meanings. σκαιόν—cf. 790: *Vesp.* 1183, ὦ σκαιὲ κἀπαίδευτε.

630. σκαλαθυρμάτι'—'scraps, trifling quibbles,' formed from σκαλαθύρω=σκάλλω, to dig (*Eccl.* 611): or, according to the scholiast, from σκαλ(εύω-ευμα) and άθυρμα-ατιον, 'a toy, trifle.'

631. ὅμως γε μήν—so 822.

632. καλῶ—future, as in 452.

633. ἕξει—=ἔξιθι. Blaydes takes it as indicative and prints a question, 'will you come out?' τὸν ἀσκάντην—i.e. the σκίμπους of 254 and 709.

635. ἀνύσας τι—cf. 506. ἰδού—'there,' taking the place of a pupil.

638. ἐπῶν—not verses but words, their right use and form, which Protagoras and Prodicus insisted on. Their ὀρθοέπεια is illustrated 658 sq.

639. ἔναγχος—*Eccl.* 823: this word is always attached to past tenses. It never occurs in tragedy, νεωστί being used (*New Phrynichus*, p. 70).

640. παρεκόπην—'I was defrauded': *Eq.* 807, οἵων ἀγαθῶν παρεκόπτου: *ib.* 859. διχοινίκῳ must be explained as instrumental, 'by means of, in the matter of, a two-pint measure.' Blaydes adopts διχοινίκου, a regular construction; but the dative can be justified by such passages as Thuc. iv. 73, 4, τῷ βελτίστῳ τοῦ ὁπλιτικοῦ βλαφθῆναι.

644. οὐδὲν λέγεις—'nonsense'; 781: *Vesp.* 75 etc. περίδου... εἰ μή—Strepsiades proposes to bet that the half-gallon is 'a four-measure.' In English we bet that a thing *is* so and so; in Greek and Latin the layer of the wager engages to forfeit the stake *unless* he prove right: cf. *Ach.* 772, περίδου μοι περὶ θυματιδᾶν ἁλῶν, αἰ μή κ.τ.λ. περί is used of the stake, as in *Eq.* 791. In Latin we have the analogous use of *ni* with sponsionem facere, pignus dare, e.g. Cic. *Off.* iii. 19, 77, cum is sponsionem fecisset ni vir bonus esset: see Lewis and Short, *ni*, III B. For περίδου cf. Hom. *Il.* xxiii. 485, τρίποδος περιδώμεθον ἠὲ λέβητος, where the stake is expressed by the genitive of price.

645. τετράμετρον...ἡμιεκτέον—the half-*ἐκτεύς* was a 'four-measure,' as it contained 4 χοίνικες. Strepsiades as usual takes the most common and material view of what is proposed to him.

646. ἐς κόρακας, ὡς—'confound it, how clownish you are': only a comma should follow ἐς κόρακας: cf. 133.

647. ταχύ γ' ἄν—ironical, 'you look like a promising student of rhythms,' a more refined subject than metres: so Dem. *Meid.* 581 § 209, ταχύ γ' ἂν χαρίσαιντο, οὐ γάρ; τάχα δ' ἄν, 'perhaps you might,' is adopted by many editors.

648. **πρὸς τἄλφιτα**—cf. 176, 'to get my living.' Strepsiades may also refer to his dealings with the ἀλφιταμοιβός (640).

649. **πρῶτον μέν**—there is no answering δέ or εἶτα, as Socrates is interrupted. **εἶναι** is loosely constructed, 'tamquam praecessisset διδάξουσι' (Blaydes). **κομψόν**—'refined, neat.' The word is sometimes used in a good sense, sometimes in contempt. Here the meaning is that Strepsiades would learn to speak in company with grace and proper modulation. In Plato's *Republic* (400 B) there is a discussion on the rhythms which should be chosen as tending to propriety of life and speech.

651. **κατ' ἐνόπλιον**—sc. ῥυθμόν, what is the rhythm of the war tune: εἶδος ῥυθμοῦ πρὸς ὃν ὠρχοῦντο σείοντες τὰ ὅπλα (schol.). **κατὰ δάκτυλον**—'dactylic.'

653. **τίς ἄλλος**—Strepsiades as usual misunderstands, and points first one finger then another at Socrates in a vulgar derisive way. **ἀντί**—'instead of,' i.e. but, except; implying comparison and preference: cf. note on *Vesp.* 210.

654. **πρὸ τοῦ**—cf. 5. There seems something wrong about this line; μέν has nothing to answer it, and the sentence does not run clearly. 'Versus fortasse interpolatus' (Blaydes).

655. **ᾤζυρέ**—the penultimate is short, as in *Vesp.* 1504, 1514.

657. **τὸν ἀδικώτατον**—Blaydes reads τὸν ἄδικον τοῦτον as in 116; Meineke suggests τὸν ἀδικώτερον.

659. **ἅττ' ἐστὶν ὀρθῶς ἄρρενα**—Cope on Arist. *Rhet.* iii. 5, 5, calls Protagoras' classification of nouns the earliest attempt at Greek grammar.

661. **ἀλεκτρυών**—after the mention of this singular 'quadruped' Bentley suspects that two lines are lost, containing a fresh question from Socrates and a list of female creatures in answer, also ending with ἀλεκτρυών. This form served for either gender, as we see from Fragments 80 and 237: Blaydes also cites Phrynichus p. 228, λέγε δὲ ἀλεκτρυὼν καὶ ἐπὶ θήλεος καὶ ἐπὶ ἄρρενος, ὡς οἱ παλαιοί.

662. **πάσχεις**—nearly = ποιεῖς, 'what folly you let yourself utter.'

663. **ἀλεκτρυόνα**—Porson suggested the contracted form ἀλεκτρυῶ to avoid the concurrence of five short syllables. Blaydes read καὶ ταὐτὸ for κατὰ ταὐτό.

666. **ἀλεκτρύαιναν**—on the analogy of λέων λέαινα, θεράπων θεράπαινα, and various proper names. This form never came into use; ἀλεκτορίς is quoted from Aristotle.

669. **διαλφιτώσω κ.τ.λ.**—as we might say, 'I'll fill your sack with flour,' a suitable offer from a farmer; cf. 1146.

670. ἰδοὺ μάλ' αὖθις—so *Pac.* 5 etc. τὴν κάρδοπον ἄρρενα κ.τ.λ.—the point is that κάρδοπος being a feminine word has no business with a masculine ending in ος.

674. ταὐτὸν δύναται—'is equivalent'; qua masculine termination they stand on the same footing. σοι—for you, = 'you make it equivalent,' so ὑμῖν, 688.

675. οὐδ' ἦν—Strepsiades apparently understands that Cleonymus 'is identical with a kneading-trough'; and replies that on the contrary he never even had one.

676. ἀλλ' ἐν θυείᾳ—Cleonymus, says the scholiast, is here satirised as a needy parasite; so a mortar was big enough for any kneading he wanted at home.

677. τὸ λοιπόν—'henceforth'; conversely τὸν ἄλλον χρόνον is nearly always 'hitherto.'

680. ἐκεῖνο δ' ἦν ἄν—'then we should have had.' Blaydes, considering that the sense of the passage ought to be 'we should, or shall have,' suggests ἐκεῖνο τἄρ' ἦν 'then it seems it is,' or οὕτω γ' ἂν εἴη. Κλεωνύμη—suggesting the man's cowardice and effeminacy. So Horace calls a person in contempt *Pediatia* (*Sat.* i. 8. 39); and Cicero calls young Curio *filiola* Curionis (*Ep. Att.* i. 14, 5).

681. ἔτι δέ γε—various alterations are given for the unmetrical ἔτι γε of the manuscripts: of these ἔθ' ἕν τι gives excellent sense, if not too much of a change. ἕν τι is 'one definite thing,' ἕν γέ τι 'any one thing.' ὀνομάτων—here 'names'; ὄνομα being either *nomen* or *nomen proprium*.

684. Κλειταγόρα—a Thessalian poetess, according to the scholiast on *Vesp.* 1246, but the scholiast on *Lys.* 1225 calls her a Laconian.

686. Philoxenus is spoken of with contempt, *Vesp.* 84; and Amynias is satirised repeatedly in the same play as an effeminate sycophant. Melesias is perhaps the father of Thucydides, the opponent of Pericles.

688. ὑμῖν—'with you'; 674.

690. Ἀμυνία—thus the vocative termination is feminine. There is of course a gibe at the man's womanish character.

692. ἥτις οὐ—'inasmuch as she does not.' ὅστις μή is the usual construction when the meaning is 'whoever'; but here, though a general notion may be implied, a definite statement is made about a definite person.

694. οὐδέν—'not at all' is the meaning of this phrase in answer to a question, as shown by quotations in Blaydes. Here it seems no

answer. Dr Merry thinks the meaning may be οὐδὲν μανθάνεις ὧν πάντες ἴσμεν, you are not learning what everybody knows, but something rare. Mr Green takes it with τί μανθάνω; 'to what end am I learning?' 'To no end indeed.' Possibly it may refer to μανθάνω only, 'Learning? you're learning nothing.' τί δρῶ;—conjunctive, 'what am I to do.'

696. ἐνθάδ'—on the σκίμπους, which seems to have been essential; see 254: Strepsiades has sufficient reason already to regard it with apprehension (634).

698. οὐκ ἔστι παρὰ ταῦτ' ἄλλα—seemingly a catchword of the day, and probably a quotation from some tragedy. It occurs *Vesp.* 1166, also followed by κακοδαίμων ἐγώ: *Pac.* 110: cf. Plat. *Gorg.* 507 A, οὐκ ἔχω παρὰ ταῦτ' ἄλλα φάναι.

Socrates now goes in, returning at 723. Strepsiades is left on his bed.

699. οἵαν—relative, as in 1158.

700—705. The chorus encourage Strepsiades 'to think out things for himself.' The *strophe* seems to have been left imperfect, as there is nothing corresponding to verses 812, 813 in the *antistrophe.*

701. πυκνώσας—'condensing yourself,' i.e. concentrating your mind, συναγαγὼν πάντα τὸν νοῦν σου (schol.). It may also suggest 'packing yourself tight' in the bed-clothes.

703. ὅταν εἰς ἄπορον πέσῃς—a cut at Socrates, says the scholiast, who when he found himself in a difficulty μεθίσταται εἰς ἕτερον. Socrates advises his pupil in the same spirit, 743.

704. πήδα—Eur. *Troad.* 67, τί δ' ὧδε πηδᾷς ἄλλοτ' εἰς ἄλλους τρόπους;

710. Κορίνθιοι—παρ' ὑπόνοιαν for κόρεις, with an allusion to the rapacity of the Corinthians, who, as the scholiast suggests, may at this time have been threatening Attica.

712. τὴν ψυχὴν ἐκπίνουσιν—'are draining my life-blood'; Soph.

El. 785, τούμὸν ἐκπίνουσ' ἀεὶ ψυχῆs ἄκρατον αἷμα. Note the rhyming ending of these lines; we have something like it 305 sq.

716. μή νυν—Blaydes compares *Pac.* 83, μή μοι σοβαρῶs χώρει λίαν.

717. καὶ πῶs—sc. οὐκ ἀλγῶ; how am I to help it?

718. φρούδη χροιά —hard thinking, he feels, tells on him already; he is on his way to be like Chaerephon (503): cf. 103 and 120.

719. ἐμβάs—see 858. He may have taken off his shoes, like his cloak (497), on entering. At any rate bare feet were philosophical; cf. 103.

721. φρουρᾶs ᾄδων—the sound of φροῦδοs suggests this phrase. The sentry proverbially 'sings on his watch' to keep himself awake, like the watcher in Aesch. *Ag.* 16. Strepsiades 'means that instead of sleeping he cries out as he is bitten by the κόρεις' (Merry). The genitive φρουρᾶs is generally explained on the analogy of νυκτόs, ἑσπέραs, like αἰθρίαs (371).

722. ὀλίγου —sc. δέων, 'all but'; *Vesp.* 829, ὀλίγου μ' ἀπώλεσας.

723. οὗτος τί ποιεῖς;—Socrates comes back, to see about his pupil's progress. In 732 he does just the same; and, as Teuffel points out, this scene is full of such inconsistencies and repetitions. Teuffel therefore assigns verses 700—706 and 731—739 to the first edition of the *Clouds*; 691—699, 707—730 and 740—745 to the second.

726. ἀπόλωλ' ἀρτίως —so the threat of ἀπολεῖ comes too late.

727. μαλθακιστέ'—Plat. *Alc.* i. 124 D, οὐκ ἀποκνητέον οὐδὲ μαλθακιστέον, ὦ ἑταῖρε. For the plural cf. *Ach.* 394, βαδιστέα: *ib.* 480, ἐμπορευτέα. Strepsiades is to face the κόρεις bravely, veiled like a neophyte initiated in the school of Pythagoras (Blaydes).

729. ἀπαιόλημ'.—Aesch. *Choeph.* 1002, ξένων ἀπαιόλημα: Eur. *Ion* 549, τοῦτο κἄμ' ἀπαιολεῖ 'puzzles.' As Mr Green says, 'the first sense would probably be to dazzle or confuse by quick motion, as one might do by sleight of hand: cf. *praestigiae, praestringere.*' 'Quickly moving' is the primary sense of αἰόλος. ἐπιβάλοι κ.τ.λ.—'invest me with—an aptitude for fleecing.'

730. ἐξ ἀρνακίδων—as if the ἀρνακίs were connected with ἀρνεῖσθαι. γνώμην—'plan, device.' ἀποστερητρίs is formed like αὐλητρίs, ὀρχηστρίs, from αὐλητήs etc.

731. ἀθρήσω—aorist subj. with φέρε. ἔρχεται πάλιν ἐπ' αὐτὸν ὁ Σωκράτηs is the scholiast's comment on this line, but it seems rather to have been meant for the master's first reappearance, as noted on 723. μὰ τόν κ.τ.λ.—'not I, by Apollo'; so *Eq.* 14 etc.

733. ἔχεις τι; —as if asking a hunter or fisher.

740. σχάσας—see note on 107. Here σχάσας seems the converse of πυκνώσας (701): 'the old man is to loosen and spread out his thoughts over various matters: not to keep them too close and concentrated' (Green).

The predicate λεπτήν shows that the thought is to spread like a thin and subtle film. 'Cutting your thought fine' is another rendering; while Merry prefers 'checking the play of your subtle thought,' like πυκνώσας, and Blaydes takes a similar view.

741. κατὰ μικρόν –'little by little': the disciple is to consider details and particulars. For περιφρόνει cf. 225.

742. διαιρῶν—'division' of genus into species, κατ' εἴδη διαιρεῖσθαι τὰ ὄντα (Plat. *Phaedr.* 273 E), was essential for true reasoning. οἴμοι τάλας—'a cimicibus morsus exclamat' (Blaydes).

743. ἔχ' ἀτρέμα see note on 261. κἂν ἀπορῇς τι—a mere repetition of the idea in 702.

744. τὴν γνώμην...αὐτό —a disputed sentence, the question being about the accusatives. Reiske cuts the knot by reading τῇ γνώμῃ, and many editors approve. Still on the whole I think Dindorf's view the best, that αὐτὸ καὶ ξυγάθρισον is put for καὶ ξυγώθρισον αὐτό. There are instances of such an order, e.g. *Pac.* 417: and this view avoids altering τὴν γνώμην κίνησον, which seems certainly right. 'Stir up your mind' is natural, but 'stir it up,' start it, 'in your mind' (i.e. τὸ νόημα, your idea), is not so probable. For suggested alterations see the critical note.

ξυγώθρισον—from ξύγωθρον, in the sense of a bar, according to Pollux, =κλεῖσον 'bar it in,' secure it. Another traditional explanation is that ξύγωθρον is the beam of a balance, like ξυγόν, giving the meaning 'weigh it.'

746. Σωκρατίδιον—cf. 80 and 222.

748. τὸ τί;—'what is it?': so *Pac.* 826, ἴθι νυν κάτειπέ μοι. ΤΡ. τὸ τί; So the article is used with ποῖος when something said before requires explanation.

749. Θετταλήν—Thessaly was the country of witches.

750. καθέλοιμι...τὴν σελήνην—Plat. *Gorg.* 513, τὰς τὴν σελήνην καθαιρούσας, τὰς Θετταλίδας: Hor. *Epod.* 5. 45, quae sidera excantata voce Thessala lunamque caelo deripit: Verg. *Ecl.* viii. 69, carmina vel caelo possunt deducere lunam.

751. αὑτήν—beginning a line, as if we had a prose sentence.

752. ὥσπερ κάτοπτρον—plainly a round mirror like the full moon. The crest-case, as Mr Green shows, was most likely round (and flat).

754. σελήνη—no article; so 626. The moon regulated the calendar, and brought on pay-day: cf. 17.

755. ότιὴ τί δή;—'because why?'; cf. 784: *Plut.* 136. Blaydes here reads τιὴ τί δή; with some manuscript authority.

757. προβαλῶ—see 489; our *problem*.

758. γράφοιτο—'if a suit were entered against you.' This is a true and reasonable passive; but γράφομαι is usually middle, 'to indict.' Hence Blaydes' note, 'corrigendum existimabam πεντετάλαντόν τις δίκην, sed obstat dativus σοι, dicebant enim γράφεσθαί τινα (non τινι) δίκην.' We may add that, though a γραφή could be called a δίκη in a general sense, γράφομαι δίκην is not a customary phrase, and could not be used of bringing a civil action (λαγχάνειν δίκην), which is meant here.

759. ὅπως ἄν—cf. 776.

761. μή νυν—a repetition of the advice in 740, as Mr Green rightly notes. What Socrates fears is narrowness and self-centred thought, and he enjoins a freer and wider range.

762. ἀποχάλα—compare what Socrates says, 227 sq.

763. λινόδετον...τοῦ ποδός—'tied to a thread by the foot': Hom. *Il.* xxiii. 853, πέλειαν δῆσεν ποδός: Hdt. v. 16, παιδία δέουσι τοῦ ποδὸς σπάρτῳ: cf. *Vesp.* 369, for gen. with ἕλκω.

ὥσπερ μηλολόνθην—as the cockchafer was tied to a thread, so the thought was to have its flight but not to stray beyond control.

766. ἤδη...ἑόρακας—cf. 370. φαρμακοπώλαις—the sellers of precious stones, says the scholiast, were anciently called φαρμακοπῶλαι, as such stones had occult virtues. Rather perhaps stones of magic or medical value would naturally be kept by φαρμακοπῶλαι.

768. ὕαλον—a crystal lens: Kuster quotes Plin. *Nat. Hist.* xxxvii. 10, 28, invenio apud medicos quae sint urenda corporum non aliter utilius uri putari quam crystallina pila adversis opposita solis radiis.

770. ὁπότε γράφοιτο—after the plaintiff had made the deposits in a civil action, it was the duty of the magistrate before whom the case came to placard the declaration on a tablet for the inspection of the public (Dict. Ant. *dike*). I do not understand the middle γράφοιτο in this passage. Surely the γραμματεύς was the person who actually made the entry on the tablet, ὁ γράφων τὰ λεγόμενα ἐν ταῖς δίκαις as the scholiast says, and the verb would be γράφω (or ἐγγράφω), not γράφομαι. γράφομαι is to get written, or to write for one's own use. The technical γράφομαί τινα, 'I indict a man,' is literally 'I get his name entered' for trial, and is properly used of the prosecutor. Thus Dem. *Dionys.* 1284,

§ 6, συγγραφήν εγράψαντο is 'they had a bond drawn up': *Vesp.* 537, μνημόσυνα γράψομαι, 'I will make notes (for my own use)'; so *ib.* 576. We should expect ὁπότε γράφοι τὰς δίκας, as the sense of the line is general, the particular case coming in afterwards.

772. τὰ γράμματα—the actual letters, or the entry generally, on the waxed tablet: see Dict. Ant. *tabulae*.

773. νὴ τὰς Χάριτας—the device being clever and pretty, Χαρίτων γὰρ ἔργα καὶ δῶρα σοφία. The scholiast also says that a sculpture of the Charites was a work of Socrates himself in his early days; but this reminiscence is somewhat out of place.

οἴμοι, which is more often used in sorrow or indignation, here expresses joy.

774. διαγέγραπται—'cancelled,' lit. 'crossed out'; Dem. *Lept.* 501, § 145, πεισθεὶς ὑπὸ σοῦ διεγράψατο.

775. ξυνάρπασον—'take in': Soph. *Aj.* 16, ξυναρπάζω φρενί. Here there seems the same idea as in ὑφαρπάσει 490.

776. ὅπως ἄν—'how you might'; see Goodwin, § 330. For the reading see the critical note, and cf. 759. Attic usage is against the 2nd sing. opt. in -σαις, which should be -σειας: so in *Vesp.* 819, Brunck proposed εἴ πως ἐκκομίσειας for ἐκκομίσαις: see *New Phrynichus* p. 439. Whatever the reading, the question was how to rebut an adverse judgment, which Strepsiades might incur from want of evidence on his side. The scholiast supposes him here to be in danger of the penalty for bringing an unsupported accusation. ἀντιδικῶν—participle.

777. ὀφλήσειν—so 34: Aesch. *Ag.* 534, ὀφλὼν...κλοπῆς δίκην.

778. φαυλότατα—i.e. most easily: see note on λόγισαι φαύλως, 'calculate roughly,' *Vesp.* 656. καὶ δὴ λέγω—*Av.* 175, βλέψον κάτω. ΕΙΙ. καὶ δὴ βλέπω. Strepsiades is now quite elated, and confident of his cleverness.

779. ἐνεστώσης—'pending,' not yet finished: Dem. *Apatur.* 896, § 13, ἐνεστηκυίας τῆς δίκης.

780. καλεῖσθαι—*Vesp.* 830, τὴν δίκην καλεῖν: *ib.* 1441, with ὁ ἄρχων: so often in Demosthenes.

781. οὐδέν κ.τ.λ.—'Nonsense.' ST. 'It's not,' cf. 644: *Vesp.* 75, οὐδὲν λέγει. ΣΩ. μὰ Δία, 'that's nonsense.' So. 'It is indeed.'

782. οὐδείς...εἰσάξει δίκην—note that εἰσάγω with δίκην expressed or understood is always used of the presiding magistrate. In Aesch. *Eum.* 580—2, Liddell and Scott unaccountably make Athene the prosecutor; she was the president of the court. But εἰσάγειν τινά is

used of the prosecutor, as in line 845. So in the other passage cited by Liddell and Scott, Dem. *Timocr.* 703 § 10, γραψάμενοι τὸν νόμον καὶ εἰσαγαγόντες εἰς ὑμᾶς, the offending νόμος is to be indicted and brought into court by the prosecutors.

783. ὑθλεῖς—φλυαρεῖς· ὕθλος γὰρ ὁ φλύαρος (schol.). The substantive is used by Plato and Demosthenes. διδάξαιμ' ἄν, a correction due to Elmsley, is accepted by most editors, the double ἄν being common enough. Reiske reads διδάξαιμεν, Kock prefers οὐ γὰρ διδάξαιμ' ἄν. διδάσκομαι, 'to get taught,' is most inapplicable here. In Plat. *Rep.* 421 E, where διδάξεται is used of the teacher, Cobet reads διδάξει.

785. ἅττ' ἂν καὶ μάθῃς—'whatever you *have* learned': Thuc. iv. 11, 4, εἴ πῃ καὶ δοκοίη δυνατὸν εἶναι σχεῖν, if at any point it *did* seem possible to land.

787. τί μέντοι—μέντοι is often used in a question, like our 'why, what was it?'

788. ματτόμεθα—trying to recollect his lesson about κάρδοπος and καρδόπη, 670 sq. Blaydes reads ᾽ματτόμεθα, which may be right, as referring to the time when the lesson was given.

789. οὐκ ἐς κόρακας ἀποφθερεῖ;—so *Eq.* 892: *Pac.* 500, οὐκ ἐς κόρακας ἐρρήσετε;

790. ἐπιλησμότατον—as if from ἐπίλησμος. Eur. *Hec.* 369 has εὐσχήμως, but εὔσχημος is actually found.

792. ἀπὸ γὰρ ὀλοῦμαι—so 1440: *Vesp.* 780, ἀνά τοί με πείθεις. γλωττοστροφεῖν—*Ran.* 892, γλώττης στρόφιγξ.

798. ἀλλ' οὐκ ἐθέλει γάρ—cf. *Vesp.* 318, ἀλλ' οὐ γὰρ οἷός τ' ἔτ' εἴμ' ᾄδειν, τί ποιήσω; τί πάθω = what am I to do? *Av.* 1432, τί γὰρ πάθω; σκάπτειν γὰρ οὐκ ἐπίσταμαι.

800. εὐπτέρων—'well-feathered,' might imply 'vigorous' as Mr Green suggests; or it may be 'high-flying,' ὑπερηφάνων, μέγα φρονουσῶν, or εὐγενῶν (schol.).

803. This verse is practically repeated in 843, and is therefore struck out here by Kock and Meineke.

805—12. 'While Strepsiades is gone after his son, the Chorus congratulate Socrates on the advantages he will get out of his dupe, advising him to make hay while the sun shines' (Green). The ode may have been consistent with the first *Clouds*; see note on 723. It is scarcely in agreement with what goes before as we now have it, for Strepsiades was not bidden by Socrates to fetch his son, but simply to take himself off, nor was he an eager scholar, but a rejected dunce.

810. ἀνδρός—the genitive is probably governed by ἀπολάψεις, but it might be absolute. ἐκπεπληγμένου—'excited,' rather than 'amazed' or 'bewildered': so in Thuc. v. 66, 1, ἐξεπλάγησαν ' were excited ': id. vii. 43, 6, ἐκπεπληγμένοι: iv. 14, 3, ὑπὸ προθυμίας καὶ ἐκπλήξεως.

811. γνούς—' seeing (this),' i.e. seizing the occasion. ἀπολάψεις—lit. 'you must lap up from him,' i.e. make the most out of him you can. The proper Attic future is λάψομαι, as shown *Pac.* 885, ἐκλάψεται, but the active form might stand in a chorus. The scholiast however gives ἀπολέψεις, 'you will skin': while a few manuscripts have ἀπολαύσεις, which suggests Hermann's ἀπολαύσαις, as the future is ἀπολαύσομαι: see *New Phrynichus* p. 393 and 409.

814. Strepsiades comes on the stage with his son, threatening to turn him out of doors if he will not go to school. οὗτοι κ.τ.λ.—cf. *Vesp.* 1442, οὔ τοι μὰ τὴν Δήμητρ' ἔτ' ἐνταυθὶ μενεῖς. Here Strepsiades swears by Mist, in imitation of the master, cf. 627.

815. ἀλλ' ἔσθ'...κίονας—the traditional explanation is that Megacles had wasted his fortune on his horses, only the pillars of his hall attesting his former magnificence. But is there any evidence of this? In lines 70 and 124 Megacles is the splendid noble; and the meaning may be 'get what you can from your uncle's pillars,' i.e. in his palace or his stable-yard.

817. μὰ τὸν Δία—the final α in Δία is lengthened by metric stress: Meineke reads μὰ τὸν Δί' οὔ.

818. ἰδού γ' ἰδού—repeating his words in contempt: *Eq.* 87, ἰδού γ' ἄκρατον: *ib.* 344, ἰδοὺ λέγειν. τῆς μωρίας—cf. 153.

819. τὸ Δία νομίζειν—for the construction see 268: for νομίζω 'to acknowledge, believe in,' cf. Xen. *Mem.* i. 1, 1, οὓς ἡ πόλις νομίζει θεοὺς οὐ νομίζων, part of the indictment of Socrates.

820. ἐγέλασας—cf. 174; and for ἐτεόν 35.

821. παιδάριον εἶ—a mere child with nursery notions, though you are old enough to know better. φρονεῖς—*Vesp.* 507, φρονῶν τυραννικά.

822. ὅμως γε μήν—so 631.

824. ὅπως δέ—the caution is an echo of 143. For the construction cf. 1177 and 1464. The greater number of examples are in the colloquial language of Aristophanes (Goodwin § 271 sq.). The earliest instance is Aesch. *Prom.* 68.

825. ἰδού—approaching, as ordered: so 255.

829. αἰβοῖ—γελῶν λέγει (schol.), in contemptuous disgust ; cf. 102.

830. ὁ Μήλιος—Diagoras of Melos was reputed an atheist, so Socrates is here called the Melian.

831. τὰ ψυλλῶν ἴχνη—see 144.

832. τῶν μανιῶν—Blaydes reads τοσουτονὶ μανιῶν, comparing Eur. *Troad.* 972, ἐς τοσοῦτον ἀμαθίας ἐλθεῖν, and many other examples. The article may however be explained as meaning 'have you got so far in your frenzies?' The plural is not uncommon: compare the old English 'lunes.'

833. χολῶσιν—cf. *Pac.* 66, where ἡ χολή means madness, μανίαι coming in the line before. εὐστόμει—=εὐφήμει: Aesch. *Choeph.* 997, κἂν τύχω μάλ' εὐστομῶν: Soph. *Phil.* 201, εὔστομ' ἔχε, ἀντὶ τοῦ σιώπα (schol.): cf. Hdt. ii. 171.

835. ὑπὸ τῆς φειδωλίας—this gibe comes in well, as Strepsiades is preaching economy. The dirty ways of the philosophers who affected hardiness are often jeered at. Socrates in particular was noted for avoiding the baths: *Av.* 1282, ἐκόμων, ἐπείνων, ἐρρύπων, ἐσωκράτων: *ib.* 1554, ἄλουτος Σωκράτης.

838. ὥσπερ τεθνεώτος—like washing a corpse. καταλόει— 'you bathe away,' spend on your bathing. Blaydes suspects that the active καταλοεῖς 'wash away, waste,' should be read, as baths were not yet an extravagant luxury. Besides the accusative following the middle looks suspicious. For the forms of λούω see *New Phrynichus*, p. 275. All the manuscripts here have καταλούει, and possibly that form should be retained, as it is quite possible to consider the diphthong short like the οι in ποιῶ and τοιοῦτος. As a rule those persons in which the ending is preceded by a short connecting vowel ε or ο are supplied as if from λόω, and contract the o of the stem with the connecting vowel. Thus λούω, λούεις, λούουσι, but λοῦμεν, ἔλουν. τὸν βίον—παρὰ προσδοκίαν instead of τὸ σῶμα.

840. καὶ μάθοι—cf. 785.

841. ἄληθες;—note the change of accent when ἄληθες is used as an exclamation.

843. ἐνταυθί—most MSS. have ἐνταυθοῖ, as in 814. ἐνταυθοῖ repeatedly occurs in manuscripts where 'here' is the meaning

required: it has mostly been altered. See Shilleto's full critical note on Dem. *Fals. leg.* 441 § 356. The father now goes in.

845. **παρανοίας...ἕλω**—'am I to indict and convict him of lunacy?': see Dict. Ant. *παρανοίας δίκη*. The construction is like *Vesp.* 1207, Φαΰλλον εἷλον διώκων λοιδορίας: cf. 591. **εἰσαγαγών**—'bringing (him) before the court,' as prosecutor: εἰσάγειν δίκην is different; see note on 782.

846. **τοῖς σοροπηγοῖς**—cf. ναυπηγός, ἀσπιδοπηγός, ἁρματοπηγός, ἅμαξαν πήξασθαι, νῆας πῆξαι and πήξασθαι. The son thinks it may be old age that has crazed his father. Strepsiades now comes back with a cock and a hen, to show his son the value of learning; see 660 sq.

850. **καλεῖν**—for 2nd person imperative; so 1080: cf. note on *Vesp.* 386.

853. **τοὺς γηγενεῖς**—'those Sons of Earth' (Merry). They were enemies of the gods, like the Giants and Titans, and moreover they dwelt underground (508).

854. **ὅ τι μάθοιμ'**—optative of indefinite frequency.

855. **ἐπελανθανόμην ἄν**—iterative, see note on 54. Some manuscripts here omit ἄν and have τῶν ἐτῶν.

857. **καταπεφρόντικα**—'I have thought it away': *Eq.* 1352, καταμισθοφορῆσαι τοῦτο, to spend it all on fees.

858. **ποῖ**—*Vesp.* 665, ποῖ τρέπεται τὰ χρήματα; **τέτροφας**— perfect of τρέπω: so apparently Soph. *Trach.* 1009, ἀνατέτροφας: Dem. *de Cor.* 324 § 296, ἀνατετροφότες.

859. **ὥσπερ Περικλῆς**—Pericles was believed to have bribed the Spartan king Pleistoanax and Cleandridas the ephor to withdraw their troops from Attica, and charged the sum to 'needful expenditure': see Plutarch, *Per.* ch. 22 and 23: cf. Thuc. ii. 21, 1. One scholiast refers the story to a charge of peculation in connivance with Phidias. **ἀπώλεσα**—for Pericles' ἀνήλωσα.

861. **πιθόμενος**—after you have complied with my wishes, by going to school. πειθόμενος, the ordinary reading, would go closely with ἐξάμαρτε, 'commit the iniquities I would have you.'

862. **οἶδ'**—joined with πιθόμενος· ὅν...'πριάμην following without a connecting word. Otherwise οἶδα is parenthetical, and κἀγώ goes with πριάμην. Kock suggests οἶσθ' parenthetically placed.

863. **ὀβολόν**—paying the dicasts was instituted by Pericles. The fee, says the scholiast, varied in amount. Apparently it was at first an obol and was raised to three obols by Cleon.

864. **τούτου**—cf. 22, 876. **Διασίοις**—see 408. **ἁμαξίδα**—

a toy waggon, as in 880. The scholiast adds ἢ πλακοῦντος εἶδος, as if it were a gingerbread horse and cart. For the diminutive termination cf. χυτρίς, μαχαιρίς etc.

866. εὖ γ'—applauding and encouraging his son who is now ready to enter the school: cf. euge tuum et belle, Pers. i. 49.

869. κρεμαθρῶν—instead of μαθημάτων, referring to 218 and 229, and giving occasion for the pun which follows. The long a in κρεμαθρῶν troubles the commentators; who to avoid it suggest καὶ τῶν γε, or κρεμαστρῶν, or οὔπω τρίβων.

τρίβων—'versed in'; *Vesp.* 1429, τρίβων ἱππικῆς. In the next line Pheidippides means an old cloak, which Socrates would look like if he were hung up. The suggestion of hanging Socrates calls forth the rebuke in line 871.

872. ἰδού—cf. 818. Socrates is shocked at the boy's broad and boorish pronunciation of the diphthong.

873. διερρυηκόσιν—διακεχηνόσι schol.; wide and gaping.

875. κλῆσιν—'summoning,' implying the act of plaintiff and accuser generally. χαύνωσιν—'invalidation,' as Mr Green suggests: making the adversary's arguments seem χαῦνοι and ἀσθενεῖς, or perhaps imposing on the jurors with such arguments.

876. Ὑπέρβολος—stupid and vulgar as he was—so no one need despair who will pay high enough.

877. ἀμέλει—cf. 422. θυμόσοφος—*Vesp.* 1280, θυμοσοφικώτατον.

878. ὄν—in agreement with παιδάριον. Blaydes shows by many examples that ὄν and ὤν are equally right in this construction: cf. 917. τυννουτονί—'only so big,' δεικτικῶς (schol.): *Ran.* 139, ἐν πλοιαρίῳ τυννουτῳί.

879. ἔπλαττεν κ.τ.λ.—cf. Hor. *Sat.* ii. 3, 247, aedificare casas.

881. πῶς δοκεῖς—lit. 'how think you?' here printed without a question as it has lost its interrogative force. *Ach.* 24, ὡστιοῦνται πῶς δοκεῖς ἀλλήλοισιν: so πῶς οἴει, *Ran.* 54.

883. This line is repeated from 113: Dobree would omit it here. Meineke and others consider the next line spurious.

885. πάσῃ τέχνῃ—'by all means'; so 1323: *Eq.* 592 etc.

887. ἀπέσομαι—Meineke follows Bentley in reading ἄπειμι as in *Them.* 277. μέμνησ', ὅπως...δυνήσεται—cf. 1107, μέμνησ' ὅπως στομώσεις. The construction with the 3rd person here, and in 882, is practically equivalent to 'see that you make him learn, see that you teach him how.'

888. δίκαι'—merely 'pleas,' arguments, according to Blaydes, but just arguments may be meant: so 1339.

Socrates and Strepsiades now leave the stage, and Pheidippides remains with the chorus. A choral ode would naturally follow; but the poet left this part incomplete when remodelling the play. The omission is thus noted by the scholiast, μέλος δὲ τοῦ χοροῦ οὐ κεῖται, ἀλλὰ γέγραπται μὲν ἐν μέσῳ χοροῦ,—τὸ τοῦ χοροῦ πρόσωπον ἐκλέλοιπεν ἐπιγραφὴ δὲ φέρεται χοροῦ, i.e. though there is no ode, the word ΧΟΡΟΥ is added as the remains of a stage direction.

889—1104. The just and unjust Arguments now appear on the stage, represented by the actors who had lately personified Socrates and Strepsiades. They are dressed, according to the scholiast, like fighting cocks, and are brought on in wicker cages. However this may have been, the δίκαιος or κρείττων λόγος bears the part of straightforward justice, and old-fashioned ways; while the ἄδικος or ἥττων λόγος personifies modern immorality, with all its tricks of sophistry and rhetoric.

This part of the play belongs to the second *Clouds*.

891. ἴθ' ὅποι χρῄζεις—from the *Telephus* of Euripides, says the scholiast. Telephus comes in again in 922.

892. ἐν τοῖς πολλοῖσι—crowds being most easily carried away by the arts of the rhetorician. There is a notable passage to this effect in Plato's *Republic*, 492 B.

893. τίς ὤν;—for this participial form of question cf. 895 and 900: so *Ach.* 45 etc. **ἥττων γ' ὤν**—'yes, the worse.' Blaydes reads ΑΔ. λόγος ἥττων ὤν.

894. σὲ νικῶ—'nunc et semper. Anglice, I'm your master' (Blaydes).

897. ἀνθεῖ—cf. 962. **διὰ τουτουσί**—pointing to the audience, 'thanks to their folly.'

905. τὸν πατέρ' αὑτοῦ—Plat. *Euthyphr.* 6 A, τοῦτον (Δία) ὁμολογοῦσι τὸν αὑτοῦ πατέρα δῆσαι: Aesch. *Eum.* 641, αὐτὸς δ' ἔδησε πατέρα πρεσβύτην Κρόνον. No editor that I know of questions the reading here, though the regular order of words is ὁ αὑτοῦ (τούτου etc.) πατήρ, but ὁ πατὴρ αὐτοῦ, ἐμοῦ etc.: see note on 515.

906. αἰβοῖ—expressing disgust.   τουτὶ κ.τ.λ.—so *Vesp.* 1483: *Ran.* 1018. Dr Blaydes has a full collection of instances of the use of καὶ δή, 'even now,' nearly equivalent to ἤδη. It is also used for 'granted that'; as in *Vesp.* 1224, καὶ δὴ γάρ εἰμ' ἐγὼ Κλέων, 'suppose me to be Cleon.'

907. χωρεῖ—'is advancing, spreading.'   λεκάνην—λείπει τὸ ἵνα ἐμέσω (schol.): cf. *Ach.* 583.

908. τυφογέρων—so *Lys.* 335: *Vesp.* 1364, τυφεδανός.   ἀνάρμοστος—μηδενὶ ἁρμοζόμενος, or ἄρρυθμος, ἄμουσος (schol.): unsuited to company, or out of tune with modern ways.

910. ῥόδα μ' εἴρηκας—so κακόν τινα λέγειν and the like.

911. κρίνεσι—irregular dative, like δένδρεσι and κλάδεσι, though no nominative κρίνος occurs: so σάββασι in Greek Test.

912. χρυσῷ πάττων—so καταχρυσοῦν, *Eccl.* 826: Lat. *inaurare*.

913. οὐ δῆτα—i.e. in old times my words would not have seemed compliments. For πρὸ τοῦ cf. 5.   μολύβδῳ—a worthless metal, contrasted with gold. Dr Merry thinks there may be an allusion to beating with a whip loaded with lead.

915. πολλοῦ—so πολλὴ πολλοῦ, *Ran.* 1046: cf. *Eq.* 822. Equivalent to πάνυ, according to Suidas. It is apparently genitive of value.

916. φοιτᾶν—'to go to school,' as in 938: Dem. *de Cor.* 315, § 265, ἐδίδασκες γράμματα, ἐγὼ δ' ἐφοίτων.

920. αὐχμεῖς κ.τ.λ.—nowadays virtue is shabby and squalid, while vice is sleek and prosperous.

922. Τήλεφος—Telephus was Euripides' pet character, or at any rate Aristophanes' pet butt, as a hero in rags with a mouth full of philosophical talk; see *Ach.* 430 sq.

924. γνώμας...Πανδελετείους—Pandeletus, says the scholiast, συκοφάντης ἦν καὶ φιλόδικος, γράφων ψηφίσματα. The ἄδικος λόγος battened on his rascally 'maxims' or 'resolutions.'

926. ἧς ἐμνήσθης—'which you speak of,' i.e. the cleverness of Telephus and Euripides. The first οἴμοι therefore expresses admiration or regret.

929. Κρόνος—cf. 928.

935. ἐπίδειξαι σύ τε...τε—so *Vesp.* 452, ἀλλ' ἄφες με καὶ σὺ καὶ σύ.

938. κρίνας φοιτᾷ—may decide on his master.

945. ἢν ἀναγρύξῃ—'if he utter a sound'; cf. 963: *Eq.* 294, εἴ τι γρύξεις: *Vesp.* 373, ἐὰν γρύξῃ τι.

948. ὑπὸ τῶν—see critical note; Meineke's suggestion is meant to avoid the repetition of ὑπό.

949—60. The chorus exhorts the champions to do their best in view of the mighty issue at stake.

949. πισύνω—*Vesp.* 385, ὑμῖν πίσυνος: *Pac.* 84, ῥώμῃ πίσυνος.

950. γνωμοτύποις μερίμναις—'maxim-coining cares': *Ran.* 877, ἀνδρῶν γνωμοτύπων: *Thesm.* 55, γνωμοτυπεῖ.

955. ἀνεῖται—'is let loose, is started,' a metaphor from hounds let loose, is Mr Green's rendering. But does this go well with κίνδυνος? The scholiast says κεῖται, δέδοται· νῦν προκεῖται ἡμῖν ὑπὲρ ἁπάσης τῆς σοφίας κινδυνεῦσαι. ἀνεῖται then seemingly means 'is allowed.' Dr Merry says 'is set going.'

957. ἀλλ', ὦ—cf. *Vesp.* 546; *Ran.* 1004.

960. ῥῆξον—357, ῥήξατε φωνήν.

962. ἤνθουν—cf. 897. **'νενόμιστο**—'was in vogue'; 1185: so νομίζειν θεούς etc. Note the use of perfect and pluperfect: νενόμισται = 'it is an established custom.'

963. πρῶτον μέν—commonly followed by εἶτα (or ἔπειτα) without δέ. **γρύξαντος**—945.

964. βαδίζειν—sc. ἔδει. **ἐς κιθαριστοῦ**—so ἐς διδασκάλου etc. The κιθαριστής took up the education of Athenian boys at the age of thirteen, and taught them music and poetry. Before that they were under a γραμματιστής. No mention is here made of this; possibly, as Teuffel suggests, because there was no great difference between old and modern ways.

965. τοὺς κωμήτας—the boys of the same κώμη, ward or quarter, *vicus*. **γυμνούς**—in the χιτών only, not muffled up like the modern boys in 987. **κριμνώδη**—'thick as barley-meal' (κρίμνον).

966. ἐδίδασκεν—sc. ὁ κιθαριστής.

967. Παλλάδα κ.τ.λ.—first words of songs written, the one by Lamprocles, the other by Cydias of Hermione. **Τηλέπορόν τι βόαμα**—'some loud strain,' sc. λύρας.

968. ἐντειναμένους τὴν ἁρμονίαν—'keeping up the key' (Merry); 'with the earnest severe harmony of the olden time' (Green). The Dorian style is meant, which was calm and serious, not passionate and excited like the Phrygian, or soft and plaintive like the Lydian; see Dr Merry's note. ἐντείνεσθαι φωνήν is 'to raise the voice.'

970. βωμολοχεύσαιτ'—'play the buffoon'; do anything unfit for serious and dignified music. **καμπήν**—'turn, flourish'; cf. 333, ᾀσματοκάμπτας.

971. κατὰ Φρῦνιν—'i,, le of Phrynis'; a Lesbian who won the prize at the P ather   ἄρχοντος Καλλίου. He was charged with spoiling th   f m   ., τὸν ἴδιον στρόβιλον ἐμβαλών τινα, 'introducing turns a..d   .es of his own.' δυσκολοκάμπτους— difficult and complicated.

972. ἐπετρίβετο—cf. 1376 and 1407. πολλάς—sc. πληγάς, cognate: Dem. *Fals. Leg.* 403 § 197, ξαίνει κατὰ τοῦ νώτου πολλάς: so S. Luc. xii. 47, δαρήσεται πολλάς. τὰς Μούσας ἀφανίζων— 'spoiling the art of music'; Thuc. vii. 69, 2, τὰς πατρικὰς ἀρετὰς μὴ ἀφανίζειν.

981. ἀνελέσθαι—*Ach.* 810, μίαν (ἰσχάδα) ἀνειλόμην: cf. Hom. *Il.* i. 449, οὐλοχύτας ἀνέλοντο, 'took up barley grains in their hands.' Hdt. iv. 128, σῖτα ἀναιρεόμενοι, 'foraging.' δειπνοῦντ'—the accusative and infinitive form the subject of ἐξῆν, a not uncommon construction. κεφάλαιον—i.e. the bulb, root: *Vesp.* 679, σκορόδου κεφαλήν. Dr Blaydes reads καὶ φυλλεῖον instead of κεφάλαιον τῆς, in order to get rid of the article. But surely the stalk of a radish is not much of a delicacy.

982. τῶν πρεσβυτέρων ἁρπάζειν—'to snatch away from'; 'senioribus praeripere' (Blaydes): cf. *Pac.* 1118, ἁρπάσομαι σφῶν αὐτά.

983. κιχλίζειν—'to giggle,' like a thrush: cf. Theocr. *Id.* xi. 78. Another rendering is 'to be dainty,' as thrushes were choice morsels.

984. ἀρχαῖά γε—old-fashioned like the following institutions. The Διπόλια (Διπόλια or Διπόλεια) was an annual festival to Zeus the protector of the city (Πολιεύς), to whom a bull was sacrificed, whence the festival was also called Βουφόνια: *Pac.* 420. The old Athenians wreathed their hair χρυσῶν τεττίγων ἐνέρσει (Thuc. i. 6, 3) as an emblem of their indigenous origin (schol.): *Eq.* 1331, τεττιγοφόρας. Κηκείδου—διθυράμβων ποιητὴς πάνυ ἀρχαῖος (schol.).

985. ἀλλ' οὖν—'well, anyhow.' ταῦτ' ἐστὶν ἐκεῖνα—so 1152: *Ach.* 41 etc.: cf. 1167.

986. Μαραθωνομάχους—the typical warrior-burgess; *Ach.* 181, etc.: *Vesp.* 711, ἄξια τοῦ 'ν Μαραθῶνι τροπαίου. The usual form is -μάχης: hence -μάχας should perhaps be read here.

987. ἐντετυλίχθαι—*Plut.* 692, αὐτὴν ἐντυλίξασα: τυλίττω, der. from τύλη, 'to muffle up.'

990. πρὸς ταῦτ'—'wherefore,' 'looking at this.'

991. βαλανείων ἀπέχεσθαι—i.e. warm baths; see 1044, and note on 837.

992. φλέγεσθαι—'to flame up,' with shame and indignation.

993. **θάκων**—seats in public pl.ces. For the construction cf. Xen. *Mem.* ii. 3, 16, ὁδοῦ παραχωρῆσαι πρεσβυτέρῳ: so Hdt. ii. 80, οἱ νεώτεροι τοῖσι πρεσβυτέροισι...ἐπιοῦσι ἐξ ἕδρης ἐνιστέαται, where Herodotus adds that such respect to the old, wh...i was observed in Egypt, was in Greece only found in Lacedaen. or authorities on the old-fashioned deference to age see Mayor's note on Juv. xiii. 55, si iuvenis vetulo non assurrexerat.

995. **ὅτι τῆς αἰδοῦς κ.τ.λ.**—'because you are to represent (form anew) the image (model) of honour (shame, modesty),' i.e. exemplify it in your own life. Blaydes quotes in illustration Plat. *Symp.* 222 A, πλεῖστ' ἀγάλματα ἀρετῆς ἐν αὑτοῖς ἔχοντας, speaking of Socrates' λόγοι: [Dem.] *in Aristog.* 780 § 35, καὶ δίκης γε καὶ εὐνομίας καὶ αἰδοῦς εἰσι πᾶσιν ἀνθρώποις βωμοί...ἐν αὑτῇ τῇ ψυχῇ ἑκάστου καὶ τῇ φύσει. This reading and rendering are adopted by most editors. A few manuscripts instead of ἀναπλάττειν have ἀναπλήσειν, which might mean 'to complete.' Some editors, however, reading ὅ τι μέλλει, give it the sense 'to defile' lit. 'infect'; but with this meaning the verb requires a genitive e.g. κακίας. A tempting reading is ὅ τι...μέλλει...ἀφανίζειν, which gives a good sense, but is mere conjecture.

996. **Ἰαπετόν**—i.e. ἀρχαῖον, μωρόν: cf. 929. Iapetus was the brother of Cronos.

997. **μνησικακῆσαι τὴν ἡλικίαν**—'quid haec significent nescio' is Dr Blaydes' comment: and certainly 'to reproach (your father) with the age from which you were reared as a chick' seems a little unintelligible. Is it to reproach him with his old age now, as some editors take it, or rather to remind him reproachfully of his earlier manhood, as ἐξ ἧς seems to suggest, μνησικακῆσαι also pointing to some past grudge?

Further, the construction is questionable. μνησικακεῖν, when it does not stand alone, as it often does, takes dative of the person and genitive of the thing, and may have a cognate (neuter) accusative, e.g. Dem. *de Cor.* 258 § 96, πόλλ' ἂν ἐχόντων μνησικακῆσαι Θηβαίοις τῶν πραχθέντων. But this does not justify taking ἡλικίαν as cognate or determinant accusative. Blaydes therefore proposes τῆς ἡλικίας. Of course we might take ἡλικίαν after καλέσαντα, 'calling his age (that of) Iapetus,' but such an order of words would be scarcely tolerable. I suspect that μνησικακῆσαι is wrong and that something like μνῆστιν (ἐᾶσαι) τῆς ἡλικίας 'to forget the early days' should be restored.

ἐνεοττοτροφήθης—formed from νεοττός, like παιδοτροφεῖν, *Lys.* 956.

1000. **ταῦτ'...πείσει**—see note on 77, and cf. 87.

1001. **Ἱπποκράτους**—the general who fell at Delium (Thuc. iv.

101, 2): he was the nephew of Pericles. His three sons Telesippus, Demophon and Pericles were jeered at as υιώδεις τινὲς καὶ ἀπαίδευτοι. Hence the joke on υἰέσιν resembling ὑσίν. For the Attic forms of υἱός see *New Phrynichus* p. 142. εἴξεις—as if from εἶκα: cf. 341. καλοῦσι is future, as it is probably in 452. βλιτομάμμαν—'a silly baby': from βλίτον a tasteless herb, and μάμμη or μαμμᾶν: hence blitea 'silly,' Plaut. *Truc.* iv. 4, 1.

1002. ἀλλ' οὖν—985. λιπαρός—shining from oil, or with a bright clear skin.

1003. στωμύλλων—*Ran.* 1310, in a choral song. The middle is generally used. τριβολεκτράπελ'—from τρίβολος, a burr (*Lys.* 576) or a caltrop, and ἐκτράπελος, 'out of the way,' strange. σκληρὰ καὶ ἀπαίδευτα is the scholiast's explanation of the first part of the word. Mr Green gives the meaning of the whole as 'far-fetched jokes, out-of-the-way subtleties and witticisms,' such as the specimen talk in *Eq.* 77-80.

1004. ἑλκόμενος—probably into court, πραγματίου meaning 'some paltry lawsuit'; but it may be simply 'worried, hustled,' as in *Vesp.* 793, κᾷθ' εἷλκον αὐτόν, where the idea of 'sc. in ius' is absurd: cf. 1218. γλισχρ.—from γλισχρός greedy, or obstinate, ἀντιλογ- and (ἐξ) ἐπίτριπτος 'rascally'; a quarrel with some greedy rogue.

1005. 'Ακαδήμειαν—the celebrated γυμνάσιον on the banks of the Cephissus, where Plato afterwards taught. It was adorned by Cimon with trees and walks and fountains. μορίαις—the olive trees sacred to Athene. ἀποθρέξει—running for exercise or practice is meant, not running away; so the compound with διά is probably better (Blaydes).

1006. καλάμῳ λευκῷ—ἦν δὲ τῶν Διοσκούρων ἴδιον στεφανοῦσθαι καλάμῳ (schol.).

1007. μίλακος—Dr Sandys on Eur. *Bacch.* 107 shows that this was a plant resembling black bryony. ὄζων—cf. 50: *Vesp.* 1060, ὄζήσει δεξιότητος: *Pax* 529, where there is the same mixture of material and immaterial things that we have here. ἀπραγμοσύνης—contrasted with 1005 and 1019. λεύκης—sacred to Heracles and furnishing the athletes' crown. φυλλοβολούσης—perhaps 'with waving leaves' (Merry); or the idea may be that the tree 'sheds its leaves' to crown the young champion.

1008. πτελέᾳ ψιθυρίζῃ—Theocr. *Id.* xxvii. 68, ἀλλάλοις ψιθύριζον: so Claudian uses *adsibilo* with dative.

1010. πρὸς τούτοις—if right, this must go with προσέχειν τὸν νοῦν, but such a construction is unknown elsewhere; though πρός τινι τὸν νοῦν ἔχειν is found, e.g. Plat. *Protag.* 324 A. It has been suggested to take πρός adverbially 'besides'; while Blaydes prefers καὶ τούτοισιν.

1013. λαμπράν—'bright and clear,' rightly I think preferred by Blaydes to λευκήν (albam), which in Aristophanes would suggest effeminate or unhealthy paleness, e.g. *Ran.* 1092.

1019. ψήφισμα μακρόν—this is what you will get from your professors of talking: cf. 1007.   σ' ἀναπείσει—sc. ὁ ἄδικος λόγος.

1022. Ἀντιμάχου—an Antimachus is mentioned *Ach.* 1150; a different man according to the scholiast.

1023. ἀναπλήσει—most probably active, sc. σε: σ' is inserted by some editors: cf. *Ach.* 847, δικῶν (σε) ἀναπλήσει. It may however be passive, though the usual future is πλησθήσομαι. The word has the idea of defiling or infecting noted on 995.

1024-35. This *antistrophe* does not exactly correspond to 949-60, having probably been left incomplete.

1024. καλλίπυργον—'lofty': 'cf. *Ran.* 1004, πυργώσας ῥήματα σεμνά, said of Aeschylus. Euripides on the other hand is κομψός: cf. 1030, κομψοπρεπῆ μοῦσαν' (Green).

1028. ἆρ'—'after all, as it seems.'

1030. πρὸς οὖν τάδ'—cf. *Vesp.* 644, δεῖ δὲ σέ κ.τ.λ.   κομψοπρεπῆ—πανοῦργον, 'rascally, knavish,' is the scholiast's explanation, but 'subtle-seeming' seems more the sense, κομψός being used of sophistical refinement and the like.

1035. εἴπερ...ὑπερβαλεῖ—'if you are going to conquer'; cf. 443.

1036. The ἄδικος λόγος responds in iambic tetrameters, the metre appropriated in Aristophanes to the more ignoble character. Thus, in the *Frogs* Euripides maintains his case in iambics (906—967), while Aeschylus rejoins in anapaests (1006—1070), the metre of the δίκαιος λόγος.   ἐπνιγόμην—Blaydes suggests πάλαι γε πνίγομαι...κἀπιθυμῶ, as being the usual construction when the thing is still going on; e.g. *Vesp.* 317, τήκομαι πάλαι: line 4 is of course different.   τὰ σπλάγχνα—'heart,' as we say; *Ran.* 1006, τὰ σπλάγχν' ἀγανακτεῖ.

1038. μέν—'displicet hoc μέν,' says Dr Blaydes. It has nothing to correspond to it, and the order γάρ...μέν is unusual: qu. ἐγὼ γὰρ οὖν, or the like.

1040. ταῖς δίκαις—judgments, awards of justice: as in Hom. *Il.* xvi. 542 etc., Hes. *Op.* 217.   ἀντιλέξαι—so Soph. *Oed. Tyr.* 409; the usual aorist is ἀντειπεῖν.

1041. πλεῖν—*Ran.* 90, πλεῖν ἢ μύρια : *Ach.* 858, πλεῖν ἢ τριάκονθ' ἡμέρας.

1042. αἰρούμενον.. ἔπειτα—*Ach.* 291, σπεισάμενος...εἶτα δύνασαι : *Ran.* 205 etc.: ἔπειτα or εἶτα marking opposition between the participle and the verb = 'after that, still.'

1043. σκέψαι—the ἄδικος λόγος first speaks to Pheidippides, and then, two lines below, turns to his opponent.

1044. ὅστις—*quippe qui*; see note on 692. θερμῷ λοῦσθαι—this shows the meaning of 991. For the form of the verb see note on 838.

1045. τίνα γνώμην ἔχων ;—'with what idea, what meaning?': γνώμη being what one has in one's mind.

1046. δειλόν—several manuscripts, including the best, have δειλότατον, hence Blaydes reads κάκιστον αὐτὰ καὶ δειλότατον ἄνδρα ποιεῖ. κάκιστον in agreement with ἄνδρα seems likely, but αὐτά as nom. is intolerable.

1047. ἐπίσχες—'hold, stay': *Eq.* 847 : common in tragedy. σ' ἔχω μέσον λαβών—with a grip like a wrestler's : *Ach.* 571, ἔχομαι μέσος : *Ran.* 469, ἀλλὰ νῦν ἔχει μέσος.

1048. τῶν τοῦ Διός κ.τ.λ.—the sentence runs awkwardly, as νομίζεις first takes the accusative ἄριστον and then an infinitive πονῆσαι. Meineke therefore suggests τῶν τοῦ Διὸς τίν' ἀνδρ' ἄριστον εἶναι.

1051. 'Ηράκλεια λουτρά—hot springs, such as were caused to rise by Athene (or Hephaestus) at Thermopylae for the weary Heracles; hence the term was generally used.

1052. ταῦτ' ἐστί κ.τ.λ.—so Aeschylus says that Euripides taught chattering and talking and thus emptied the παλαίστραι, *Ran.* 1069. For the wording cf. 26. δι' ἡμέρας—all day long.

1055. ἐν ἀγορᾷ κ.τ.λ.—this order, for τὴν ἐν ἀγορᾷ, is suspicious.

1057. ἀγορητήν—λιγὺς Πυλίων ἀγορητής is the regular title of Nestor, *Il.* i. 248 etc.; 'and in *Il.* i. 490 the ἀγορά is called κυδιάνειρα, an epithet generally of μάχη ; the two faculties, fight and council, being thus put in equal honour' (Green). The ἄδικος λόγος, while fallaciously assuming that one ἀγορά is as good as another, relies on the old belief that Homer was the teacher of all excellence.

1058. ἄνειμι ἐντεῦθεν—cf. 1075, 1408; Hdt. vii. 239, ἄνειμι δὲ ἐκεῖσε τοῦ λόγου. γλῶτταν—Mr Green in an excellent note shows that good speaking was recognized on every hand as essential in Athenian public life. It was the cruel and overbearing Cleon who inveighed against it (Thuc. iii 38, 4), because, as Bacon says, 'he was on the bad side in causes of estate, knowing that no man can speak fair of causes sordid and base.' In this case the ἄδικος gives no proof, as a mere assertion is sufficient.

1061. ἤδη—cf. 767.

1063. τὴν μάχαιραν—his (legendary, well known) sword. Peleus resisted the charms of Hippolyte, who falsely accused him to her husband Acastus. Acastus therefore left him unarmed in the desert, but the gods bestowed on him a sword for his protection against wild beasts.

1064. ἀστεῖον—'nice,' ironical; cf. χρηστός, v. 8.

1065. οὐκ τῶν λύχνων—'he of the lamp-market'; 551: cf. *Av.* 13, οὐκ τῶν ὀρνέων: *Vesp.* 789, ἐν τοῖς ἰχθύσιν, 'in the fish-market.'

1068. κᾆτ' ἀπολιποῦσά γ'—'yes, and then she left him, for his want of spirit.' The story was that Thetis put her child Achilles in the fire to burn away his mortal nature. Peleus seeing it cried out in terror, and Thetis fled back to her sister Nereids.

1073. κοτταβῶν—*Pac.* 343, ἑστιᾶσθαι, κοτταβίζειν. κιχλισμῶν—983: R has καχασμῶν=καγχ. 'loud laughter,' which is adopted by some editors.

1075. εἶεν—often before a question; 176: Soph. *Oed. Col.* 476, εἶεν· τὸ δ' ἔνθεν ποῖ τελευτῆσαί με χρή; πάρειμ' ἐντεῦθεν—cf. 1058.

1077. ἀπόλωλας—'you are a ruined man': the perfect denoting 'future certainty' (Goodwin § 51). ὁμιλῶν—cf. 1399: *Plut.* 776, ἀξίους τῆς ἐμῆς ὁμιλίας: cf. *Vesp.* 1028, τὰς Μούσας αἷσιν χρῆται 'is intimate with.' Here the association is that of pupil and master.

1080. ἐς τὸν Δί' ἐπανενεγκεῖν—sc. τὴν αἰτίαν: Eur. *Ion* 827, ἀνέφερ' ἐς τὸν δαίμονα: so with acc. expressed id. *Or.* 76, ἐς Φοῖβον ἀναφέρουσα τὴν ἁμαρτίαν. For infinitive in imperative sense, cf. 850: see Goodwin § 784: in the case of the 2nd person the subject is in the nominative.

1081. ὡς—'saying that.' ἥττων—common with words implying passion, ἔρωτος, οἴνου, ἡδονῆς, κέρδους, and the like.

1102. ἡττήμεθα κ.τ.λ.—the δίκαιος λόγος is utterly beaten, and, throwing his cloak aside, runs off the stage among the audience.

1103. θοἰμάτιον—for speedier exit: *Vesp.* 408,
ἀλλὰ θαἰμάτια βαλόντες ὡς τάχιστα, παιδία,
θεῖτε καὶ βοᾶτε καὶ Κλέωνι ταῦτ' ἀγγέλλετε.

1105. Socrates and Strepsiades reappear in a scene which no doubt belonged to the first *Clouds*. It might come in after line 881, but goes most awkwardly with all that now intervenes.

1106. διδάσκω—interrogative subjunctive.

1107. μέμνησ' ὅπως—cf. 887.

1108. στομώσεις—'sharpen, put an edge to,' also implying sharp speaking: Soph. *Oed. Col.* 795, τὸ σὸν στόμα πολλὴν ἔχον στόμωσιν: Eur. *Suppl.* 1206, ὀξύστομον μάχαιραν. Mr Green notes that the same metaphor was used in Hebrew, 'the edge of the sword' being literally 'the mouth of the sword.' He prefers Gesenius' explanation 'that the figure is taken from the teeth, and the idea of biting' to Liddell and Scott's view, that στόμα is the foremost part, front, and so of weapons the point or edge.

ἐπὶ μὲν θάτερα—'on the one side' i.e. one jaw.

1109. οἶον—'fit for.' οἶος with the dative alone is unusual. In Thuc. vi. 12, 2, οἶον νεωτέρῳ βουλεύσασθαι, an infinitive follows, and there Classen adopts the emendation νεωτέρους: in Plat. *Euthyd.* 272 A, we have λέγειν...λόγους οἵους εἰς τὰ δικαστήρια, but there it is easy to understand λέγουσι or the like: so Soph. *Phil.* 273, οἷα φωτὶ δυσμόρῳ ῥάκη προθέντες. If the text be sound it is, I suppose, equivalent to ὅπως στομώσεις αὐτὸν (τοιοῦτον) οἶον (στομώσεις) δικιδίοις.   **δικιδίοις**—petty suits, 'suitlets'; *Eq.* 347: *Vesp.* 511.

αὐτοῦ stands as it does because of the additional ἑτέραν: so γνώσεσθε τὴν ἄλλην αὐτοῦ πονηρίαν, Isocr. 18, 52: cf. note on 905.

1110. τὰ μείζω πράγματα—affairs of state, as well as important trials.

1113. ὠχρὸν μὲν οὖν, οἶμαί γε—so most editors, giving the line as an 'aside' to Pheidippides, who certainly had shown distaste enough for the philosophical complexion (103, 120). Dindorf however follows R and V in reading ἔγωγε for οἶμαί γε, when of course Strepsiades is the speaker. He too knew the disfiguring effects of learning (718, φρούδη χροιά), but preferred sacrificing his son's appearance to paying his debts; see 1171.

1114. χωρεῖτέ νυν—to Socrates and Pheidippides, who now leave the stage. The chorus then turn to Strepsiades, warning him that his experiment may turn out badly. Here at any rate they have no sympathy with the ἄδικος λόγος.

1115—1130. Part of a parabasis consisting of a second *epirrhema* (575), in which the Clouds warn the judges to secure their favour by deciding for them.

1115. **τοὺς κριτάς**—the subject of the subordinate verb is made the object of the main verb; as in 145 and 1148. The construction is common enough, but this is a peculiarly ugly instance of it, and Blaydes not unnaturally says 'annon τοῖς κριταῖς? cf. *Av.* 1101,

τοῖς κριταῖς εἰπεῖν τι βουλόμεσθα τῆς νίκης πέρι,
ὅσ' ἀγάθ', ἢν κρίνωσιν ἡμᾶς, πᾶσιν αὐτοῖς δώσομεν,

cf. *Eccl.* 1154.' The judges in comedy were five in number, in tragedy ten.

1116. **ἐκ τῶν δικαίων**—'from (in accordance with) the rights of the case,' or quasi-adverbial, as *Av.* 1435, ἐκ τοῦ δικαίου (=δικαίως), which Cobet would read here.

1117. **νεᾶν**—cf. Hes. *op.* 462, θέρεος δὲ νεωμένη οὔ σ' ἀπατήσει. **ἐν ὥρᾳ**—in due season, i.e. in spring.

1119. **καρπόν**—especially corn; 282: *Eccl.* 14, στοάς τε καρποῦ βακχίου τε νάματος πλήρεις.

1120. **ἄγαν ἐπομβρίαν**—taken together by Blaydes and Krüger (*Grammar* § 50. 8, 19): Thuc. i. 122, 4, οὐκ ἄλλο τι φέροισαν ἢ ἄντικρυς δουλείαν, 'downright slavery': Dem. *Fals. leg.* 385 § 141, γέγονεν...ἄρδην ὄλεθρος. No similar instance is however given of ἄγαν without the article; and it may go with πιέζειν.

1125. **σφενδόναις**—with hail like sling-stones, as the scholiast explains. **παιήσομεν**—so *Lys.* 459: τυπτήσω, *infr.* 1444.

1126. **πλινθεύοντ'**—sc. the τις in 1121.

1127. **κέραμον**—'the tiling': Thuc. iv. 48, 2, ἔβαλλον τῷ κεράμῳ: ἄμπελος is used in the same collective way *ib.* 100, 2.

1128. **ξυγγενῶν τις**—τις ἢ φίλων is read by Blaydes (with Cobet) for ἢ τῶν φίλων, which without τις would be a most exceptional partitive genitive, not to be justified by e.g. 104.

1129. **τὴν νύκτα πᾶσαν**—as the bride was brought home in procession at night, this would spoil the whole affair.

1130. **ἐν Αἰγύπτῳ**—where there was no rain, Hdt. iii. 10: or, according to another view, even in Egypt, though it was a distant country and overrun with thieves.

1131. Strepsiades reappears on the stage, with a bag of meal, which he intends for Socrates in accordance with his promise (669). He is counting up the days which remain till his interest must be paid.

πέμπτη—sc. φθίνοντος, i.e. the 25th or 26th, according as the month contained 29 or 30 days. This is counting backwards from the last of the month, as was commonly done in its third decade: see Dict. Ant. i. 338, *Calendarium*: Lid. and Scott, μήν.

1134. ἔνη καὶ νέα—'the old and new': so the last day of the lunar month was called by Solon, because at the beginning of the day the moon was waning, but before the close had begun to wax again. See Lid. and Scott, ἔνος.

1135. πᾶς...οἷς—the plural may be joined with such words as πᾶς, ἕκαστος, ὅστις, which have a collective force.

1136. θείς μοι πρυτανεῖα—lit. depositing court-fees, i.e. instituting proceedings, against me; cf. 1180, and see Dict. Ant. i. 629, *dike*.

1137. κἀμοῦ μέτρι' ἄττα—some such correction as this is required to connect the sentence: ἐμοῦ τε μέτρια (Green) is good and near the MSS.

1138. μὲν λαβέ—(μοι λαβέ Naber), a correction which commends itself. The old man offers to pay a part down, if the rest may stand over and something be remitted. How could μὴ λάβῃς be called 'a just and reasonable offer'?

1141. δικάσεσθαι—most manuscripts have -σασθαι, as in 35 (see note).

1145. παῖ, ἠμί—*Ran.* 37, παιδίον, παῖ, ἠμί, παῖ: *Av.* 57, etc. Except in this phrase ἠμί is mostly found in the imperfect, ἦ, καί (Hom.), ἦν δ' ἐγώ, ἦ δ' ὅς, in Attic dialogue. Instead of a servant Socrates himself appears with his pupil. Teuffel has what seems to me a strange notion, that ἀσπάζομαι was a new-fashioned greeting, χαῖρε being the older style. This is founded on *Plut.* 322,

χαίρειν μὲν ὑμᾶς ἐστίν, ἄνδρες δημόται,
ἀρχαῖον ἤδη προσαγορεύειν καὶ σαπρόν·
ἀσπάζομαι δ', κ.τ.λ.

There however the speaker is greeting friends who were ground down with poverty; and the meaning surely is that to bid them χαίρειν was a silly old form and destitute of meaning in their case: cf. *Ach.* 832, ΔΙ. καὶ χαῖρε πολλά. ΜΕ. ἀλλ' ἁμὶν οὐκ ἐπιχώριον. D. I wish you joy. M. It's not our country's fashion.

1146. τουτονί—the sack of meal (θύλακος). Socrates, it is said, though he refused fees, would accept presents of wine or eatables from his disciples.

1147. ἐπιθαυμάζειν—δώροις τιμᾶν (schol.), 'to compliment,' i.e. reward; so θαυμάζω.

1148. τὸν υἱόν...εἴφ'—cf. 115.

1149. ὅν—some editors refer this to υἱόν, others to the unjust λόγος which Socrates had lately 'brought on the stage' (886) or 'taken into' the Contemplatory. The run of the words is certainly in favour of ἐκεῖνον being antecedent to ὅν, and this gives rather more point to the rest of the line.

1150. μεμάθηκεν—a comic exaggeration, says Teuffel, of the Sophists' promises to teach all wisdom in a few lessons. ἀπαιόλη—cf. 728; and for the personification see note on 424.

1153. κἂν παρῶσι—'even if you find a thousand appearing': some manuscripts having κἂν παρῆσαν, Blaydes reads κεἰ παρῆσαν.

1154. βοάσομαί τἄρα—from the *Peleus* of Euripides. 'Strepsiades in his wild delight breaks into tragic metre and dialect' (Merry). ὑπέρτονον (γήρυμα) occurs Aesch. *Eum.* 569.

1155. ὀβολοστάται—usurers, lit. 'penny-weighers,' from ἱστάναι.

1156. τἀρχαῖα—'the principal.' τόκοι τόκων—'compound interest': Theophr. *Char.* 10, of the μικρολόγος, δεινὸς δὲ καὶ ὑπερημερίαν πρᾶξαι καὶ τόκον τόκου. ἀνατοκισμός, says Teuffel, was not forbidden at Athens, but regarded as mean. The line also suggests, 'may you perish, yourselves, your ancestors and your children's children.'

1158. οἷος=ὅτι τοῖος: cf. 699: and note on *Vesp.* 187, ὦ μιαρώτατος ἵν' ὑποδέδυκεν, 'abominable wretch for having crept in there.'

1160. ἀμφήκει—'gleaming with two-edged tongue'; his tongue cut both ways, for he had learned, we suppose, both arguments and could maintain right or wrong.

1161. πρόβολος—προστάτης, τεῖχος, ἀσφάλεια (schol.): in Xenophon 'a fortress.' Mr Green inclines to 'a spear, a lance in rest,' which is the meaning in Herodotus.

1163. Λυσανίας—λύων τὰς τοῦ πατρὸς ἀνίας (schol.): Soph. Fr. 765, νόστον ἄγοι τὸν νικομάχαν καὶ παυσανίαν: so λυσίπονος, Pind.

1165. ὦ τέκνον, ὦ παῖ—a parody of Euripides, *Hec.* 172, ὦ τέκνον, ὦ παῖ...ἔξελθ' οἴκων, ἄιε ματέρος αὐδάν. This being a mother's cry, possibly the words should be assigned to Strepsiades rather than to Socrates. All this part is a cento or parody of tragedy.

1168. ὦ φίλος—Soph. *Oed. Col.* 1698, ὦ πάτερ, ὦ φίλος. Socrates now hands the son over to his father and retires from the stage.

1170. ἰοῦ ἰοῦ—a shout of joy: 'Strepsiades dances round his son, shouting with delight to see the true philosophic pallor on his face' (Merry).

1171. χροιάν—103, 1113.

1172. νῦν μέν γ'—'now, at any rate.' πρῶτον—with νῦν, nunc demum (Teuffel): or 'to begin with,' as in 1044 (Blaydes). ἰδεῖν εἶ κ.τ.λ.—'you have a repudiative and contradictious look' (Merry).

1173. τοῦτο τοὐπιχώριον—'that true Attic expression is in full bloom upon you (which asks), What's that you say?': a look ready to question and contradict; cf. 207.

1174. ἐπανθεῖ—cf. 1024, τοῖς λόγοις ἔπεστιν ἄνθος. καὶ δοκεῖν—'to look injured when you're in the wrong.' For οἶδ' ὅτι Blaydes follows Bentley in reading εὖ ποιεῖν (sc. δοκεῖν), 'to seem to be serving a man when you are cheating him': Green suggests καὶ κακουργεῖσθαι δ' ἔτι.

1176. Ἀττικὸν βλέπος—πανοῦργον or δριμύ, says the scholiast: sharp and keen, at any rate.

1177. κἀπώλεσας—we should say 'since you destroyed me, do you also save me' (Green). So in comparisons, as Jowett says, in Greek the word καί commonly adheres to the standard of comparison (ὥσπερ καί), in English the corresponding word adheres to the person or thing compared, e.g. Thuc. iv. 62, 3, τιμωρία οὐκ εὐτυχεῖ ὅτι καὶ εὐέλπι.

1180. εἰς ἥν γε—'yes, the day for which' etc. 'The γε in the answer proves τις preferable to τίς in the line before' (Green). For θήσειν κ.τ.λ. cf. 1136.

1181. The argument is that the summons would be void, not being laid for one definite day.

1183. εἰ μή...γένοιτ' ἄν—'unless (it were the case that) the same woman *could* become' etc.: γένοιτ' ἄν being equivalent to γενέσθαι δύναιτο.

1185. καὶ μὴν νενόμισταί γ'—'anyhow it's the established custom.'

1186. ὅ τι νοεῖ—'what it means.'

1187. ὁ Σόλων—such praises of Solon as an ideal legislator were a stock thing in speeches : e.g. Dem. *de Cor.* 227 § 6, οὓς (νόμους) ὁ τιθεὶς ἐξ ἀρχῆς Σόλων, εὔνους ὢν ὑμῖν καὶ δημοτικός.

1189. τὴν κλῆσιν—the calling into court (780) i.e. the procedure generally. **ἐς δύ' ἡμέρας κ.τ.λ.**—assuming that 'the old and new' are two days, the son lays down that 'the old' (ἕνη) must be the 30th and therefore the νέα the 1st of the next month or νουμηνία.

1190. ἐς γε τὴν ἕνην τε καὶ νέαν—Cobet would read εἴς τε τὴν ἕνην καὶ τὴν νέαν, to show that two distinct days are meant.

1191. αἱ θέσεις—αἱ καταβολαὶ τῶν πρυτανείων (schol.), and the actual beginning of the suit.

1192. ἵνα δὴ τί—sc. γένοιτο : *Pac.* 409, ἵνα δὴ τί τοῦτο δρᾶτον; τὴν ἕνην προσέθηκεν—why add in that 'back-day' (Merry) : why not have it all on the νουμηνία (or νέα) ? **ἵν', ὦ μέλε**—that the parties sued might have a clear day in which to arrange a compromise.

1193. ἡμέρᾳ μιᾷ πρότερον—'one day sooner.'

1194. ἀπαλλάττοιντο—sc. τοῦ δικάζεσθαι, 'settle the matter, get rid of it,' as in *Pac.* 293, πραγμάτων τε καὶ μαχῶν : so Buttman explains ἀπαλλαγῆναι Dem. *Meid.* 563, and ἀπήλλαγμαι, *ib.* 578. Teuffel cites Plat. *legg.* 915 C, ἀπαλλάττωνται πρὸς ἀλλήλους τῶν ἐγκλημάτων : *ib.* 936 E, ἀπαλλαττέσθω τῆς δίκης. Meineke and others read διαλλάττοιντο 'might get reconciled.'

1196. Then why do the magistrates expect the fees to be paid on the 30th instead of waiting for the 1st?

1197. ἀρχαί—as we say 'the authorities,' using abstract for concrete. Strictly ἡ ἀρχή = οἱ ἐν τῇ ἀρχῇ, αἱ ἀρχαί = οἱ ἐν ταῖς ἀρχαῖς.

1198. προτένθαι—lit. 'fore-eaters'; either rich men who secure beforehand dainties in the market, or, according to Brunck, certain officials who tasted the meat beforehand for sacrificial banquets. τένθης occurs *Pac.* 1009, 1120 : τενθεία, *Av.* 1691 : derived from τένδω (Hes. *Op.* 524).

1199. ὑφελοίατο—α for ν metri gratia : so ἐργασαίατο, *Av.* 1147 and *Lys.* 42 : *Eq.* 662, γενοίαθ' etc. and trag.

1200. προὐτένθευσαν —'they forestalled them by one day': construction as in 1193, and such phrases as Thuc. vii. 80, 4, προὔλαβε πολλῷ, 'got far ahead.'

1201. εὖ γε—'capital!' says Strepsiades in ecstasy; and then turns to the audience in tones of exultation; cf. *Lys.* 1217, ὑμεῖς τί κάθησθε; **ἀβέλτεροι**—*Ran.* 989, ἀβελτερώτατοι κεχηνότες καθῆντο.

1202. ἡμέτερα τῶν σοφῶν—*Ach.* 93, τόν γε σὸν τοῦ πρέσβεως : Eur.

El. 366, πόσις ἐμὸς τῆς ἀθλίας.   λίθοι—for stupidity: Ter. *Hec.* ii. 1, 17, me omnino lapidem non hominem putas: for hardness, Theocr. *Id.* x. 7, τὸ πᾶν λίθος.

1203. ἀριθμός—Eur. *Troad.* 475, οὐκ ἀριθμὸν ἄλλως etc.: Hor. *Epist.* i. 2, 27, nos numerus sumus.   ἄλλως—'merely': Eur. *Hel.* 1421, ἄλλως πόνος.   ἀμφορῆς νενημένοι—the audience, seated in rows on the sloping sides of the theatre, looked like wine-jars stowed in tiers: Thuc. vii. 87, 2, τῶν νεκρῶν ὁμοῦ ἐπ' ἀλλήλοις ξυννενημένων.

1204. εἰς—expressing relation, 'addressed to'; with ᾄδω, *Lys.* 1243, see next note.

1205. ἐπ'—'for, on the ground of.'   μοὔγκώμιον—i.e. μοι ἐγκ.: Frag. 414, ᾄδωμεν ἐς τὸν δεσπότην ἐγκώμιον.

1206. Στρεψίαδες—ὡς ἄγροικος περὶ τὴν κλητικὴν ἐσφάλη, 'made a mistake in the vocative' which should be Στρεψιάδη (schol.). He gives a vocative like Σώκρατες (219), which is of a different declension.

1207. ὡς...χοῖον—'so wise art thou and so clever is thy son'; cf. 1158.

1211. νικᾷς κ.τ.λ.—cf. 99, 432 etc.

1214. Pasias the money-lender comes on the stage with his summons-witness (κλητήρ), Strepsiades being still in the house.   εἶτ'—'after this' *then*, with surprise and indignation: *Vesp.* 1133, ἔπειτα παῖδας χρὴ φυτεύειν; so *Ach.* 126.   προϊέναι—'to part with': Hdt. i. 24: common in middle in Dem. of advancing money.

1215. κρεῖττον ἦν—so *Vesp.* 219: this construction without ἄν denotes what would have been better, but has not been done; so εἰκὸς ἦν etc., also ἐνῆν, ἐχρῆν and the like: see Goodwin § 415 sq. τότε—'at the time' when Strepsiades applied for a loan.

1216. ἀπερυθριᾶσαι—ἀπαναισχυντῆσαι (schol.), to have refused unblushingly.   σχεῖν—to incur (aor.).

1217. ὅτε—see note on 7.   ὅτε and γε are to be taken together: cf. *Pac.* 1251, ὅτ' ἀντέδωκά γ'; Plat. *Phaed.* 84 D, ὅτε γε μηδ' ὑμᾶς δύναμαι πείθειν.

1218. ἕλκω σε κλητεύσοντα—'have to drag you to be my witness,' to prove due service of the summons: cf. *Vesp.* 1415,

οδί τις ἕτερος, ὡς ἔοικεν, ἔρχεται
καλούμενός σε· τόν γέ τοι κλητῆρ' ἔχει.

ib. 1413, γυναικὶ κλητεύειν, to be her witness.

1220. οὐδέποτέ γε κ.τ.λ.—litigation being a pride and glory: so the συκοφάντης, *Av.* 1451, declines to disgrace his family by taking up a decent trade,

τὸ γένος οὐ καταισχυνῶ·
παππῷος ὁ βίος συκοφαντεῖν ἐστί μοι.

1221. καλοῦμαι—perhaps future, as in *Vesp.* 1416, quoted above, where too the word is used for summoning, like προσκαλοῦμαι. Pasias speaks in a loud voice, which Strepsiades hears and comes out.

1223. τοῦ χρήματος;—so *Vesp.* 1417, προσκαλοῦμαι ὕβρεως; cf. 22, where the loan is mentioned.

1225. ψαρόν—roan or iron-grey, from ψάρ, a starling.

1226. ὅν—'when you all know me' etc.; the sense supplies the antecedent. A noteworthy instance of such elliptic construction is found Thuc. iv. 26, 3, ἀθυμίαν πλείστην ὁ χρόνος παρεῖχεν, οὓς ᾤοντο κ.τ.λ.: so ii. 44, 2.

1228. μὰ τὸν Δί' οὐ γάρ—to be taken together, as μά in negation must be connected with a negative expressed or implied. The sense is, '(very likely) for' etc.

1232. ἀπομόσαι τοὺς θεούς—the power appealed to is in the accusative; as in 246 and 1227: *Eq.* 424, τοὺς θεοὺς ἀπώμνυν.

1233. ποίους θεούς;—this is often a contemptuous question, expecting no reply, as in 367: still it does not lose its interrogative form, and Pasias gives a literal answer: cf. 1377.

1234. τὸν Δία—it was the Athenian custom to swear by three gods, of whom Zeus was always one. Thus Socrates too has his three deities to whom he appeals, 627.

1235. κἂν προσκαταθείην γ'—'yes, and I would give three obols in for the privilege,' his day's pay as a juryman.

1236. ἀπόλοιο...ἔτι—'yet, some day': *Thesm.* 887, κακῶς ἄρ' ἐξόλοιο κἀξολεῖ γ' ἔτι.

1237. ἁλσίν κ.τ.λ.—Strepsiades looks contemplatively at his creditor, and remarks that a dressing with salt would do him good. Possibly he was a fat wine-bibbing fellow, who would make a good wine-skin if cleaned with salt. Such men indeed were called ἀσκοί, as we learn from a fragment of Antiphanes. Another view is that drunkards or lunatics were rubbed with salt. ὄναιτ' ἄν—*Plut.* 1062, ὄναιο μεντἄν εἴ τις ἐκπλύνειέ σε. διασμηχθείς should be -σμηθείς according to Rutherford, *New Phrynichus,* p. 321: σμάω is Attic, σμήχω Homeric and late Greek.

1238. ἓξ χόας χωρήσεται—'he will take six gallons' i.e. I suppose, hold that quantity of wine, the χοῦς being a liquid measure; but it might be, he will require that amount of salt to cure him. For χωρέω, 'to contain,' cf. Hdt. i. 51, χωρέων ἀμφορέας ἑξακοσίους etc.

1240. καταπροίξει—an 'isolated future always used with a preceding negative and in Attic Greek never found outside of Comedy' (*New Phrynichus,* p. 254): cf. *Vesp.* 1396, οὔτοι καταπροίξει Μυρτίας.

1241. Ζεὺς γέλοιος ὀμνύμενος—'swearing by Zeus is absurd': so Plat. *Phaedr.* 236 D, γέλοιοι ἔσομαι...αὐτοσχεδιάζων, 'extemporising on my part will be ridiculous': Ar. *Eth.* i. 12, 3, γέλοιοι φαίνονται (οἱ θεοὶ) πρὸς ἡμᾶς ἀναφερόμενοι, 'referring the gods to a human standard': ib. x. 8, 7, γέλοιοι φανοῦνται (οἱ θεοὶ) συναλλάττοντες, 'the notion of the gods making contracts': so *occisus Caesar*, 'Caesar's murder.' 'Ridiculous,' of a person, is usually καταγέλαστος, sometimes γέλοιος, e.g. Plat. *Rep.* 517 D, where however participles follow. For the accent see Lid. and Scott.

τοῖς εἰδόσιν—'sic fere loquuntur qui aliquid soli vel cum paucis scire videri cupiunt' (Blaydes): Eur. *Rhes.* 973, σεμνὸς τοῖσιν εἰδόσιν θεός.

1242. ἦ μήν κ.τ.λ.—cf. 865: *Vesp.* 1332, ἦ μὴν σὺ δώσεις αὔριον τούτων δίκην.

1244. ἔχ' ἥσυχος—'keep quiet'; *Plut.* 127: so with adverbs, ἠρέμα, ἀτρέμας, αὐτοῦ etc.; see 261. Strepsiades now goes in to fetch a kneading-trough.

1246. ἀποδώσειν σοι δοκεῖ;—Pasias says this to his witness. Another reading makes the witness say 'I think he will pay you'; but the witness is most likely a κωφὸν πρόσωπον. The compound with ἀπό means to pay what is due; so *reddo*, and our 'render.'

1248. ὅ τι—sc. do you ask what? For the master's lesson about κάρδοπος see 670—680.

1249. ἔπειτα—cf. 1214: *Av.* 911, ἔπειτα δῆτα δοῦλος ὢν κόμην ἔχεις; τοιοῦτος ὤν—when you know no better than this.

1251. ὅστις καλέσειε—the optative in the relative clause is assimilated to the optative in the antecedent clause, as in English we say, 'I would not pay a penny to one who *was* so ignorant'; see examples in Goodwin §§ 531 and 558; e.g. Plat. *Men.* 92 C, πῶς ἂν εἰδείης περὶ τούτου τοῦ πράγματος οὗ παντάπασιν ἄπειρος εἴης;

1252. οὐκ ἄρ' ἀποδώσεις; 'you are not going to pay then?' ἄρα expresses an inference, with some anxiety. Blaydes with slight authority adopts ἆρ', an interrogative expressing indignation: *Av.* 91, οὐκ ἄρ' ἀφῆκας; ὅσον γέ μ' εἰδέναι—(or ὅσον γ' ἔμ') lit. 'so far as my knowing goes.' For this 'absolute infinitive, expressing a limitation or qualification of some word or of the whole sentence,' see Goodwin §§ 776—783. Compare ὡς ἔπος εἰπεῖν, 'to put it in a word': ὡς ἐμοὶ δοκεῖν, 'as it seems to me': *Pac.* 857, ὅσα γ' ὧδ' ἰδεῖν.

1253. ἀνύσας τι—cf. 506. ἀπολιταργιεῖς—ἀποδραμεῖ, ἀποσκιρτήσεις (schol.), 'skip off': *Pac.* 562, λιταργιοῦμεν. The scholiast derives the word from λίαν and ἀργός (swift): see λῖ- in Lid. and Scott.

1256. ταῖς δώδεκα—sc. μναῖς, 1224.

1258. τὴν κάρδοπον—'because you called it in your silly way τὴν κάρδοπον.' The money-lender now goes off.

1259. ἰώ μοί μοι—Amynias, from whom the racing car had been bought (31), enters lamenting, and perhaps bruised. It is not clear whether he has literally been thrown from his chariot or is using tragic metaphors.

1260. ἔα—of surprise, hah!: Eur. *Hec.* 501, ἔα, τίς οὗτος; Aesch. *Prom.* 298, ἔα, τί χρῆμα; often put as here extra versum.

1261. τῶν Καρκίνου τις δαιμόνων—some tragic hero or demigod in trouble; παρ' ὑπόνοιαν for παίδων (schol.). Carcinus was a tragic poet with three small sons, one of them, Xenocles, a poet too: *Vesp.* 1511,
ὁ σμικρότατος, ὃς τὴν τραγῳδίαν ποιεῖ.
It is one of the son's plays, according to the scholiast, that is here parodied or quoted.

1263. κατὰ σεαυτὸν τρέπου—go your own way; keep your calamities to yourself; the same line, *Ach.* 1019.

1266. Τληπόλεμος—son of Heracles. He accidentally slew his uncle Licymnius (Hom. *Il.* ii. 661), which seems to have been the subject of the play of Xenocles. We do not know how far the tragic lines are parody, or if a chariot accident came in.

1269. ἄλλως τε μέντοι—Blaydes reads πάντως for μέντοι, comparing Aesch. *Prom.* 636 etc.

1270. τὰ ποῖα—'which be they?': cf. 748.

1271. κακῶς ἄρ' ὄντως εἶχες—according to Blaydes = 'you *are* then in a bad way'; like *Av.* 280, οὐ σὺ μόνος ἄρ ἦσθ' ἔποψ, 'you are not then (as I thought) the only hoopoe,' ἄρα with the imperfect, usually ἦν, implying present recognition of an existing fact: see Goodwin § 39, and my note on *Vesp.* 3. I am not sure that this is a case of the idiom noted. The sense may be simply 'you were unlucky then' (inference), as in 1476.

1272. ἐξέπεσον—lit. 'I was thrown out': so *Vesp.* 1427: Hom. *Il.* xxiii. 467 etc. The scholiast considers that χρημάτων is understood = 'I was ruined.' 'I came to grief' represents either meaning, as well as the sense of 'failing, being rejected,' = explodi.

1273. ἀπ' ὄνου καταπεσών—said to be a proverbial phrase for stupid awkwardness, with a pun on ἀπὸ νοῦ.

1276. τὸν ἐγκέφαλον—'you seem to have a sort of concussion of the brain'; due, Strepsiades seems to think, to his accident.

1277. προσκεκλήσεσθαι—but for the following clause in the future, one would incline to προσκεκλῆσθαι, the reading of R and V, which as it is is adopted by Hermann, Green and Teuffel. It corresponds closely to the line before; 'you look like a man with a crack on the head,' 'you look like a man with a summons into court.'

1283. δίκαιος εἶ—cf. 1434: *Plut.* 1030, ἀγαθὸν δίκαιός ἐστ' ἔχειν.

1284. μετεώρων—see 228 and 333.

1286. ἀπόδοτε—speaking to father and son. ὁ τόκος—Strepsiades pretends to understand τόκος only in the sense of 'offspring.' Dr Merry wittily renders:

'Pay me the interest that the money bears.'
'What sort of creature is it that it bears?'

1287. τί δ' ἄλλο γ' ἤ—'why, of course'; 1448, 1495.

1288. πλέον πλέον—'more and more': so μᾶλλον μᾶλλον, *Ran.* 1001.

1289. ὑπορρέοντος—'slipping away.'

1291. πρὸ τοῦ—cf. 5.

1292. οὐ γὰρ δίκαιον—'reasonable.' Blaydes suspects δίκαιον, and suggests οὐ γὰρ δύνατ' αὐτήν, or οὐδ' ἔστιν αὐτήν.

1296. ἀποδιώξει—the Attic future of διώκω is διώξομαι, as with 'all verbs expressing the exercise of the senses, or denoting any functional state or process'; see *New Phrynichus* p. 377. Here the following σ made the corruption easy: so *Eq.* 969. 'Will you not sue yourself away?' is Blaydes' rendering, Amynias having threatened prosecution. For the whole line cf. *Av.* 1020, οὐκ ἀναμετρήσει σαυτὸν ἀπιὼν ἀλλαχῇ; For ἀπό most manuscripts have ἐκ, the two prepositions being perpetually confounded.

1297. ταῦτ' ἐγὼ μαρτύρομαι—calling on the bystanders to witness the assault; *Vesp.* 1436 etc. : μαρτύρομαι alone l. 1222 etc.

1298. οὐκ ἐλᾷς—'move on, come up'; repeated from *Eq.* 603: cf. *ib.* 243, οὐκ ἐλᾶτε; For σαμφόρα see 122.

1299. ἄξεις; ἐπιαλῶ—sc. τὸ κέντρον, 'will you be off? I'll lay the whip about you': cf. Hom. *Od.* ix. 288, ἑτάροις ἐπὶ χεῖρας ἴαλλεν. ἐπιαλῶ is adopted by most editors, the manuscripts having ἐπεὶ ἀλῶ or the like.

1301. ἔμελλον ἄρα—'I thought I should make you move'; lit. 'I was, it seems, going to move you': cf. *Ach.* 347, ἐμέλλετ' ἄρα πάντως ἀνήσειν τῆς βοῆς: *Ran.* 268, ἔμελλον ἄρα παύσειν ποθ' ὑμᾶς τοῦ κοάξ, 'I thought I should presently stop your croaking': so *Vesp.* 460.

1302. αὐτοῖς τροχοῖς—cf. αὐτοῖς ἀνδράσι, 'men and all': *Vesp.* 119, αὐτῷ τυμπάνῳ. It is a form of the dative of accompaniment (Madv. § 42), sometimes with the article, sometimes without.

Amynias now goes off, and Strepsiades returns indoors to his interrupted banquet.

1303—20. The chorus, now openly siding with the Cause of right, predict that Strepsiades will soon be sorry for the lessons of knavery which his son has learned.

1303. πραγμάτων ἐρᾶν φλαύρων—cf. 1459. ἐξαρθείς, besides avoiding tautology, corresponds in scansion to the antistrophic ἐζήτει in 1312. With the manuscript reading ἐρασθείς 'thereof' is to be supplied.

1305. ἀποστερῆσαι — ἀποστερεῖν is generally 'to keep back, defraud.'

1307. οὐκ ἔσθ' ὅπως—cf. 1275: with οὐκ following. *Ach.* 116.

1312. ἐζήτει—the reading of most manuscripts, though R has

ἐπεζήτει. From the latter Dindorf, retaining ἐρασθείς in 1304, gives ἐπέζει, 'was hot on,' a conjecture more ingenious than probable. Blaydes reads ἐδίζητ' (Epic and Ionic) and suggests ἐθήρα etc.

1313. εἶναι—'that his son should be' etc.

1314. ἐναντίας—see 888, 1040, 1339.

1318. ἴσως δ' ἴσως—the repetition has a tone of solemn warning.

1321. Strepsiades rushes out, beaten by his son. The son avows his conduct, and is ready to prove that it is right.

1323. ἀμυνάθετε—an aorist form of ἀμύνω (see Lid. and Scott). πάσῃ τέχνῃ = παντὶ τρόπῳ, πάσῃ δυνάμει (schol.) : cf. 885 : *Thesm.* 65.

1324. τῆς κεφαλῆς—words of felicitation and the opposite take the genitive.

1329. χαίρω—like the ἄδικος λόγος, 910.   ἀκούων—having said to me, or of me : *Eq.* 1276, πόλλ' ἀκοῦσαι καὶ κακά: *Vesp.* 621, ἀκούω ταῦθ' ἅπερ ὁ Ζεύς.

1337. ποίοιν λόγοιν;—here, as Mr Green says, is another instance of a question asked by ποῖος, no doubt with indignation and astonishment, to which yet an answer is given : see note on 1233.

1338. ἐδιδαξάμην—in its proper middle sense, 'I had you taught.' μέντοι—'indeed, in truth,' with an ironical intonation. In 1342 = tamen.

1344. ὅ τι καὶ λέξεις—'what you *are* going to say'; cf. 528, and 840: Thuc. iv. 11, 4, εἰ πῃ καὶ δοκοίη δυνατὸν εἶναι σχεῖν, 'if at any point it *did* seem possible to force a landing.'

1347. 'πεποίθειν—most of the manuscripts have πέποιθεν, R has πεποίθει. The correction is due to Dawes, who first pointed out that -ει(ν) is the termination of the third person pluperfect, -η that of the first person : see *New Phrynichus*, p. 229.

1349. ἔσθ' ὅτῳ θρασύνεται—*Ach.* 330, ἦ 'πὶ τῷ θρασύνεται; cf. Soph. *Oed. Col.* 1031, ἀλλ' ἔσθ' ὅτῳ σὺ πιστὸς ὢν ἕδρας τάδε.

1352. πάντως δέ—'and you will certainly do so.'

1353. λοιδορεῖσθαι—'to quarrel,' lit. 'rail mutually,' as in 62. The middle with this meaning takes the dative; the active 'to rebuke' the accusative.

1356. τὸν κριὸν ὡς ἐπέχθη—'the shearing of the ram': the accusative is the object of the preceding active clause, as noted on 1115. The scholiast says that this is the beginning of an ode by Simonides on Krius, a wrestler of Aegina,

ἐπέξαθ' ὁ κριὸς (or Κριὸς) οὐκ ἀεικέως
ἐλθὼν εἰς εὔδενδρον ἀγλαὸν Διὸς τέμενος·

and explains that Krius came out with added lustre, resplendent like a new-shorn ram.

1357. ἀρχαῖον—'antiquated'; 985. κάχρυς...ἀλοῦσαν—the editors give a 'mill song' from Plutarch: ἄλει μύλα, ἄλει· καὶ γὰρ Πιττακὸς ἀλεῖ, μεγάλας Μιτυλάνας βασιλεύων· whether Pittacus was a mill-owner or, as Mr Green suggests, 'ground' his people by tyranny.

1360. τέττιγας—who lived on dew and air and did nothing but sing: Plat. *Phaedr.* 259 C, τὸ τεττίγων γένος...μηδὲν τροφῆς δεῖσθαι γενόμενον ἀλλ' ἄσιτόν τε καὶ ἄποτον εὐθὺς ᾄδειν.

1363. ἠνεσχόμην—note the double augment, as in 1373; ἀνέχομαι is one of the eleven verbs so augmented in Attic (*New Phrynichus*, p. 85).

1364. ἀλλά—'at least, at any rate'; as in 1369. μυρρίνην—when catches (σκόλια) or poetic recitations were given at banquets the leader held a spray of myrtle, and passed it to another guest to continue in his turn: cf. *Vesp.* 1220 sq.

1366. ἐγὼ γάρ—according to the text this is an indignant question on the part of the son, who in the next line gives his reasons for not thinking Aeschylus chief of poets. This arrangement is adopted by most editors, but it is not quite satisfactory; see critical note. Green suggests that πρῶτον ἐν ποιηταῖς may be 'above all other poets for empty sound' etc.: so Merry. ἐγὼ γάρ κ.τ.λ. seems genuine praise in the father's mouth, so perhaps Hermann's transposition should be adopted; unless indeed a line or so is lost. Blaydes suggests ἦ γάρ... νομίζεις; spoken by the son.

1367. ψόφου πλέων—compare the very outspoken criticism of Aeschylus by Euripides, *Ran.* 909 sq. ἀξύστατον—'unconnected,' ill put together; without the compactness and logical sequence of Euripides; *Ran.* 1119 etc. Blaydes quotes Quintilian's judgment, 'sublimis et gravis et grandiloquus usque ad vitium, sed rudis in plerisque et *incompositus.*'

στόμφακα—'mouthing,' bombastic; see the kindred words: *Vesp.* 721, στομφάζοντας. κρημνοποιόν—cf. *Ran.* 929, ῥήμαθ' ἱππόκρημνα: *Eq.* 628, κρημνοὺς ἐρείπων (of Cleon), 'precipice-words,' rugged and huge: cf. ἀγριοποιός, *Ran.* 837.

1368. ὀρεχθεῖν—κινηθῆναι καὶ ταράττεσθαι (schol.). In Homer the word occurs once, *Il.* xxiii. 30, where Leaf discusses the traditional explanations, and inclines to connect it with ὀρέγομαι, meaning 'stretched themselves out' in death. Theocritus, *Id.* xi. 43, uses it of the sea, apparently connecting it with ῥοχθεῖν ' roar.' Here it may denote the heart's beating or throbbing.

1369. τὸν θυμὸν δακών—here='curbing my temper': *Ran.* 43, δάκνω γ' ἐμαυτόν : *Vesp.* 778, δακνῶν σεαυτόν, 'galling.'

1371. ῥῆσιν—'passage': *Vesp.* 581 : *Ran.* 151.

1372. ἀδελφός...ἀδελφήν—τὴν Κανακὴν ὁ Μακαρεύς, in the *Aeolus* (schol.). The appeal to Apollo or Heracles ἀλεξίκακος, 'heaven preserve us,' is thrown in parenthetically. For the word cf. *Vesp.* 1043.

1373. ἐξαράττω—'buffet him,' κρούω, λοιδορῶ, πλήττω (schol.): Meineke reads εὐθέως ἤραττον, as an imitation of Soph. *Phil.* 374, κἀγὼ χολωθεὶς εὐθὺς ἤρασσον κακοῖς: so *Aj.* 725.

1375. ἔπος πρὸς ἔπος ἠρειδόμεσθ'—'we hurled against each other word for word, exchanged angry words' (Blaydes). ἐρείδω, to 'pour forth' or 'pile up,' implies force and effort; *Eq.* 627, ἀναρρηγνὺς ἔπη ἤρειδε κατὰ τῶν ἱππέων. Here the middle denotes mutual exchange of hard words.

1376. ἔφλα με κ.τ.λ.—*Pac.* 1306, φλᾶν ταῦτα πάντα καὶ σποδεῖν. ἐπέτριβεν—972 and 1407.

1377. ὅστις οὐκ—cf. 692.

1378. σοφώτατον—σοφός being the special praise of Euripides and his school. ὦ τί σ' εἴπω ;—Dem. *de Cor.* 232 § 22, εἴτ' ὦ—τί ἂν εἰπών σέ τις ὀρθῶς προσείποι ;

1381. σου πάντα κ.τ.λ.—'the meaning of all your baby cries': τραυλίζω denotes lisping and imperfect talk generally.

1382. βρῦν—from this is derived βρύλλειν 'to drink,' *Eq.* 1126. εἴποις—the optative indicates indefinite frequency, and is followed by the iterative construction with ἄν ; cf. 54. ἐπέσχον—Hom. *Il.* ix. 489, οἶνον ἐπισχών.

1392. πηδᾶν ὅ τι λέξει—'are beating, to hear what' etc. : so *Ach.* 361, ἐμέ γε πόθος ὅ τι φρονεῖς ἔχει : cf. Eur. *Bacch.* 1289, καρδία πήδημ' ἔχει.

1395. λάβοιμεν...ἐρεβίνθου—*Pac.* 1223, οὐκ ἂν πριαίμην οὐδ' ἂν ἰσχάδος μιᾶς. For ἀλλ' οὐδ', 'nay not even,' cf. Dem. *Fals. leg.* 352 § 41, ὑπὲρ δὲ Φωκέων...ἀλλ' οὐδὲ μικρόν : id. *Meid.* 551 § 147, ἀλλ' οὐδ' ὁτιοῦν.

1397. κινητὰ καὶ μοχλευτά—perhaps a parody of Eur. *Med.* 1317, τί τάσδε κινεῖς κἀναμοχλεύεις πύλας ; we have had μοχλευτήν, 567.

1399. καινοῖς πράγμασιν—cf. 515, νεωτέροις πράγμασι.

1400. τῶν καθεστώτων κ.τ.λ.—Socrates according to Xenophon was really charged with teaching his pupils ὑπερορᾶν τῶν καθεστώτων νόμων (*Mem.* i. 2, 9).

1402. τρία ῥήμαθ'—Mart. vi. 54, 2, iunget vix tria verba miser. Note that ἦ is the proper Attic form of the 1st person imperfect, which has generally been altered into the later ἦν.

1403. αυτός—his father, who had forced the new learning upon him.
1404. γνώμαις κ.τ.λ.—cf. 101 and 950; and for ξύνειμι, *Vesp.* 1460, ξυνόντες γνώμαις ετέρων.
1405. Socrates, said his accuser, professed to make sons wiser than their fathers, and declared that they might justly proceed against them for incompetence (*Mem.* i. 2, 49).
1406. ίππευε—see note on 15.
1407. τέθριππον—sc. ἄρμα, a four-in-hand. τυπτόμενον επιτριβήναι—'to be beaten to death'; cf. 972.
1408. εκείσε κ.τ.λ.—lit. 'I will pass to that point in my argument at (from) which you cut me off' i.e. at which you interrupted me. τοῦ λόγου probably depends on εκείσε (though it might go with the verb): Hdt. vii. 239, άνειμι δὲ εκείσε τοῦ λόγου τῇ μοι τὸ πρότερον εξέλιπε. For μέτειμι Blaydes would prefer 'πάνειμι or (τῶν λόγων) άνειμι as in 1058.
1409. ἔτυπτες—here the two best manuscripts have the unclassical and unmetrical form ετύπτησας, an instance of the way in which copyists replaced genuine forms by words better known at the time when the manuscript was made (*New Phrynichus*, p. 106).
1415. κλάουσι κ.τ.λ.—traditionally a parody of Eur. *Alc.* 694, χαίρεις ὀρῶν φῶς πάτερα δ' οὐ χαίρειν δοκεῖς; a verse which is quoted in full *Thesm.* 194. Here the iambic line seems out of place; it is accordingly bracketed by Blaydes.
1416. τοῦτο τοὔργον—sc. τὸ τύπτεσθαι or τὸ κλάειν τυπτόμενον.
1417. δὶς παῖδες—the scholiast quotes from Theopompus, δὶς παῖδες οἱ γέροντες ὀρθῷ τῷ λόγῳ, and other passages.
1420. ἀλλ' οὐδαμοῦ—even if old men should be beaten, the principle is nowhere extended to fathers.
1421. οὔκουν κ.τ.λ.—but law, urges the son, is a mere matter of regulation; it can be altered. ὁ...θείς—the original proposer. R and V have τιθείς, the tense referring to the time when the enactment was made: Dem. *de Cor.* 227 § 6, ὁ τιθεὶς ἐξ ἀρχῆς Σόλων etc.
1423. τὸ λοιπόν—'henceforward': cf. 676.
1426. ἀφίεμεν—'we remit, and grant them (the fathers) a free gift of the beatings we have had'; i.e. we will start fair without retrospective retaliation. This is plainly the sense; but it involves a harsh omission of ἡμᾶς (ὑπ' αὐτῶν) before συγκεκόφθαι. Blaydes suggests that αὐτούς, ἡμᾶς or αὐτοί should be read for αὐτοῖς: R has αὐτούς.
1429. ψηφίσματ'—cf. 1018: *Av.* 1038, ψηφισματοπώλης, 'a bill-hawker,' who comes round with his wares in the new republic.

11—2

1433. πρὸς ταῦτα—990. σαυτόν ποτ'—you will some day have yourself to thank that your son won't let you beat him.
1436. ἐμοὶ κεκλαύσεται—'I shall have had my sufferings in vain.' σὺ δ' ἐγχανών—not 'you will die of laughing at me' (Merry), but 'you will have had the laugh of me when you are dead'; the participle as usual being the important word. For ἐγχανεῖν, 'to scoff at,' cf. *Eq.* 1313, ἐγχανεῖται τῇ πόλει: *Vesp.* 721, ἐγχάσκειν σοι. τεθνήξεις—the active form is right, as is shown by Aesch. *Ag.* 1279, τεθνήξομεν: cf. *Vesp.* 654: τεθνήξομαι is late Greek.
1438. τούτοισι—'these younger men,' the son and his fellows.
1440. ἀπὸ γὰρ ὀλοῦμαι—sc. if I don't listen (schol.): but is it not rather deprecatory, 'no more, pray, for 'twill be the death of me' (Green)? For the *tmesis* cf. 792.
1441. καὶ μήν κ.τ.λ.—i.e. apparently, you will find some comfort for your recent beating when you hear what I mean to do. Bergler however takes παθὼν ἅ κ.τ.λ. to mean 'if you yield again to my arguments, as you have already.'
1443. τυπτήσω—the regular Attic future of τύπτω, meaning 'to strike': 'I will wound' is πατάξω or παίσω. For ὥσπερ καί see note on 1177.
1444. μεῖζον κακόν—the father's common sense and human feeling are at length revolted by this further step in philosophical teaching, and he turns upon his son in righteous wrath. We have here a caricature of Euripides, who made Orestes excuse himself for matricide on the ground that he was less closely related to his mother than to his father (*Or.* 552). Mr Green points out that the same plea is urged by Apollo in Aesch. *Eum.* 658—666. τί δ' is answered by τί δ' ἄλλο below.
1449. ἐς τὸ βάραθρον—*Eq.* 1362, ἐς τὸ βάραθρον ἐμβαλῶ: *Ran.* 514 etc.
1452. ταυτὶ δι' ὑμᾶς—after his burst of rage Strepsiades turns to the Clouds, and appeals to them in expostulation for leading him astray.
1453. ἀναθείς—*Av.* 546, ἀναθείς σοι ἐμαυτόν: Thuc. viii. 82, 1, τὰ πράγματα πάντα ἀνετίθεσαν.
1454. μὲν οὖν—cf. 71.
1455. στρέψας—a pun on his name Strepsiades: cf. 434, στρεψοδικῆσαι.
1457. ἐπῄρετε—42: imperf. 'kept egging on' (Merry).
1466. μετ' ἐμοῦ 'λθών—Hermann suggests μετελθών: as μετέρχομαι, from the idea of pursuing, means prosecuting or visiting with vengeance.
1467. ἀλλ' οὐκ ἄν—cf. 871.

1468. πατρῷον Δία—a tragic line, as is shown by the long α in πατρῷον, and the title of the god. Apollo, not Zeus, was the special Athenian πατρῷος, but Ζεὺς πατρῷος is often appealed to by the characters in tragedies.

1469. ἰδού γε—cf. 818: and for ἀρχαῖος 984, 1357.

1471. δῖνος—see 828.

1473. διὰ τουτονὶ τὸν δῖνον—'because of that confounded dinus' (Blaydes): he means the whirl or vortex about which Socrates has taught him. τουτονί does not necessarily imply actual presence; see 1427, and note on 83. But the word δῖνος suggests another meaning, and in the next line Strepsiades suddenly sees its personification in an earthen pot, and vents his scorn upon it, literally turning his deity to clay.

1474. χυτρεοῦν—cf. *Vesp.* 618, τοῦ σοῦ δίνου, a wine-jar. Dindorf, Kock and Meineke reject this line, which they consider an interpolation due to taking τουτονί of something actually there. It seems however intended for the sake of the pun, and also as showing the old man's muddle-headedness, which is one of his strong points, e.g. 236 and 645.

1475. φληνάφα—'twaddle, babble'; *Eq.* 664, ἐφληνάφα. Pheidippides turns from his father and leaves the scene.

1476—1510. Strepsiades, repenting of his folly and enraged against philosophy and philosophers, attacks and burns the school. This scene was added in the second edition of the play.

1476. οἴμοι παρανοίας—for gen. cf. 925. **ὡς...ἄρα**—here certainly of past time, see 1271.

1477. ἐξέβαλλον—i.e. 'was for casting out.'

1478. ὦ φίλ' Ἑρμῆ—he turns to a bust of Hermes standing near the house, and asks for counsel and advice.

1480. ἐμοῦ κ.τ.λ.—gen. absol. **ἀδολεσχίᾳ** –'idle prating': Plat. *Parm.* 135 D, διὰ τῆς δοκούσης...ἀδολεσχίας: *Crat.* 401 B, μετεωρολόγοι καὶ ἀδολέσχαι τινές, the stock word of contempt for philosophers.

1481. εἴτ' αὐτούς—'whether I am to prosecute them by indictment'; the accusative depending on both verb and participle, as with νικᾶν λέγων: *Vesp.* 907, τῆς γραφῆς ἣν ἐγραψάμην τουτονί.

1482. διωκάθω—interrogative aorist, in form like ἀμυναθεῖν, 1323.
1483. ὀρθῶς παραινεῖς—after putting his ear to the statue's lips, to hear the god's decision.   δικορραφεῖν—Av. 1435: so ῥάπτω in the sense of devising or concocting.
1489. ἐμβάλῃς—Ach. 510, καὐτοῖς Ποσειδῶν ἐμβάλοι τὰς οἰκίας.
1492. ἀλαζόνες—for all their proud theories and impious boasts; cf. 102.   ἰού—a disciple rushes out of the house as the flames catch it.
1496. διαλεπτολογοῦμαι—'I am discoursing subtly (chopping logic) with the beams of your house' (Blaydes): cf. 320. Strepsiades is now introducing the house-beams to a subtle element (Green).
1498. θοἰμάτιον—see 497 and 856.
1502. οὗτος—Socrates himself is at length alarmed and comes out.
1503. ἀεροβατῶ—the master's own words, 225.
1506. τί γὰρ μαθόντες—this is the best supported reading. Some manuscripts have μαθόντ' ἐς, as in Plut. 899, ὑβρίζειν εἰς ἔμ'. The dual would refer to Socrates and Chaerephon only; but the plural is better, as all the disciples are meant. They are a godless lot, and deserve to be included in the common ruin. Some editors read παθόντες or παθόντ' ἐς: see 340 and 402.
1507. τὴν ἕδραν—ἐπὶ τίνος ὀχεῖται καὶ πῶς καὶ διὰ τί μένει (schol.): cf. Hdt. vii. 37, ὁ ἥλιος ἐκλιπὼν τὴν ἐκ τοῦ οὐρανοῦ ἕδρην ἀφανὴς ἦν: Eur. *Iph. T.* 193, ἀλλάξας δ' ἐξ ἕδρας ἱερὸν μετέβαλεν ὄμμα Ἅλιος. We have τὰς ὁδούς of the moon in 171 and 584.
1508. δίωκε—assigned by Meineke and others to the chorus. R and V prefix 'Ἑρμ(ῆς), from 1478, as if the god himself led the attack. The words are spoken to the slave, but meant for everyone.

'Mr Grote (*History of Greece*, part ii. chap. 37, ad fin.) is probably right in suggesting that Aristophanes took this idea from the actual circumstances attending the subversion of the Pythagorean order in Croton, where their school was set on fire, and very many perished in the flames, among whom, according to one tradition, was the αὐτός, the great master himself' (Rogers).

1509. A line most damaging to Socrates, as Hermann points out, coming thus at the end of the play when the poet spoke his real convictions, and leaving its sting in the minds of the spectators.

1510. τό γε τήμερον—'for the day.' Meineke adopts (from Moeris) εἶναι for ἡμῖν. No doubt τό γε τήμερον εἶναι is a good prose phrase; e.g. Plat. *Crat.* 273 C, τὸ μὲν τήμερον εἶναι: ib. 396 D, τὸ νῦν εἶναι etc. But there is not sufficient reason to alter the text; and besides, the pronoun is needed; cf. *Thesm.* 1227, πέπαισται μετρίως ἡμῖν.

INDEX I

Academia 1005
accusative, adverbial 55
,, anticipatory of subject 95, 145, 479, 493, 1115
,, cognate 99, 115, 131, 439
adverb with subst. 1120
Amynias 31, 686, 1259
Anaxagoras 378
aor. inf. of future time 35, 1141
Athamas 257
Athenian love of law 208, 1220

Byzantium 249

calendar 615
Carcinus 1261
Chaerephon 104, 144, 156, 503 etc.
Cleitagora 684
Cleon 549, 582, 1058
Cleonymus 353, 400, 680
Coesyra 48, 800
Colias 52

dative with subst. 305
Democritus 377
Diagoras 830
diminutives 80, 222, 746
Dionysia 508, 609
Doric forms 30, 249, 276

Electra 534
Ephesus, temple at 599
Euboea 211
Eupolis 553

gender of words 659 sq.
Genetyllis 52
genitive of exclamation 153, 364, 818
,, partitive 59, 107, 138

genitive of price 22, 31, 473, 864
,, ,, time 9, 371, 721
,, with words of congratulation 166, (1324)

Hermes 1234, 1478
Homer 1056
Hyperbolus 551, 876, 1065

Iapetus 998
infinitive for imper. 850, 1080

Leogoras 109
Lucretius 371, 378, 392, 404

Maeotis, lake 273
Maricas 553
Megacles 46, 124, 815
Memnon 622
Mimas 273
Months, reckoning of, 17, 1131

Panathenaea 386
Pandeletus 924
participle 381, 1241
Pasias 21, 1214
Peleus 1063
Pericles 859
pluperf. term. 380, 1347
Prodicus 361

Sarpedon 622
Socrates misrepresented 98, 140, 703, 1400, 1405
Solon, ideal law-giver 1187
Sunium 401

Theorus 400
Thessalian witches 749
Thetis 1067
Trophonius 508

INDEX II

ἀβέλτερος 1201
ἄγομαι, φέρομαι 241
ἀγορά 991, 1055
ἀγορητής 1057
ἀδολέσχης 1485
ἀδολεσχία 1480
ἀεροβατῶ 225, 1503
ἀήρ 230, 264
ἀθῷος 1413
-αι inf. elided 7, 42, 550, 780, 988, 1140, 1341, 1357
αἰβοῖ 102, 829
αἰγίδος ἡνίοχος 602
Αἰδώς 995
αἰθήρ 264, 570
ἀκαρῆ 496
ἀκόρητος 44
ἀκούω 529, 1329
ἀλαζών 102, 1492
ἀλεκτρυών 4, 661, 664
ἀληθές 841
ἀλλά repeated in dialogue 123—7
,, 'still' 'at least' 1364, 1369
ἀλλ' οὐ 'and not' 132
ἀλλ' οὐδέ 1396
ἀλλ' οὖν γε 1002
ἄλλο τι (ἤ) 423
ἄλλως 1203
ἄλλως τε καί 1269
ἀμαξίς 864
ἀμέλει 422, 488, 877
ἀμυναθεῖν 1323
ἀμφί μοι 595
ἀμφορῆς 1203
ἄν iterative 54, 855, 1382, 1402
,, omitted 426
,, repeated 118, 783, 840, 1056 etc.
ἀναγεύω 523
ἀνάγκη 377, 405

ἀναπείθω with double acc. 77 (cf. 999)
ἀναπιμπλάναι 995, 1023
ἀναπλάττειν 995
Ἀναπνοή 627
ἀνάρμοστος 908
ἀνατιθέναι τὰ πράγματα 1453
ἀνεῖται κίνδυνος 955
ἀνθεῖν 897, 962, (1174)
ἄνθος 1026
ἀνόητα 417
ἀντιγραφή 472
ἀνυπόδητος 103
ἀνύσας (τι) 181, 506, 635, 1253
ἄξιος with dat. 474
ἀξύστατος 1367
ἀπαιολή 1150
ἀπαιόλημα 729
ἀπαλλάττομαι 1194
ἀπαστίαν ἄγειν 621
ἀπεριμερίμνως 136
ἀπερυθριᾶσαι 1215
ἀπ' ὄνου 1273
ἀποστερεῖν 1305
ἀποφεύγω 167
ἀπραγμοσύνη 1007
ἆρα 319, 410, 1027, 1252, 1271, 1301, 1476
ἄρα 465
ἀράττειν 1373
ἀρνακίδες 730
ἁρπάζω with gen. 982
ἀρχαί 1197
ἀρχαῖος 915, 984, 1156, 1469
ἀσκάντης 633
-ατο = -ντο 1199
ἀτάρ 382, 403
ἀτραπός)(ὁδός 76
ἀτρέμας 390
ἀτρεμεί 261

INDEX II

Ἀττικὸν βλέπος 1176
αὑτοῖς τροχοῖς 1302
αὑτοῦ)(αὐτοῦ, position of 515, 905, 1109
ἀφανίζειν 542, 972
ἄφυκτος 1047

βαλανεῖα 837, 991, 1054
βάραθρον 1449
βεκκεσέληνος 398
βλιτομάμμας 1001
βολβοί 188
Βουφόνια 985
βρενθύεσθαι 362
βρῦν 1382
βρίω with dat. 45
βωμολοχεύεσθαι 960
βωμολόχος 910

γάρ 331, 679, 868, 1359
,, in a question 191, 218, 248
γελοῖος 1241
γηγενεῖς 853
γλισχραντιλογεξεπίτριπτος 1004
Γλῶττα 424, 1058
γραμματεύς 770
γράφεσθαι 758, 770
γρύζειν 963
γυμνός 498, 965

δαί, τί; 491, 1275
Δαιταλῆς 529
δάκνειν τὸν θυμόν 1369
δάκτυλον, κατά 651
δ' οὖν 39
δέδοικα μή with ind.)(subj. 493
δεινὰ ποιεῖν 388, 583
δήμαρχος 37
δῆμος = ἐκκλησία 432
δημότης 210
διαγράφω 774
διαιρεῖν 741
διακεκναισμένος 120
διαλεπτολογεῖσθαι 1496
Διάσια 408, 864
διατρέχω 1005
διδάσκομαι 111, 127, 783, 1338
διεντέρευμα 166
διερρυηκώς 873
Διιπόλια 984

δίκαι, νόμοι καί 1040
δῖνος 380, 1473
διφθέρα 72
διωκαθεῖν 1481
δρόμος 25, 28
δυσβουλία 587

ἐγκεκορδυλημένος 10
ἐγχάσκειν 1436
ἔδρα, τῆς σελήνης 1507
εἰ δὲ μή 1433
εἶεν 1075
εἰκάδες 17
εἰ μή with particip. 229
εἴλλω 761
εἴξασι 341
εἴξεις 1001
εἰσάγειν δίκην 782, (845)
εἴσοδος of the stage 326
εἶτα, ἔπειτα 524, 860, 1042, 1214, 1249
εἶτα without δέ 66, 581, 609, 963
εἴτε, εἴτε 1243, 1481
,, ἤ 271
ἐκλείπω 584
ἐκπίπτειν 1272
ἐκπλήττεσθαι 810
ἐκστρέφω 88, 554
ἐκτιθέναι 531
ἐλαύνω 25, 28, 29, 1298
ἕλκω 540 (553), 1004
ἔμελλον ἄρα 1301
ἐμπλησθείς 386
ἐν δίκῃ 1332
ἔν τι 681
ἐνεχυράζω 35, 241
ἔνη καὶ νέα 1134, 1178, 1222
ἐνόπλιον, κατ' 651
ἐνταῦθα, -θοῖ 814, 843
ἐντεινάμενος 968
ἐντυλίττω 987
ἐξαλίσας 32, 33
ἐξαμβλόω 137
ἐξαράττειν 1373
ἕξει 633
ἐξεκόπην 24
ἔξοδος 579
ἐπαίρω 42
ἐπακούω 263

ἐπαναφέρω 1080
ἐπέχω 1382
ἐπί with dat. 1205
ἐπιάλλω 1299
ἐπιθαυμάζω 1147
ἐπιμαρτύρομαι 495
ἐπίσχες 1047
ἐπισχών 495
ἐπιχαλκεύειν 422
ἐρείδω 558, 1375
ἐς κόρακας 123, 133, 646, 789, 871
ἐτεόν 35, 93, 1502
εὐθύ with gen. 162
εὔπτερος 800
εὑρίσκω, augment of 137
εὐστόμει 833
ἔχων with verb 131

Ζεὺς βασιλεύς 2, 153
,, πατρῷος 1468
ζύγιος 122
ζυγωθρίζω 745

ἤ...ἤ 622
ἦ, 1st pers. 530, 1402
ἤδη 'ever' 370, 766, 1061
ἡμέτερος with gen. 1202
ἠμί 1145
ἡμιεκτέον 643
ἤν without ἄν 1215
Ἡράκλεια λουτρά 1051
ἥσθην 174
ἥττων 1081

θέσεις 1191
Θουριομάντεις 332
θυμβρεπίδειπνος 421
θυμόσοφος 877

ἰατροτέχνης 332
ἰδέα 'form' 344
ἰδού 82, 635, 670, 818
ἱερομνημονεῖν 624
ἱμάτιον 987 (266)
ἵνα τί; 1192
ἰού 1, 1321
ἰοῦ 1170
ἱππάζυμαι 15
ἵππερος 74
ἱππῆς, οἱ 120

ἱππική 27, 107
ἵππος, names compounded with 63
ἴτης 445

καί emphatic 785, 840
,, δή 778, 906
κακόν, τό 26
καλεῖν δίκην 780
καλῶ fut. 452, 632, 1001
καμπή 969
κἄπειτα following particip. 409
κατὰ μῆνα 756
,, σεαυτὸν τρέπου 1263
,, σελήνην 626
καταλόει 838
καταπροίξει 1240
κεῖμαι 126, 550
κέντρων 450
κέραμος tiling 1127
κεφαλήν, ἐς τήν 40
κιχλίζω 983
κλάω 58, 1415
κληρουχική 203
κλῇσις 1189
κλητεύω 1218
κομᾶν 545
κόμην ἔχων 14
κομμάτιον 510
κοππατίας 23, 438
κόρδαξ 540
κορίζομαι 68
κότταβος 1073
κρεμάθρα 218, 869
κριμνώδη κατανίφει 965
κρίνεσθαι 66
Κρόνια 398
Κρόνιππος 1070
κρόταλον 260
κροῦσις 318
κύκλιοι χοροί 333
κινῇ 268
κύρβις 448
κωμήτης 965

λαβή 551
λάρος 591
λεπτός 230
λεπτότης 153
λημᾶν 327
λινόδετος with gen. 763

INDEX II

λιπαρός 300, 1002
λόγος δίκαιος (κρείττων), ἄδικος (ἥττων) 113, 116, 883, 889 sq.
λόγω, ἄμφω τώ 112, 882
λοιδορεῖσθαι 62
λοιπόν, τό 677, 1423
λούω, forms of 838
λοφεῖον 751

μά 330, 1291
μανίαι 832
Μαραθωνόμαχοι 985
μαρτύρομαι (495), 1222, 1297
ματτυολοιχός 451
μελιτοῦττα 507
μέν with ἐγώ etc. 29, 563
μὲν οὖν 71, 221, 1113, 1454
μέντοι 787, 1338
μεριμνοφροντισταί 101
μέσον ἔχω 1047
μετέρχομαι 1466
μετέωρος etc. 228, 333, 360
μηλολόνθη 763
μή μοί γε 84, 433
μῖλαξ 1007
μνησικακῶ 999
μοι eth. 57, 107
μου ,, 74
μορίαν 1005
μυρρίνη 1364
μυστοδόκος 303

νεοττοτροφεῖν 999
νομίζεται 498, 962, 1185, 1416, 1420
νομίζω 423, 819
νόμισμα 248
νουμηνία 1191, 1195
νύκτες 2

ξύλον 592, 1431
ξυμβαίνειν 67
ξυνωρικεύομαι 15
ξυστίς 70

ὀβολοστάται 1155
ὄζειν with gen. 50, 1007
οἰμώζειν 217
οἷος = ὅτι τοιοῦτος 699, 1158
,, with dat. 1109

ὀλίγου 722
ὄμμα αἰθέρος 285
ὀμνύναι constr. 248, 1241
ὀνειροπολῶ with acc. 16, 27
ὀνομάζω with two acc. 847
ὅπως 'when' 60
,, with fut. 257, 489, 824, 882 etc.
ὅπως ἄν 759, 776
ὀρεχθεῖν 1368
ὁ with τίς etc. 748, 1270
ὅς with antecedent implied 1226
ὅστις 1044
,, οὑ 692, 1377
ὅτε giving reason 7, 1217
οὐ μή 296, 367, 505
οὐδέ 'also not' 126
οὐδ' ὥς 527
οὐδὲν λέγω 644, 781
οὐκ ἄν ellipt. 5, 108, (1379)
οὗτος 83, 97, 723, 1473
οὑτοσί 84
οὕτω...ὡς in prayer 520
ὀφλισκάνω 34, 777, 1035
ὀψοφαγεῖν 983

παιπάλη 260
παλαίστρα 177, 1054
πάνθ' ὅ τι 328
παρ' αὑτοῖς 112
παρακόπτω 640
παρανοίας ἑλεῖν 845
παρατείνω 212
παρέλκω 553
παρέχω with inf. 422, 441
πάσχω)(ποιῶ 234, 662, 798, 1198
πέκεσθαι 1356
περιδίδομαι 644
περίοδος γῆς 206
περιορᾶν constr. 125
περιφρονεῖν 225
περσικαί 151
πηδᾶν with καρδία 1392
πνιγεύς 96
ποιεῖν εἰς 557
ποῖος 247, 367, 1232, 1337
πολεμιστήρια 28
πολιοῦχος 602
πόλις, the acropolis 69
πολλάς sc. πληγάς 972
πολλοῦ 915

πότης 57
πράγματα 515, 1399
πραγμάτιον 1004
πράττομαι with double acc. 246
πράττων καὶ βουλεύων 419
προβάλλω 489, 757
πρόβολος 1161
προδιδάσκω 476
προϊέναι 1214
προμνήστρια 41
πρόπολος 436
πρόσσχετε 575
προσφύω 372
προτένθαι 1198
πρὸ τοῦ 5, 654, 1291
πρυτανεῖα 1136, 1180, 1255
πῶς δοκεῖς 881

ῥέγκω 5, 11
ῥηγνύναι φωνήν 357, 960
ῥιγῶν 416, 442

σαμφόρας 23
σειραφόρος 122
σελήνην καθαιρεῖν 750
σιδάρεοι 249
σκίμπους 254
σμῆνος 297
σοφός 520, 1370, 1378
σπαθᾶν 53, 55
στέμφυλα 45
στέφανος 256, 625
στομοῦν 1108
στρεβλοῦν 620
συγγίγνεσθαι 252, 1317
σχάζω 107, 740
σχινδάλαμοι 130

ταῦτα adv. acc. 319
τάχυ γ' ἄν 647
τεθνήξω 1436
τερατεία 318
τέττιγες 984, 1360
τί acc. cogn. 202, 1147
τίθεσθαι of names 65, 67

τί μαθὼν)(παθών; 340, 402, 1506
τίς ὤν; 893
τόκος 18, 20, 1285
„ τόκου 1156
τριβολεκτράπελος 1003
τρίβων 869
τρίμμα 260, (447)
τρυγοδαίμων 296
τρύμη 448
τυπτήσω 1445

ὕαλος 768
ὕειν 368, 370, 1118
ὑπακούω 263
ὑπανίσταμαι 993
ὑπολύω 152
ὑψικέρατα 597

φαλακρός 540
φαρμακοπῶλαι 766
φασιανοί 109
φελλεύς 71
φέρομαι 376, 406
φλέγεσθαι 992
φοιτᾶν 916
φορτικός 524
φροντίζω with gen. 75, 125
φροντιστήριον 94
φρουρᾶς ᾄδων 721
φύσις 'appearance' 503
φωρᾶν 499
φῶς, πρὸς τό 632

χάος 424
χαύνωσις 875
χολᾶν 833
χοῦς 1238
χρέος, τί ἔβα με; 30
χρῆμα with gen. 2
χρηστός 8
χωρεῖν 18, 906, 1238

ψαρός 1225

ὥρας, ἐς τάς 562

THE PITT PRESS SERIES

AND THE
CAMBRIDGE SERIES FOR SCHOOLS AND TRAINING COLLEGES.

Volumes of the latter series are marked by a dagger †.

COMPLETE LIST

GREEK

Author	Work	Editor	Price
Aeschylus	Prometheus Vinctus	Rackham	2/6
Aristophanes	Aves—Plutus—Ranae	Green	3/6 each
,,	Nubes, Vespae	Graves	3/6 each
,,	Acharnians	,,	3/-
Demosthenes	Olynthiacs	Glover	2/6
,,	Philippics I, II, III	G. A. Davies	2/6
Euripides	Alcestis	Hadley	2/6
,,	Hecuba	Hadley	2/6
,,	Helena	Pearson	3/6
,,	Heraclidae	Pearson	3/6
,,	Hercules Furens	Gray & Hutchinson	2/-
,,	Hippolytus	Hadley	2/-
,,	Iphigeneia in Aulis	Headlam	2/6
,,	Medea	,,	2/6
,,	Orestes	Wedd	4/6
,,	Phoenissae	Pearson	4/-
Herodotus	Book V	Shuckburgh	3/-
,,	,, IV, VI, VIII, IX	,,	4/- each
,,	,, IX 1—89	,,	2/6
Homer	Odyssey IX, X	Edwards	2/6 each
,,	,, XXI	,,	2/-
,,	,, XI	Nairn	2/-
,,	Iliad VI, XXII, XXIII, XXIV	Edwards	2/- each
,,	Iliad IX and X	Lawson	2/6
Lucian	Somnium, Charon, etc.	Heitland	3/6
,,	Menippus and Timon	Mackie	3/6
Plato	Apologia Socratis	Adam	3/6
,,	Crito, Euthyphro	,,	2/6 each
,,	Protagoras	J. & A. M. Adam	4/6
Plutarch	Demosthenes	Holden	4/6
,,	Gracchi	,,	6/-
,,	Nicias	,,	5/-
,,	Sulla	,,	6/-
,,	Timoleon	,,	6/-

THE PITT PRESS SERIES, ETC.

GREEK continued

Author	Work	Editor	Price
Sophocles	Oedipus Tyrannus	Jebb	4/-
Thucydides	Book III	Spratt	5/-
,,	Book VI	,,	6/-
,,	Book VII	Holden	5/-
Xenophon	Agesilaus	Hailstone	2/6
,,	Anabasis I, II	Pretor	4/-
,,	,, I, III, IV, V	,,	2/- each
,,	,, II, VI, VII	,,	2/6 each
† ,,	,, I, II, III, IV, V, VI	Edwards	1/6 each
	(With complete Vocabularies)		
,,	Hellenics I, II	,,	3/6
,,	Cyropaedeia I	Shuckburgh	2/6
,,	,, II	,,	2/-
,,	,, III, IV, V	Holden	5/-
,,	,, VI, VII, VIII	,,	5/-
,,	Memorabilia I, II	Edwards	2/6 each

LATIN

The volumes marked * contain Vocabulary

Author	Work	Editor	Price
Bede	Eccl. History III, IV	Mayor & Lumby	7/6
Caesar	De Bello Gallico		
	Com. I, III, VI, VIII	Peskett	1/6 each
,,	,, II–III, and VII	,,	2/- each
,,	,, I–III	,,	3/-
,,	,, IV–V	,,	1/6
*† ,,	,, I, II, III, IV, V, VI, VII	Shuckburgh	1/6 each
,,	De Bello Gallico. Bk I	,,	-/9
	(With Vocabulary only: no notes)		
,,	De Bello Gallico. Bk VII		-/8
	(Text only)		
,,	De Bello Civili. Com. I	Peskett	3/-
,,	,, ,, Com. III	,,	2/6
Cicero	Actio Prima in C. Verrem	Cowie	1/6
,,	De Amicitia, De Senectute	Reid	3/6 each
,,	De Officiis. Bk III	Holden	2/-
,,	Pro Lege Manilia	Nicol	1/6
,,	Div. in Q. Caec. et Actio Prima in C. Verrem	Heitland & Cowie	3/-
,,	Ep. ad Atticum. Lib. II	Pretor	3/-
,,	Orations against Catiline	Nicol	2/6
*† ,,	In Catilinam I	Flather	1/6
,,	Philippica Secunda	Peskett	3/6
,,	Pro Archia Poeta	Reid	2/-
,,	,, Balbo	,,	1/6
,,	,, Milone	Reid	2/6
,,	,, Murena	Heitland	3/-
,,	,, Plancio	Holden	4/6
,,	,, Roscio	J. C. Nicol	2/6
,,	,, Sulla	Reid	3/6
,,	Somnium Scipionis	Pearman	2/-

LATIN continued

Author	Work	Editor	Price
*Cornelius Nepos	Four parts	Shuckburgh	1/6 each
*Erasmus	Colloquia Latina	G. M. Edwards	1/6
,,	Colloquia Latina (*With Vocabulary only: no notes*)	,,	-/9
* ,,	Altera Colloquia Latina	,,	1/6
Horace	Epistles. Bk I	Shuckburgh	2/6
,,	Odes and Epodes	Gow	5/-
,,	Odes. Books I, III	,,	2/- each
,,	,, Books II, IV; Epodes ,,		1/6 each
,,	Satires. Book I		2/-
Juvenal	Satires	Duff	5/-
Livy	Book I	H. J. Edwards	*In the Press*
,,	,, II	Conway	2/6
,,	,, IV, XXVII	Stephenson	2/6 each
,,	,, V	Whibley	2/6
,,	,, VI	Marshall	2/6
,,	,, IX	Anderson	2/6
,,	,, XXI, XXII	Dimsdale	2/6 each
*,,	(adapted from) Story of the Kings of Rome	G. M. Edwards	1/6
*,,	,, Horatius and other Stories	,,	1/6
,,	,, ,, (*With Vocabulary only: no notes*)		-/9
Lucan	Pharsalia. Bk I	Heitland & Haskins	1/6
,,	De Bello Civili. Bk VII	Postgate	2/-
Lucretius	Books III and V	Duff	2/- each
Ovid	Fasti. Book VI	Sidgwick	1/6
,,	Metamorphoses, Bk I	Dowdall	1/6
,,	,, Bk VIII	Summers	1/6
* ,,	Phaethon and other stories	G. M. Edwards	1/6
*† ,,	Selections from the Tristia	Simpson	1/6
*†Phaedrus	Fables. Bks I and II	Flather	1/6
Plautus	Epidicus	Gray	3/-
,,	Stichus	Fennell	2/6
,,	Trinummus	Gray	3/6
Pliny	Letters. Book VI	Duff	2/6
Quintus Curtius	Alexander in India	Heitland & Raven	3/6
Sallust	Catiline	Summers	2/-
,,	Jugurtha	,,	2/6
Tacitus	Agricola and Germania	Stephenson	3/-
,,	Hist. Bk I	Davies	2/6
,,	,, Bk III	Summers	2/6
Terence	Hautontimorumenos	Gray	3/-
Vergil	Aeneid I to XII	Sidgwick	1/6 each
*†,,	,, I, II, III, V, VI, IX, X, XI, XII	,,	1/6 each
,,	Bucolics	,,	1/6
,,	Georgics I, II, and III, IV	,,	2/- each
,,	Complete Works, Vol. I, Text	,,	3/6
,,	,, ,, Vol. II, Notes	,,	4/6
,,	Opera Omnia	B. H. Kennedy	3/6

THE PITT PRESS SERIES, ETC.

FRENCH

*The volumes marked * contain Vocabulary*

Author	Work	Editor	Price
About	Le Roi des Montagnes	Ropes	2/-
Balzac	Le Médecin de Campagne	Payen Payne	3/-
*Biart	Quand j'étais petit, Pts I, II	Boïelle	2/- each
Boileau	L'Art Poétique	Nichol Smith	2/6
Corneille	Polyeucte	Braunholtz	2/-
,,	Le Cid	Eve	2/-
De Bonnechose	Lazare Hoche	Colbeck	2/-
,,	Bertrand du Guesclin	Leathes	2/-
* ,,	,, Part II	,,	1/6
D'Harleville	Le Vieux Célibataire	G. Masson	2/-
Delavigne	Louis XI	Eve	2/-
,,	Les Enfants d'Edouard	,,	2/-
De Lamartine	Jeanne d'Arc	Clapin & Ropes	1/6
De Vigny	La Canne de Jonc	Eve	1/6
*Dumas	La Fortune de D'Artagnan	Ropes	2/-
*Enault	Le Chien du Capitaine	Verrall	2/-
Erckmann-Chatrian	La Guerre	Clapin	3/-
,,	Waterloo, Le Blocus	Ropes	3/- each
,,	Madame Thérèse	,,	3/-
,,	Histoire d'un Conscrit	,,	3/-
Gautier	Voyage en Italie (Selections)	Payen Payne	3/-
Guizot	Discours sur l'Histoire de la Révolution d'Angleterre	Eve	2/6
Hugo	Les Burgraves	,,	2/6
,,	Selected Poems	,,	
Lemercier	Frédégonde et Brunehaut	G. Masson	2/-
*Malot	Remi et ses Amis	Verrall	2/-
* ,,	Remi en Angleterre	,,	2/-
Merimée	Colomba (*Abridged*)	Ropes	2/-
Michelet	Louis XI & Charles the Bold	,,	2/6
Molière	Le Bourgeois Gentilhomme	Clapin	1/6
,,	L'École des Femmes	Saintsbury	2/6
,,	Les Précieuses ridicules	Braunholtz	2/-
,,	,, (*Abridged Edition*)	,,	1/-
,,	Le Misanthrope	,,	2/6
,,	L'Avare	,,	2/6
*Perrault	Fairy Tales	Rippmann	1/6
,,	,,	,,	-/9
	(*With Vocabulary only: no notes*)		
Piron	La Métromanie	Masson	2/-
Ponsard	Charlotte Corday	Ropes	2/-
Racine	Les Plaideurs	Braunholtz	2/-
,,	,, (*Abridged Edition*)	,,	1/-
,,	Athalie	Eve	2/-
Saintine	Picciola	Ropes	2/-
Sandeau	Mdlle de la Seiglière	,,	2/-
Scribe & Legouvé	Bataille de Dames	Bull	2/-
Scribe	Le Verre d'Eau	Colbeck	2/-
Sédaine	Le Philosophe sans le savoir	Bull	2/-

4

THE PITT PRESS SERIES, ETC.

FRENCH continued

Author	Work	Editor	Price
Souvestre	Un Philosophe sous les Toits	Eve	2/-
,,	Le Serf & Le Chevrier de Lorraine	Ropes	2/-
*Souvestre	Le Serf	Ropes	1/6
,,	,, (*With Vocabulary only: no notes*)	,,	-/9
Spencer	A Primer of French Verse		3/-
Staël, Mme de	Le Directoire	Masson & Prothero	2/-
,,	Dix Années d'Exil (Book II chapters 1—8)	,,	2/-
Thierry	Lettres sur l'histoire de France (XIII—XXIV)	,,	2/6
,,	Récits des Temps Mérovingiens, I—III	Masson & Ropes	3/-
Voltaire	Histoire du Siècle de Louis XIV, in three parts	Masson & Prothero	2/6 each
Xavier de Maistre	La Jeune Sibérienne. Le Lépreux de la Cité d'Aoste	Masson	1/6

GERMAN

*The volumes marked * contain Vocabulary*

Author	Work	Editor	Price
*Andersen	Eight Stories	Rippmann	2/6
Benedix	Dr Wespe	Breul	3/-
Freytag	Der Staat Friedrichs des Grossen	Wagner	2/-
,,	Die Journalisten	Eve	2/6
Goethe	Knabenjahre (1749—1761)	Wagner & Cartmell	2/-
,,	Hermann und Dorothea	,, ,,	3/6
,,	Iphigenie auf Tauris	Breul	3/6
*Grimm	Twenty Stories	Rippmann	3/-
Gutzkow	Zopf und Schwert	Wolstenholme	3/6
Hackländer	Der geheime Agent	E. L. Milner Barry	3/-
Hauff	Das Bild des Kaisers	Breul	3/-
,,	Das Wirthshaus im Spessart	Schlottmann & Cartmell	3/-
*,,	Die Karavane	Schlottmann	3/-
*,,	Der Scheik von Alessandria	Rippmann	2/6
Immermann	Der Oberhof	Wagner	3/-
*Klee	Die deutschen Heldensagen	Wolstenholme	3/-
Kohlrausch	Das Jahr 1813	Cartmell	2/-
Lessing	Minna von Barnhelm	Wolstenholme	3/-
Lessing & Gellert	Selected Fables	Breul	3/-
Raumer	Der erste Kreuzzug	Wagner	2/-
Riehl	Culturgeschichtliche Novellen	Wolstenholme	3/-
*,,	Die Ganerben & Die Gerechtigkeit Gottes	,,	3/-
Schiller	Wilhelm Tell	Breul	2/6
,,	,, (*Abridged Edition*)	,,	1/6

5

THE PITT PRESS SERIES, ETC.

GERMAN continued

Author	Work	Editor	Price
Schiller	Geschichte des dreissigjährigen Kriegs. Book III.	Breul	3/-
,,	Maria Stuart	,,	3/6
,,	Wallenstein I.	,,	3/6
,,	Wallenstein II.	,,	3/6
Sybel	Prinz Eugen von Savoyen	Quiggin	2/6
Uhland	Ernst, Herzog von Schwaben	Wolstenholme	3/6
	German Dactylic Poetry	Wagner	3/-
	Ballads on German History	,,	2/-

SPANISH

Le Sage & Isla	Los Ladrones de Asturias	Kirkpatrick	3/-
Galdós	Trafalgar	,,	4/-

ENGLISH

Author	Work	Editor	Price
	Historical Ballads	Sidgwick	1/6
	Old Ballads	,,	1/6
Bacon	History of the Reign of King Henry VII	Lumby	3/-
,,	Essays	West	3/6
,,	New Atlantis	G. C. M. Smith	1/6
Burke	American Speeches	Innes	3/-
Chaucer	Prologue and Knight's Tale	M. Bentinck-Smith	2/6
,,	Clerkes Tale and Squires Tale	Winstanley	2/6
Cowley	Prose Works	Lumby	4/-
Defoe	Robinson Crusoe, Part I	Masterman	2/-
Earle	Microcosmography	West	3/- & 4/-
Goldsmith	Traveller and Deserted Village	Murison	1/6
Gray	Poems	Tovey	4/-
† ,,	Ode on the Spring and The Bard	,,	8d.
† ,,	Ode on the Spring and The Elegy	,,	8d.
Kingsley	The Heroes	E. A. Gardner	1/6
Lamb	Tales from Shakespeare. 2 Series	Flather	1/6 each
Macaulay	Lord Clive	Innes	1/6
,,	Warren Hastings	,,	1/6
,,	William Pitt and Earl of Chatham	,,	2/6
† ,,	John Bunyan	,,	1/-
† ,,	John Milton	Flather	1/6
,,	Lays and other Poems	,,	1/6
,,	History of England Chaps. I—III	Reddaway	2/-
Mayor	A Sketch of Ancient Philosophy from Thales to Cicero		3/6
,,	Handbook of English Metre		2/-
Milton	Arcades	Verity	1/6
,,	Ode on the Nativity, L'Allegro, Il Penseroso & Lycidas	,,	2/6
† ,,	Comus & Lycidas	,,	2/-
,,	Samson Agonistes	,,	2/6
,,	Sonnets	,,	1/6
..	Paradise Lost, six parts	,,	2/- each
More	History of King Richard III	Lumby	3/6

THE PITT PRESS SERIES, ETC.

ENGLISH *continued*

Author	Work	Editor	Price
More	Utopia	Lumby	2/-
Pope	Essay on Criticism	West	2/-
Scott	Marmion	Masterman	2/6
,,	Lady of the Lake	,,	2/6
,,	Lay of the last Minstrel	Flather	2/-
,,	Legend of Montrose	Simpson	2/6
,,	Lord of the Isles	Flather	2/-
,,	Old Mortality	Nicklin	2/6
,,	Kenilworth	Flather	2/6
,,	The Talisman	A. S. Gaye	2/-
,,	Quentin Durward	Murison	2/-
Shakespeare	A Midsummer-Night's Dream	Verity	1/6
,,	Twelfth Night	,,	1/6
,,	Julius Caesar	,,	1/6
,,	The Tempest	,,	1/6
,,	King Lear	,,	1/6
,,	Merchant of Venice	,,	1/6
,,	King Richard II	,,	1/6
,,	As You Like It	,,	1/6
,,	King Henry V	,,	1/6
,,	Macbeth	,,	1/6
Shakespeare & Fletcher	Two Noble Kinsmen	Skeat	3/6
Sidney	An Apologie for Poetrie	Shuckburgh	3/-
Spenser	Fowre Hymnes	Miss Winstanley	2/-
Wordsworth	Selected Poems	Miss Thomson	1/6
West	Elements of English Grammar		2/6
,,	English Grammar for Beginners		1/-
,,	Key to English Grammars		3/6 *net*
Carlos	Short History of British India		1/-
Mill	Elementary Commercial Geography		1/6
Bartholomew	Atlas of Commercial Geography		3/-
Robinson	Church Catechism Explained		2/-
Jackson	The Prayer Book Explained. Part I		2/6

MATHEMATICS

Ball	Elementary Algebra		4/6
†Blythe	Geometrical Drawing		
	Part I		2/6
	Part II		2/-
Euclid	Books I—VI, XI, XII	H. M. Taylor	5/-
,,	Books I—VI	,,	4/-
,,	Books I—IV	,,	3/-
	Also separately		
,,	Books I, & II; III, & IV; V, & VI; XI, & XII		1/6 *each*
,,	Solutions to Exercises in Taylor's Euclid	W. W. Taylor	10/6
	And separately		
,,	Solutions to Bks I—IV	,,	6/-
,,	Solutions to Books VI. XI	,,	6/-

THE PITT PRESS SERIES, ETC.

MATHEMATICS continued

Author	Work	Editor	Price
Hobson & Jessop	Elementary Plane Trigonometry		4/6
Loney	Elements of Statics and Dynamics		7/6
	Part I. Elements of Statics		4/6
,,	,, II. Elements of Dynamics		3/6
,,	Elements of Hydrostatics		4/6
,,	Solutions to Examples, Hydrostatics		5/-
,,	Solutions of Examples, Statics and Dynamics		7/6
,,	Mechanics and Hydrostatics		.1/6
Smith, C.	Arithmetic for Schools, with or without answers		
,,	Part I. Chapters I—VIII. Elementary, with or without answers		
,,	Part II. Chapters IX—XX, with or without answers		
Hale, G.	Key to Smith's Arithmetic		

EDUCATIONAL SCIENCE

†Bidder & Baddeley	Domestic Economy		
†Bosanquet	{ The Education of the Young from the *Republic* of Plato }		
†Burnet	Aristotle on Education		
Comenius	Life and Educational Works	S. S. Laurie	
Farrar	General Aims of the Teacher	} 1 vol.	
Poole	Form Management		
†Hope & Browne	A Manual of School Hygiene		
Locke	Thoughts on Education	R. H. Quick	
†MacCunn	The Making of Character		
Milton	Tractate on Education	O. Browning	
Sidgwick	On Stimulus		
Thring	Theory and Practice of Teaching		

†Woodward	A Short History of the Expansion of the British Empire (1500—1902)		
† ,,	An Outline History of the British Empire (1500—1902)		1

CAMBRIDGE UNIVERSITY PRESS

𝔏ondon: FETTER LANE, E.C.

C. F. CLAY, MANAGER

𝔈dinburgh: 100, PRINCES STREET

www.ingramcontent.com/pod-product-compliance
Lightning Source LLC
Chambersburg PA
CBHW020847160426
43192CB00007B/818